The Hoover Library on War, Revolution, and Peace
Publication No. 19

Raymond Poincaré and
the French Presidency

Raymond Poincaré and the French Presidency

By

GORDON WRIGHT

1967

OCTAGON BOOKS, INC.

New York

PREFACE

GENERATIONS of schoolboys have puzzled over a hypothetical clash between an irresistible force and an immovable object. The Poincaré presidency bears some resemblance to that paradox, transported into the field of government. What happened when a man of strong character found himself confined within the limits of a weak office? Were those limits expanded, temporarily or permanently, to allow room for action? Or did the office remain rigid, forcing its occupant into the ordinary mold for seven years?

The purpose of this study is to examine and appraise the activity of Raymond Poincaré from 1913 to 1920. The task of evaluation would be easier if the careers of Poincaré's predecessors had been analyzed in detail. But French presidents have never drawn much attention from historians; obscure cogs in the political machine, they have usually been dismissed with a contemptuous phrase. Only the ill-fated Millerand experiment (1920–1924) has hitherto been placed under the microscope of scholarship.[1] It may be that history has not been quite fair toward the other residents of the Elysée. Intensive research might show that such a chief magistrate as Jules Grévy, for example, was not quite so powerless as posterity has supposed. Sufficient evidence exists, however, to show that most presidents of the Third Republic were really little more than decorative officials. It was with considerable justice that Frenchmen quoted the witticism of Jean-Jacques Weiss: "The fundamental principle of the constitution is, or ought to be, that the president hunts rabbits and does not govern."

It would be foolhardy to maintain that a definitive account of the Poincaré presidency can yet be written. Any study of

[1] Ragnar Simonsson, *Millerands Presidentur; en Studie över Presidentmakt och Parlamentarism i Frankrike* (Uppsala, 1938).

v

recent political history suffers from a scarcity of source material. At the same time, it is doubtful if much more information will ever be available on this particular topic. Access to the archives will mean little, for the president's signature on an official document had no more significance than a rubber stamp. A few memoirs remain to be published (notably those of Joseph Caillaux); and collections of personal papers may some day contribute a flood of new light. Aside from these things, it is difficult to see what time may add to our present knowledge.

Even though most of the evidence is already in, the fact remains that this evidence is relatively meager. French presidents have seldom left any material trace of their passage at the Elysée. Piles of documents may attest the activity of a minister; but the chief magistrate's work was usually done behind the scenes. His influence was exercised through personal conversations or in the course of cabinet sessions, and his words there were very seldom recorded. Weighing such evidence is a risky business, comparable to the task of analyzing the legendary smoke-filled hotel room as a force in American history.

More details have come to light on Raymond Poincaré's presidency than on that of any other man. No doubt the war of 1914–1918 is partly responsible for this fact. Another reason is the public controversy which surrounded his election in 1913 and which led both friends and enemies to keep a close watch upon the Elysée. Poincaré himself wrote an eight-volume account of his stewardship—something that no other president has done. If the problem of the French presidency is to be attacked, therefore, the years from 1913 to 1920 would seem to be the point of least resistance. Perhaps some valid conclusions can be drawn about Poincaré the statesman as well as about the office which he held.

The author owes a special debt of gratitude to Professor Ralph Haswell Lutz for advice and encouragement since the inception of this study. He is under no less an obligation to Professors David Harris, H. H. Fisher, and Albert Guérard, who undertook the burden of reading and criticizing the manuscript. Professor Guérard's suggestions, the fruit of a keen understanding of French affairs, have been of particular value. The author would also acknowledge the aid of the American Field Service Association, whose grant of a fellowship made possible eighteen months' study in France.

G. W.

TABLE OF CONTENTS

CHAPTER I

THE OFFICE

In the governmental structure of the Third French Republic no official occupied a more peculiar position than did its president.[1] Established in royal splendor in the Elysée palace, he ranked as the highest magistrate of the regime. His powers, as outlined by the constitution of 1875, were more extensive than those of the president of the United States. Yet during most of the republic's sixty-five-year life, the presidency was a favorite target for irony and derision. Condemned for seven years to the "prison of the Elysée," the head of the state has been called "a useless machine which costs money but produces nothing," "a phantom," "King Log," "the emaciated shadow of a do-nothing king," "a signing machine."[2] In the words of a royalist critic, "the constitution takes away from the president of the republic all means of real action, cuts off his arms and legs, and leaves at the Elysée a derisory trunk, provided only with a tongue to complain."[3]

This presidential weakness had a double source: the provisions of the constitution itself, and the men who occupied the Elysée.

[1] Strictly speaking, the Third Republic had two presidents: *le président de la république* and *le président du conseil*. The latter official is usually referred to by foreigners as "premier." Although premier is a term never used in France, it will be employed throughout this study in order to make for greater clarity. The presidential title will be reserved for the president of the republic.

[2] James W. Garner, "The Presidency of the French Republic," *North American Review*, CXCVII (March 1913), 347.

[3] Léon Daudet, *La pluie de sang, nouveaux souvenirs 1914–1918* (Paris, 1932), p. 113.

1

During the four years which preceded the adoption of the constitutional laws of 1875, the National Assembly felt no need to discuss the merits of a strong or a weak executive. The fundamental issue in those years was the very nature of the regime to be established. Monarchists had a clear majority in the Assembly, but they were sharply divided into Legitimist and Orleanist camps. Unable to compromise their differences, they set up a stop-gap regime headed by Adolphe Thiers as "president of the republic." It was easy to see that this so-called republic depended upon the doubtful mercies of the monarchist majority. So did the president; Thiers functioned as a responsible premier, subject to repudiation by the Assembly at any time. His downfall came in 1873 when he openly avowed his support of a permanent republic. The royalists joined to force Thiers out of office and to replace him by Marshal MacMahon.

This overturn made it seem that a restoration of the monarchy was in sight. Legitimists and Orleanists worked out a successful compromise, but their scheme collapsed when the Count of Chambord flatly refused to rule France under the tricolor flag. There seemed to be no solution but to wait for the Count's death. The Assembly therefore voted MacMahon a fixed term of seven years, during which time they expected him to "warm the throne." But seven more years of temporary government did not appeal to most Frenchmen. They wanted stability, a permanent constitution; and popular demand forced the Assembly to act. The royalists still hoped to avoid the name "republic"; but M. Wallon's amendment, adopted by a one-vote majority, brought it in through the back door. Three rather sketchy fundamental laws were approved, and the Third Republic thereby came into being.

The powers entrusted to the president of the republic in 1875 were impressive enough at first sight. They may be summarized as follows:

The president was elected for a seven-year term by a majority of the National Assembly (the Chamber and Senate combined), and was eligible for re-election.

He might introduce bills in the legislature.

He supervised and assured the execution of laws.

He had the right of pardon.

He disposed of the armed forces.

He nominated to all civil and military offices.

He presided at national solemnities.

The envoys and ambassadors of foreign powers were accredited to him.

He might dissolve the Chamber with the consent of the Senate.

He might convoke the chambers, or prorogue them for one month.

He might communicate with the chambers by message.

He might return laws to the chambers and request a second deliberation.

He negotiated and ratified treaties without the consent of the legislature, except in certain special cases.

He presided over the council of ministers.

His official acts required the countersignature of a responsible minister.[4]

This list of powers was extensive enough to rank with that of any constitutional monarch. The king of England, for example, could neither preside over the council of ministers nor confer privately with ambassadors of foreign countries. It is true, of course, that royal tradition and life tenure made the king's moral influence greater. Yet the contrary could also be true; for a weakling might inherit a throne, while an elected magistrate was unlikely to come into power without a degree of ability. In contrast to the president of the United States, the French president was privileged to nominate to all offices without the consent of the Senate, to conclude certain treaties without legislative sanction, and to dissolve the lower house with the approval of the upper.

The men who adopted the laws of 1875 believed that they

---

[4] The laws may be found in Léon Duguit and Henri Monnier, *Les constitutions ... de la France depuis 1789* (Paris, 1908), pp. 319–25. The right to preside over the council of ministers does not appear in the text of the constitution.

4 RAYMOND POINCARÉ AND THE PRESIDENCY

were creating a strong presidency.[5] Monarchists hoped that the Orleanist pretender would succeed MacMahon at the Elysée; therefore they wanted to invest the president with the powers of royalty. Conservative republicans like Jules Dufaure and Edouard de Laboulaye desired an executive strong enough to assure public order and to resist an excess of democracy. Most of the republicans in the Assembly, particularly those of the Left wing, voiced exaggerated fears that the new president might be a kind of disguised dictator. But the Assembly did not fully realize that by making the chief magistrate irresponsible, they were placing him under a serious handicap. "The constitution-makers of 1875 intended the president of the republic to be an oak and . . . . they gave him the roots of a reed."[6] This fundamental weakness lay in Article 3 of the law of February 25, 1875: ". . . . every act of the president of the republic must be countersigned by a minister." Since a cabinet could be overthrown at any moment by the legislature, ministers would seldom take responsibility for a presidential act which might displease the Chamber.

Thus the broad powers granted to the president were largely vitiated from the start by the constitutional provision for ministerial countersignature and responsibility. It was still conceivable, however, that the president might be something more than "King Log." To comprehend the true status of the office as Poincaré found it in 1913, one must recall briefly the troubled history of the presidency until that time. Seven men resided in the Elysée between 1875 and 1913. Three were forced

---

[5] Joseph Barthélemy, *Le rôle du pouvoir exécutif dans les républiques modernes* (Paris, 1907), p. 627. Cf. also statements made by both supporters and opponents of the constitutional laws in the Assembly: *Annales de l'Assemblée Nationale*, XXXVI, 401 (Dufaure, February 2, 1875); *ibid.*, p. 501 (Gambetta, February 12, 1875); *ibid.*, XXXIX, 69–71 (Louis Blanc, June 21, 1875); *ibid.*, pp. 464 and 471 (Marcou, Buffet, and Laboulaye, July 7, 1875); Vicomte de Meaux, *Souvenirs politiques 1871–1877* (Paris, 1905), p. 319.

[6] Barthélemy, *Le pouvoir exécutif*, pp. 632–36, 657.

to resign, one was assassinated, one died in office; three served out a full term.[7]

Marshal MacMahon, although elected two years before the constitution went into effect, was the first to serve under its provisions. His term brought the *seize mai* incident, which probably did more than any other single occurrence to shape the presidency. MacMahon had been placed in office by the monarchist group in the National Assembly. The new Chamber of Deputies elected in 1876 was much more republican in tone; MacMahon therefore found it necessary to work with a ministry which was too liberal for his taste. Egged on by his royalist advisers, who wished to control the administrative machinery during the approaching departmental elections, MacMahon seized a pretext to request the resignation of the Jules Simon cabinet on May 16, 1877. He then used his constitutional prerogative to dissolve the Chamber, with the consent of the Senate. In the election which followed, a solid bloc of republicans was returned to the Chamber, ready to force on MacMahon a ministry of its own choosing. MacMahon tried once more to set up a conservative ministry, then inclined before the verdict of the country. He remained at the Elysée for two more years, resigning in 1879.[8]

The *seize mai* incident was fatal to the president's right of dissolution. No attempt was made to use it after 1877, for it had come to be identified with opposition to the republic. Mac-Mahon exceeded none of his constitutional powers in this affair; he was given the right to consult the country, and he did so. There was nothing illegal about his act; it simply did not succeed. But it was not mere failure of the experiment which condemned it for future use. MacMahon killed the power of

---

[7] Grévy, re-elected for a second term, was soon forced to resign (1889).

[8] On the *seize mai* incident, see: Hanotaux, *Contemporary France*, IV, chapters 1 and 3; Charles Seignobos, *L'évolution de la troisième république* (Paris, 1921), pp. 20–44; Alexandre Zévaès, *Au temps du seize-mai* (Paris, 1932).

dissolution by the anti-republican spirit in which he used it. Ever after, the taint of monarchism clung to this article of the constitution.

Two different interpretations of the president's powers were also involved in the *seize mai* crisis. MacMahon regarded himself as a sovereign chief of state, capable of choosing his ministry and governing through it.[9] He implied, in forcing out the Simon cabinet, that the president was responsible to the nation if not to the Chambers. This doctrine he was forced to abandon in December 1877. The president could no longer presume to govern; he could not appeal to the country over the heads of an obstreperous legislature. Along with these questionable pretensions, certain genuine constitutional prerogatives almost disappeared. The right of communicating with the Chambers by message, used frequently by MacMahon, was henceforth exercised only on formal occasions. In fact, any attempt to utilize presidential powers in public after 1877 aroused suspicion among pure republicans. Not only was dissolution dead but presidential influence of any kind was in bad odor. MacMahon left the presidency a narrower office than he had found it.

MacMahon's successor, Jules Grévy, was hardly the type to raise the prestige of the presidency. As a matter of fact, back in 1848 Grévy had tried to eliminate the office of president because he considered it dangerous to the republic. The coup d'état of Louis-Napoleon only confirmed his suspicion. Elected to the office himself at the age of seventy-two, Grévy tried to harmonize the presidency with his lifelong attitude. He announced in his inaugural message: "I will never enter into a struggle against the national will, expressed through its constitutional organs."[10] Essentially negative in character, he

---

[9] Message of May 18, 1877, *Annales du Sénat et de la Chambre des Députés, session ordinaire de 1877*, III, 230–31. (The parliamentary proceedings will be cited hereafter as *Chamber Debates* or *Senate Debates*.)

[10] *Chamber Debates*, February 6, 1879, p. 10.

shut himself up in the Elysée and refrained even from his
formal function of officiating at national festivities.[11] This
"most energetic champion of presidential effacement" made the
average Frenchman almost forget that a president existed.[12]

In the shadowy realm of intrigue, however, Grévy was not
so disinterested as most people supposed. He furnished an excellent example of how much a president could do while seem-
ing to do nothing. His personal influence over a large group
of moderate republicans was great. They continued to look to
him for guidance when he became president, so that men acquainted with politics spoke currently of a "policy of the
Elysée" distinct from that of the ministry.[13] The party situation was such that Grévy was able to keep his bitter rival
Gambetta out of power for three years, despite the fact that
the latter was the Chamber's outstanding leader. Forced at
last to name a Gambetta ministry, Grévy endured rather than
supported his government. The president helped to wreck the
Gambetta cabinet by influencing prominent men not to enter it
and by favoring parliamentary opposition to it.[14] After Gambetta's death Jules Ferry faced similar opposition; he once
complained that he was being "shot in the back" by the Elysée
group.[15]

It was the Schnaebelé affair of 1887 that occasioned Grévy's
most direct intervention in the conduct of government. Schnaebelé was a French border official whom the Germans accused
of espionage in Alsace. They lured him across the frontier
and there placed him under arrest. French patriots were furious. Premier Goblet and War Minister Boulanger demanded

[11] Henri Leyret, Le président de la république (Paris, 1913), p. 101.

[12] Barthélemy, Le pouvoir exécutif, p. 669.

[13] Seignobos, La troisième république, p. 108; Edgar Zévort, Histoire
de la troisième république (Paris, 1892–1904), III, 142–45, 188.

[14] Zévort, op. cit., III, 192–93, 270; Joseph Reinach in Le Matin, September 25, 1920. Reinach was Gambetta's chef de cabinet in 1881.

[15] Zévort, op. cit., III, 273–74.

that an ultimatum be sent to Germany. But Grévy resisted and carried with him a majority of the cabinet. He then helped establish a legal case which forced Bismarck to release Schnaebelé.[16] Thus the president deserved more credit than any other man for the maintenance of peace. Nor did he stop there. He began at once to intrigue against the cabinet in order to force the belligerent Boulanger out of power. When the Goblet government fell a month later, Grévy privately informed the German ambassador that the overthrow had been his handiwork.[17]

Grévy was certainly a stronger president than appearances indicated; but that fact added no strength to the office itself. He actually diminished the presidency; his nine years at the Elysée furnished a precedent which his successors could not easily break. Henceforth their influence had to be exercised behind the scenes, as Grévy's had been. Jules Grévy must bear much of the responsibility for forcing presidents to choose between passivity or conspiracy.

Most parliamentarians were pleased by Grévy's interpretation of the presidency, for it strengthened the legislature at the expense of the executive. They were willing to play the game, and did so by electing a series of second-rate politicians who were likely to prefer pomp to power. The sole exception was Jean Casimir-Périer in 1894, named during the emotional reaction which followed President Carnot's assassination by an anarchist. A wealthy bourgeois of authoritarian temperament,

[16] Reinach, *loc. cit.*; René Goblet, "Souvenirs de ma vie politique," *Revue Politique et Parlementaire*, CXXXVII (November 10, 1928), 187–90; Münster to Bismarck, June 16, 1887, *Die Grosse Politik der Europaischen Kabinette 1871–1914* (Berlin, 1926), VI, 197–98 (this series will be cited hereafter as *G.P.*). Grévy told Münster, "I know well enough that they take me for an old man who never interferes and neglects everything; that is a mistake; I hold the rudder with a firm hand, and I intervene when I judge that the time has come for it." Münster admitted that Grévy made a much more profound impression in private conversation than in public appearances, where the president seemed to be a "worn-out old man."

[17] Münster to Bismarck, July 17, 1887, *G.P.*, VI, 204–5.

Casimir-Périer was not likely to sink quietly into obscurity. His opponents of the Left did not wait to see; they started a campaign of political abuse and personal slander which caused him to resign at the end of six months. Some of their fears were doubtless justified. Casimir-Périer had never concealed his dislike of radicalism and socialism, and he admittedly planned to use his influence against them while at the Elysée. He was not a man to sign and promulgate measures which might be adopted over his contrary advice. The fact that he chose to resign rather than put up a fight was a deadly blow to the already staggering presidential prestige. The experiment seemed to prove that a strong man was out of place at the Elysée. Casimir-Périer made the situation still worse by heaping scorn on the office which he had just quitted. In letters to a newspaper he described the president as "only a master of ceremonies," and complained that the ministers had kept him in ignorance of current affairs.[18] His opinion seemed authoritative; it became widely accepted during the years that followed.

The remaining prewar presidents of France left little mark on the office. Sadi Carnot, the ill-fated predecessor of Casimir-Périer, has received some credit for the negotiation of the Franco-Russian accord; but his part was purely secondary.[19] In domestic affairs Carnot's chief contribution was to play the role of pseudo-monarch, as the German ambassador put it. He traveled indefatigably and presided over public celebrations everywhere—a duty which Grévy had neglected. Carnot's successors continued and extended this practice, until the presence of the president could be expected at every event from battle-

---

[18] Leyret, Le président, p. 13. Yet the cabinet of which Casimir-Périer complained was dominated by Moderates, one of whom was Raymond Poincaré as minister of finance. Casimir-Périer was very careful not to overstep his constitutional powers; he hesitated even to converse with ambassadors. See Münster's dispatch to Hohenlohe, January 6, 1895, G.P., IX, 394–95.

[19] Ribot to Carnot, August 7, 1891, Documents diplomatiques français, 1ère série, VIII, 631; Carnot to Ribot, August 8, 1891, ibid., p. 633; Ribot to de Montebello, August 9, 1892, ibid., IX, 693.

ship launchings to rural cattle shows. An exaggerated amount of his time was taken up in this purely decorative capacity, so that there was justification for the gibes at "France's first layer of cornerstones."

Presidential authority reached its nadir during the era 1895–1913. Félix Faure, in office until 1899, was a vain but mediocre man who loved popular applause. He sought the public eye on all occasions but made little effort to use his influence. Some Frenchmen called upon him for a gesture during the Dreyfus affair, but he excused himself by remarking to Poincaré: "I am reproached for not acting. What can I do? I am the queen of England."[20]

From the very first months of his term Faure often called in members of the diplomatic corps and freely expressed his opinions on European affairs. At least twice he transacted minor business without the premier's knowledge.[21] The German chancellor actually hoped for a time that a Franco-German rapprochement might be carried out through the president.[22] But this soon proved to be an empty dream. It became clear that Faure's activity was chiefly an outlet for his sense of self-importance. Ambassador Münster wrote in disgust that Faure was satisfied to be an "actor-sovereign."[23]

Emile Loubet and Armand Fallières were Faure's successors; each occupied the Elysée for seven years. No chief magistrates have been more colorless than this pair of ex-senators. Elected by the Left-wing parties, they had to conform to the Leftists' concept of the presidency. Except for formal journeys to foreign countries and to the provinces, they became forgotten men. Foreign diplomats seldom sought interviews at

[20] Raymond Poincaré, *Au service de la France* (Paris, 1926–33), III, 34. This work will be cited hereafter under the name of the author only.

[21] Münster to Kaiser Wilhelm II, January 22, 1897, *G.P.*, XIII, 93–94; Münster to *Auswärtige Amt*, December 3, 1898, *G.P.*, XIII, 246–47.

[22] Hohenlohe to Münster, January 1, 1896, *G.P.*, XI, 69–71.

[23] Münster to Hohenlohe, December 18, 1898, *G.P.*, XIII, 315.

the Elysée and rarely so much as mentioned the president in their dispatches. During the long tenure of Delcassé at the Quai d'Orsay, President Loubet gave the foreign minister steady moral support; but he knew little more than the general outlines of Delcassé's diplomacy. The secretive minister shared the details with no one.[24] And Fallières, after his election, assured the cabinet that for seven years there would never be a "policy of the Elysée."[25] He kept his word. Like his two predecessors, Fallières was more interested in the name than in the reality of power. It is no wonder that the presidency came to be considered a place of retirement for elderly parliamentarians worn out in the service of the republic.

But there were some in France who did not accept this condition as either ideal or inevitable. Even in the days of MacMahon a certain number of conservatives who valued public order above civil liberty welcomed the authoritarian implications of the *seize mai*. The monarchist flavor of MacMahon's experiment, added to memories of Louis-Napoleon, caused the main body of republicans to shy away. Partisans of a strong presidency were dealt another severe blow by the Boulanger fiasco. General Boulanger won the support of all those who desired executive leadership as contrasted to what they called parliamentary disorder. His failure to seize power at the opportune moment caused his bubble to collapse; and when the news got out that royalists had financed Boulanger few republicans any longer dared confess a hope for a presidency *à l'américaine*. French politics suffered from this scare for two decades thereafter.

Every year that passed, however, brought increasing stability to the republican regime. MacMahon and Boulanger gradually were pushed farther out of the memories of French-

[24] Premier Rouvier told the German ambassador in 1905 that Loubet had been kept completely in the dark by Delcassé (Radolin to Bülow, June 11, 1905, *G.P.*, XX, 408). A recent study has shown the error of this statement (see Charles W. Porter, *The Career of Théophile Delcassé* [Philadelphia, 1936], pp. 111–12, 249). [25] Leyret, *Le président*, p. 37.

men. A growing number of conservative and Moderate republicans, dissatisfied with the functioning of the government, began to express their criticisms openly. They held that the
legislature, by overthrowing ministries at will, had so completely usurped the powers of the executive branch as to make
any continuity of policy impossible. They suggested that this
"legislative despotism" might be offset by increasing the authority of the president. The best solution, they held, would be
a constitutional amendment providing for election of the president by a broader electoral college or even by popular vote.

The republicans of the Left wing viewed these proposals
with deep suspicion. They could not free their minds of the
example of Louis-Napoleon, who had used his presidential powers to destroy the Second Republic. In 1875 they had fought
the establishment of an irresponsible presidency, and had come
to tolerate that office only because it had grown progressively
weaker. Their hostility meant that a constitutional amendment
had little chance of success.

In the early years of the new century, another solution began to win converts in Moderate circles. It was argued that
the constitution really needed no revision; that it did not condemn the president to impotence; that a statesman supported by
public opinion and willing to use his powers could revive the
presidency. Waldeck-Rousseau, Paul Deschanel, and Louis
Barthou were among the politicians who spoke out for this
theory, but the clearest exposition of it was given by Deputy
Alexandre Ribot. In an address delivered in 1902 he declared:

> The action of public opinion, if it were to make itself felt with
> strength and continuity, would be far more effective than any revision.
> Do you not believe that, simply by the power of opinion and without
> any revision, we could derive from the constitution of 1875 something
> entirely different as regards . . . . the office of president of the republic
> which everyone considers too effaced as a result of historical prece-
> dents ?[26]

[26] Alexandre Ribot, *Quatre années d'opposition. Discours politiques de
M. A. Ribot* (Paris, 1905), I, 324.

Another expression of this argument came from the pen of an able young political theorist, Joseph Barthélemy, in 1907. He admitted that it was constitutionally difficult for a president to exercise much power, but concluded that it was not impossible. The chief obstacle, as Barthélemy saw it, was public opinion; if that were altered, the Elysée might cease to be a prison. "Why despair of a change of opinion?" he asked. "The functioning of our institutions could be changed if a president of the strong type were placed in the highest office."[27]

Here again the Left-wing politicians saw a threat to democracy and the rights of parliament. A Socialist-Radical newspaper warned: "If the president of the republic should ever seek to substitute his own will for the will of the nation, by using the means which the monarchical constitution of 1875 puts at his disposal, the presidential office would become intolerable to the republicans, who would demand constitutional revision and the suppression of the presidency." And a senator of the same party added: "What we need is a president of the paternal type, and not a president of the strong type."[28] It was clear that the Radicals and Moderates would never see eye to eye on the question of presidential powers.

This debate continued in rather desultory fashion during the years that followed. The eminent critic, Emile Faguet, writing also in 1907, attributed the weaknesses of the French government to the unlimited sovereignty of the legislature. But he disagreed with those who would offset it by increasing the powers of the president; he found that the constitutional prerogatives of that official were already "enormous." The fault, Faguet said, belonged to the men who had been president; for they had adopted the custom of never using their rights. Their failure to act sprang in part from fear of public opinion but more directly from the fact that the president was elected by the

[27] Barthélemy, *Le pouvoir exécutif*, pp. 698–99.

[28] *Ibid.*, pp. 677 and 697, quoting Senator Ernest Vallé, December 31, 1905, and *La Lanterne*, January 23, 1906.

National Assembly. The Assembly was not likely to name a popular or superior man, for he might recapture some of the power which the legislative branch had annexed.[29] Thus Barthélemy and Faguet agreed that the power was there if the man were willing to use it. Faguet simply added his doubt that such a man could attain the Elysée without a change in the mode of election.

A similar argument was presented by the publicist Henri Leyret in 1909. He emphasized the abyss between theory and practice which made the constitution a "legal lie" where the president was concerned. Leyret believed that only a man with an outstanding record, character, and personality could overcome the obstacles which blocked the use of the presidential powers. Like Faguet he saw little hope that anyone of this type could be elected, and concluded pessimistically that any crisis would cause the suppression of the presidency as a useless cog in the machine.[30]

Two factors contributed to a remarkable increase in the attention paid to the presidency in 1912. In the first place, the septennate of Fallières was nearing its end. Only two other presidents under the Third Republic had served out a full term; and in one of those instances, that of Grévy, the incumbent had been quietly re-elected. In every other case sudden death or resignation had caused hasty elections which left no time for electioneering, agitation, or publicity. In 1912 the new election could be seen approaching from afar; journalists and critics seized the opportunity to make copy and to give the French people some forgotten details about their obscure chief magistrate. In the second place, France was passing through a period of patriotic emotion—some have called it an era of spiritual regeneration—in 1912. It is difficult to find the exact origin of this outburst of enthusiasm; but all observers, foreign-

[29] Emile Faguet, *Problèmes politiques du temps présent* (Paris, 1907), pp. 41, 50.

[30] Henri Leyret, *La république et les politiciens* (Paris, 1909), pp. 285, 299.

ers as well as Frenchmen, remarked it. The series of diplomatic crises which culminated in the Agadir affair doubtless had much to do with it; feelings were already keyed up when Germany demanded a slice of French territory in Africa. Bitterness over the Dreyfus case was also beginning to recede, and many people were glad to forget their domestic differences in favor of national unity. The idea of strong and effective leadership was sure to spread in such an atmosphere.

First to make reference to the president who would succeed Fallières was the weekly *L'Opinion*. In November 1911 it published a prophetic item containing what it hoped would be a presidential message to the Chambers in 1914.[31] In this hypothetical message the president was to inform the legislature that the mutilated constitution ought to be be restored in all its original vigor. "My predecessors," continued the article, "oppressed by the intimidation of parties and the license of controversies, honestly mistaken as well, ... permitted several articles of the organic laws to fall into desuetude." The resulting lack of governmental balance, according to this phantom president, would be corrected if the powers of dissolution, message, prorogation, suspensive veto, and negotiation of secret treaties were all restored to full working order. *L'Opinion* sounded the keynote of a campaign which was to continue during ensuing months: the constitution is there; it is strong enough; let it be used!

Most of the agitation came from republicans of the Center or Right. Periodicals like *L'Opinion* and newspapers like *Le Figaro* and the *Journal des Débats* were the ones which lent it support. Radicals and Socialists, hostile to a strong executive ever since the republic was founded, generally kept silent. Apparently they hoped that all this talk would blow over, leaving the legislature still predominant. The only attempt to compare varying opinions was made in the monthly *Revue des Français*.

[31] *L'Opinion*, November 4, 1911, pp. 579–80.

From November 1912 to January 1913, Henri Mazel conducted a "national inquiry" in the pages of that magazine.[32] Several dozen scholars, politicians, and other prominent men contributed their views on the presidency. The general conclusion seemed to be that a strong man at the Elysée could revive the office somewhat but could not make it a real controlling agency. The investigation proved in striking fashion that the presidency had suddenly become vital and interesting to Frenchmen in many walks of life.

With the election barely a month away, Henri Leyret published a little volume that attracted widespread attention and summarized the hopes of the strong-presidency agitators. In 1909 Leyret had expressed doubt that a striking personality could ever attain the Elysée. In 1912 his pessimism was tempered by growing hope: "Are we truly condemned forever to septennates of sleep?" he asked. "The presidency which will begin with the year 1913 will decide." Leyret felt confident that he knew the wishes of the French people: "What opinion desires today is a president of the republic who will conduct himself neither as a paralytic nor as a parasite but who on the contrary will make use of his rights and act as a true head of the state." Leyret pointed out that the public was aroused as never before over a presidential election. In his opinion this was the moment for the strong man whom the presidency had been awaiting. The constitution was there, offering adequate powers. The people of France were thirsting for a leader who would make use of all his rights.[33]

Leyret's book was really a piece of campaign literature. As such it drew a reply. Another publicist, Guy de Lubersac, took issue with the idea that presidential authority lay ready in the constitution for someone to take and use. De Lubersac conceded

[32] "La présidence de la république; enquête nationale dirigée par Henri Mazel," *Revue des Français*, November 23, 1912, pp. 192–205; December 25, 1912, pp. 280–96; January 25, 1913, pp. 24–37.

[33] Leyret, *Le président*, pp. xv–xvi, 4.

that the president might become a useful and important cog in the public machine but declared that, if he did so, it would be in spite of the constitution and not with its aid. The end was desirable, but to achieve it the president would have to be " . . . . endowed with an unrivalled intelligence, feeling himself supported by the nation. . . . . The advice which he gives in the councils of government will then acquire its full weight, not because of the organic laws of 1875, but because of his popularity and his personal worth." De Lubersac feared that such a combination of circumstances was too much for which to hope; he believed therefore that the constitution should be altered, at least to permit popular election of the president.[34]

There were others who agreed with de Lubersac. Conservatives like the Progressist deputy Jules Roche and the publicist André Chéradame thought that the president could never escape legislative tutelage unless he were elected by the country at large.[35] Despite their pessimism, all these men were in full sympathy with the agitation for presidential revival. When 1913 arrived, this idea had fixed itself in the minds of many Frenchmen of the Center and Right. It was widely believed that the government stood at a crossroad and that the coming presidential election would determine the course by which France would proceed. Could a strong personality in the Elysée really direct that course? Many thought so. Then could that strong personality be elected under the system in force? And, if so, where could he be found? It remained for the events of January 1913 to answer these questions.

[34] Guy de Lubersac, *Les pouvoirs constitutionnels du président de la république* (Paris, 1913), pp. 54–55.

[35] Jules Roche, "La révision de la constitution," *Le monde économique,* March 30, 1912, pp. 383–90; André Chéradame, *La crise française; faits— causes—solutions* (Paris, 1912), pp. 638–42.

CHAPTER II

THE MAN

Raymond-Nicolas-Landry Poincaré was born in Bar-le-Duc, Lorraine, in 1860. At the moment of his birth the bells in his native town were announcing the results of an election to the Corps Législatif. "It is an omen," remarked the attending physician with a smile to Madame Poincaré; "your son will be a deputy."[1]

Legends regularly cluster about the early years of statesmen, and to this Poincaré was no exception. Always known as a prudent man, that trait in his character could be traced back to boyhood days. The citizens of Bar recalled that young Raymond had always carried an umbrella to the lycée, no matter how fine the weather.[2] His scholarship was brilliant; he stood so consistently at the top of his class that the professors began to omit his name when the weekly list was read.[3] Raymond's most important childhood experience came at the age of ten. In that year of 1870 German troops marched into Bar-le-Duc on their victorious way to Paris. They occupied the town for three years, while the German authorities proceeded to rend in two Raymond's native Lorraine. Bar-le-Duc itself remained within the boundaries of France; but only a few kilometers away lay territory once French, now German. The scar of mutilated Lorraine was too near at hand ever to be forgotten by Raymond Poincaré.

Raymond's father, a civil engineer in the service of the gov-

[1] Poincaré, VIII, 319.

[2] Henry Girard, *Raymond Poincaré* (Paris, 1913), p. 39.

[3] Martial Massiani, "M. Raymond Poincaré," *Fortnightly Review*, XCIII, n.s. (May 1913), 858. Cf. Fernand Payen, *Raymond Poincaré, l'homme, le parlementaire, l'avocat* (Paris, 1936), p. 22.

ernment, was prosperous enough to give his son a higher education. Young Poincaré received his law degree at Paris, dabbled for a time in journalism, then entered political life at the age of twenty-six as *chef de cabinet* of Minister Jules Develle. Soon after, he was elected to the general council of the Meuse, his native department.[4] A special election in the Meuse in 1887 sent him to the Chamber of Deputies with tenfold the votes of his nearest competitor.[5] Poincaré stayed in the background at the Palais-Bourbon; for three full years he did not once mount the tribune. His silence at the height of the Boulanger crisis almost cost him re-election in 1889, and did lead to a duel with one of his rivals. But his first speech before the Chamber, an able defense of the budget, retrieved his position. He was marked at once as a rising star in the political sky.[6]

His precocious advance continued when Premier Charles Dupuy made him minister of public instruction in 1893. Aged thirty-three at the time, he was one of the youngest men ever to hold a portfolio under the Third Republic. On his arrival at the ministry two officials actually mistook him for the president of the student association.[7] The Dupuy cabinet was shortlived, but it permitted Poincaré to establish his reputation. A few months later he was back in office as minister of finance, after which came a second brief period in the ministry of public instruction. In 1899 President Loubet called him to form a Poincaré cabinet, but he gave up the task rather than accept one Socialist minister.[8]

[4] Thereafter he continued to be re-elected without opposition (Payen, *Poincaré*, p. 63).

[5] At one of Poincaré's campaign meetings in 1887, Louis Madelin overheard a workingman in the audience remark: "He speaks well; he doesn't hesitate; they say he knows everything." (L. Madelin, "Un Lorrain: M. Raymond Poincaré," *Revue Hebdomadaire*, February 8, 1913, p. 249.)

[6] Girard, *Poincaré*, pp. 87–100; Payen, *Poincaré*, pp. 76–79.

[7] Payen, *Poincaré*, pp. 87–88.

[8] Abel Combarieu, *Sept ans à l'Elysée avec le président Emile Loubet* (Paris, 1932), pp. 21–22; Georges Adam de Villiers, *M. Poincaré parle* (Paris, 1933), p. 35.

There followed a ten-year period during which Poincaré virtually withdrew from active public life. His reasons for doing so have never been made entirely clear. On the threshold of power, recognized as one of the leading politicians in the Chamber, nevertheless he refused to join any ministry except for one brief period in 1906. He remained in the legislature but aroused the wrath of his political allies by refusing to vote on important measures. Once, as he was hastening toward the Palais-Bourbon, an acquaintance remarked scornfully: "He is in a hurry to abstain."[9] He emphasized his withdrawal from an active role when, in 1903, he accepted a seat in the rather somnolent Senate. Poincaré now turned his attention from politics to his hitherto neglected law practice. Before long he had become one of the wealthiest and most successful lawyers in France. Meanwhile his literary talents earned him membership among the forty immortals of the *Académie Française*.

This decade of quiet in Poincaré's political career eventually redounded to his benefit. These were the years of the Dreyfus affair, which split all France into two warring parties. Any man in public life was certain to make enemies on one side or the other. Poincaré kept as aloof from the struggle as possible. He had been a minister at the time of Dreyfus' arrest in 1894, but had known nothing about the case at the time. By 1897 he became convinced that justice had not been done, and privately began to urge revision. Yet he hesitated to speak out openly, for fear that the army's prestige might be shaken and from loyalty to his anti-Dreyfusite political allies. At last, late in 1898, he "liberated his conscience" by declaring in the Chamber that new evidence necessitated a revision of the Dreyfus judgment.[10] His speech was acclaimed by the Dreyfusites, but it split his own party and won him a number of enemies. Thereafter he scrupulously avoided any active connection with the

9 Payen, *Poincaré*, p. 251.
10 *Chamber Debates*, November 28, 1898, pp. 247–49.

Dreyfus case. When *l'Affaire* was over, Poincaré might have made the same reply which Sieyès gave to a questioner after the Reign of Terror: "I lived." There were few politicians who survived the storm so well.[11]

Poincaré's political doctrines changed little from the beginning to the end of his career. When he entered the Chamber in 1887 its numerous parties could be grouped into three major divisions. On the Right wing there still existed a bloc of royalists, Bonapartists, and ultraclericals, all hostile to the republic. On the Left, the Radicals considered themselves the true exponents of democratic progress. They were violently anticlerical, and demanded such dangerous reforms as an income tax, lay schools, and abolition of both the Senate and the presidency. Their reading of French history convinced them that a strong and independent executive would endanger the very existence of the republic. In the Center sat the Moderates, who took Léon Gambetta and Jules Ferry as their patron saints. Middle-class, conservative republicans, they clung to the nineteenth-century liberal tradition in economics and politics. The Radical program seemed to them excessive both in its *étatisme* and in its intolerance toward the Church.

Poincaré quickly found his place among the Moderate deputies. It was not long before his public statements came to be regarded as definitive expositions of the Moderate creed. His cast of mind was conservative without being reactionary. For example, he fought the proposed income tax for many years but eventually came to accept it in a limited form.[12] His anticlericalism, while not flamboyant, was deep-rooted.[13] He was not a

[11] Emile Zola assertedly said to Poincaré regarding his role in the Dreyfus affair, "Vous êtes un petit homme" (Charles Paix-Séailles, *Jaurès et Caillaux, notes et souvenirs* [Paris, n.d.], p. 76). For an account more favorable to Poincaré, see Payen, *Poincaré*, pp. 214–26.

[12] Payen, *Poincaré*, p. 310.

[13] Poincaré once said publicly to the clerical deputy Charles Benoist, "between you and me lies the whole breadth of the religious question" (Charles Benoist, *Souvenirs* [Paris, 1933–34], III, 180).

practicing Catholic, but neither was he a Freemason like most of the Radical politicians. He simply believed that the Church belonged in a sphere of its own and should not be permitted to interfere in politics or in public education. The sincerity of his republican faith was never questioned. His ideas had been formed in the 'seventies and 'eighties, when the reaction against the Empire was strongest. Finally, his patriotism was of the Lorraine variety, which all Frenchmen held to be the purest and most stubborn type that existed.

Although Poincaré's doctrines remained almost constant between 1887 and 1913, the balance of political power shifted around him. The rapid rise of a strong Socialist party on the extreme Left considerably altered the center of gravity in the legislature. Poincaré continued to describe himself as a Left republican, but by 1913 all the Moderates had been pushed from Left Center to Right Center in the Chamber. Flanking them on the Right were the so-called *progressistes,* who in turn sat next to a shrunken remnant of political and religious reactionaries. *Progressistes* and Moderates had been a single group until 1899, when a schism created a permanent division between them. Poincaré, Louis Barthou, and others kept the Moderate label, and represented a policy of mild progress and anticlericalism.[14] Their aim was to defend the republic against any menace from either Right or Left; "neither reaction nor revolution" was their motto. The *progressistes,* on the other hand, leaned perceptibly to the Right.[15]

---

[14] The schism of 1899 was hastened by Poincaré's pro-Dreyfus speech of November 1898. He and a number of others seceded from the *progressiste* parliamentary group and chose the name *républicains de gauche.* In 1901 they expanded their organization into a full-fledged party, the *alliance républicaine démocratique.* The members of the *alliance* were generally called Moderates in contradistinction to their former colleagues, the *progressistes.* (See Léon Jacques, *Les partis politiques sous la IIIᵉ république* [Paris, 1913].)

[15] The line between *progressistes* and extreme Right became difficult to draw, for the royalists had adopted the innocuous title "conservative," and the clericals had likewise abandoned their open hostility to the republic at the Pope's suggestion.

Poincaré's political ideology early led him to criticize the French governmental system. Like most of his fellow Moderates, he complained that the Radicals' doctrine of legislative supremacy had left the executive weak and anemic. In a series of public addresses delivered between 1896 and 1898 he bluntly expressed his dissatisfaction:

> The evil, the growing and redoubtable evil, arises from the fact that the Chamber has little by little arrogated to itself most of the prerogatives of government. We have unconsciously arrived at such a falsification of the parliamentary regime and such a violation of the spirit of the constitution that the deputies govern . . . . under the pseudonym of the ministers. . . . .[16]

Poincaré's words did not evaporate like those of many political speeches; they were loudly praised and often quoted during the decade that followed. Some critics protested that while he had accurately diagnosed the disease he had failed to prescribe a remedy. Poincaré hinted at an answer in 1898 when he declared: "Before revising the constitution, we might perhaps try to apply it." And in 1902, speaking at Rouen, he became more specific: "We must first draw from the constitution of 1875 the unused resources concealed within it: henceforth the president of the republic must freely exercise the powers of which he has been deprived by custom."[17] This statement placed Poincaré squarely in the ranks of the strong-presidency advocates. By it he implied that an able statesman could restore the office to its pristine vigor without changing one letter of the constitution. In the decade that followed he continued to remind the people of France that he stood for an end to legislative "despotism" and a revival of executive authority.[18]

The personality of a politician is sometimes as important

[16] Raymond Poincaré, *Questions et figures politiques* (Paris, 1907), pp. 78–79.

[17] *Ibid.*, p. 197.

[18] Payen, *Poincaré*, pp. 187–92, 308; *Le Petit Parisien*, April 28 and June 23, 1907, June 17, 1908.

as his political ideas. Poincaré's success was achieved in spite of, rather than because of, his personality. One of his glorifiers has been forced to ask the question: "How could Poincaré raise himself so high in the republic of comrades where, having admirers, he had no comrades or, having partisans, he had no friends?"[19] Almost every Frenchman or foreigner with whom he came in contact was struck by his cold, distant, unemotional attitude. A few of those who knew him well have attempted to argue that his coldness was merely a mask that covered a truly warm heart. Even though this may have been true, he never revealed these hidden qualities in public life; so far as his political career was concerned, his frigidity was virtually complete. As Philippe Berthelot of the Quai d'Orsay caustically remarked, "Poincaré is perfection—nothing more."[20]

Perhaps this deficiency made his qualities stand out in higher relief. His refusal to slap backs in the Chamber left little room for insinuations about his sincerity in political issues. His "systematic intransigeance" made Frenchmen look upon him as a man who would drive straight to his goal no matter what the cost. The younger Dumas assertedly exclaimed on seeing Poincaré, "*Sacrebleu,* when that fellow gets hold of a bone, he won't let go!"[21] Endowed with a prodigious memory and a tremendous capacity for work, free of all vices except occasional indulgence in dominoes, he could demand of his colleagues and of France a similar degree of concentration and application. Paradoxically, Frenchmen esteemed him not for his political promises but for the sacrifices which he asked of the nation.[22]

[19] Samné, *Poincaré,* pp. 376–77.

[20] Auguste Bréal, *Philippe Berthelot* (Paris, 1937), p. 66.

[21] Girard, *Poincaré,* p. 83. Hostile critics called this mere stubbornness. One of them remarked that nothing could change Poincaré's mind, "not even a good reason" (Léopold Marcellin, *Le règne des harangueurs,* [Paris, 1928], p. 249).

[22] Samné, *Poincaré,* p. 377.

Poincaré's long abstention from power came to an end in January 1912. Then was formed his "national ministry" that was destined to infuse a new spirit into France—a spirit of confidence and pride and, some have said, chauvinism. Several factors interacted to make him seem the logical leader of a resurgent nation. By his frequent refusals of portfolios since 1899 Poincaré had not only avoided making enemies; he had also established himself as no mere self-seeker but a statesman who would take power only in time of crisis. Such a crisis seemed imminent after the Agadir affair of 1911. The people of France, their patriotism ruffled, were in the mood for a new premier who would speak out fearlessly and would represent something more than a political clique. In the second place, the fact that Poincaré was a Lorrainer was cited as evidence that he deserved the nation's confidence.[23] And, thirdly, he had keynoted the new spirit in France in his recent public addresses.

Two speeches in particular attracted notice; both were delivered in August 1911 in his native Lorraine. At Verdun he told a national teachers' congress that "the first duty of a good citizen, in the present state of Europe and of the world, is to be a courageous and disciplined soldier." "Two steps away from a grievous frontier," he continued, "in a province which is the bulwark of France, how could one find a teacher who would listen to the enervating counsels of the internationalists or who would yield to the insidious suggestions of a gaping pacifism?"[24]

A few days later, in opening the session of the Meuse general council, Poincaré issued another manifesto. He emphasized the need for a strong and authoritative government in domestic affairs, and added: "But it is not only internally that the government of the republic must make its legitimate authority felt. We all expect it to be employed abroad to defend with as much resolution as courtesy the interests and dignity of France . . . ."

[23] Madelin, *loc. cit.*, p. 249.   [24] *Le Temps,* August 8, 1911.

Summarizing the nation's desires, he declared: "The whole country has no other pretension than to sacrifice none of its rights, and to give no more than it receives."[25] This address drew much attention, coming as it did during the Agadir crisis, and occurring in a council session where political questions were customarily avoided. Influential newspapers like *Le Temps* gave it their full approval.

When the Caillaux cabinet fell in January 1912, Poincaré rode into office on a wave of patriotic enthusiasm. During the year which followed he increased the intensity of this enthusiasm by his evident determination to maintain the place of France in Europe. His ministerial declaration pointed with pride to the fact that the new cabinet represented every republican group.[26] An outline of his program followed: reform of the electoral system, faithful maintenance of France's alliances and friendships, and a sincere desire for peace. But the declaration ended on a warning note. "Profoundly pacific though our country may be, it is not master of every eventuality, and it intends to remain equal to all its duties. The army and the navy will be the object of our attentive solicitude . . . ."[27] The Chamber's vote of confidence, 440 to 6 with 123 abstentions, was a smashing victory for the new government.[28]

The degree of success with which Poincaré carried out his program from January 1912 to January 1913 is beyond the scope of this study. At the same time, he who would analyze Poincaré's presidential career must pay some attention to the events of 1912, which prepared his entrance into the Elysée. More than one polemicist has attempted to extract from the tangled diplomacy of this period the essence of the French

[25] *Le Temps*, August 23, 1911.

[26] No Socialist minister was included. The cabinet won a half-hearted kind of support from the Socialists, however, by sponsoring proportional representation.

[27] *Chamber Debates*, January 16, 1912, pp. 22–23.

[28] *Ibid.*, pp. 36–37.

premier's activity. Some have tried to prove that Poincaré was carrying out a *revanche* policy, desirous or careless of war. Others have replied that he adopted a stiff attitude because he considered it the best way to avoid a conflict. Both sides have often resorted to careful selection of speeches or documents and have interpreted events to fit their theses. Even where they have used absolute good faith in examining all the sources at hand, they have faced the more subtle danger of reading into Poincaré's acts meanings which he may not have given them at the time.

The evidence now available has completely destroyed the extreme-revisionist theory that Poincaré desired and worked for a war of revenge. The published French documents have not contributed a shred of proof that he was a warmonger.[29] Most of Poincaré's critics have drawn heavily upon the dispatches of Izvolsky, the Russian ambassador in Paris.[30] According to these reports, the premier approved Russian intrigues in southeastern Europe and freely offered the support of France in all contingencies. Poincaré has flatly denied having made any such promise, and has pointed out that he always regarded Izvolsky as untrustworthy.[31] His assertion that he lacked confidence in the Russian ambassador has since been confirmed.[32] The old charge that Poincaré was an accomplice or tool of Iz-

[29] Cf. G. P. Gooch, *Before the War, Studies in Diplomacy* (London, 1938), II, 197. Gooch has made the most successful attempt at compressing Poincaré's activity as premier into a brief essay. The accurate and dispassionate nature of his analysis is confirmed by a study of the published documents and memoirs.

[30] Edited by René Marchand as *Un livre noir* (Paris, 1922–31) and by Friedrich Stieve as *Der Diplomatische Schriftwechsel Iswolskis 1911–1914* (Berlin, 1925). (These works will be cited hereafter as *Livre noir* and *Iswolski*, respectively.)   [31] Poincaré, I, 322–27.

[32] The French diplomatic documents reveal that during a conversation with Kokovtsov in August 1912 Poincaré criticized Izvolsky severely (Poincaré's notes on his voyage to Russia, *Documents diplomatiques français 1871–1914*, 3ᵉ série [Paris, 1929–1936], III, 344; this series will be cited hereafter as *D.D.F.*).

volsky simply does not hold water. As a matter of fact he usually tried to restrain the Russian government for fear that it would precipitate a crisis.

Poincaré's policies in 1912 were not beyond criticism, however. He has been absolved from war "guilt," that is, a conscious scheme to bring about a conflict. But the charge of war "responsibility" has not been destroyed. In other words, his activity contributed to the growth of a dangerous situation in Europe and helped to destroy hope of a pacific solution. Poincaré was no advocate of peace at any price. In his oft-quoted Nantes speech in October 1912 he suggested that the French should be "a people which does not want war and at the same time does not fear it."[33] His highest aim was to affirm the dignity and prestige of France; and, to achieve that end, Poincaré believed it was necessary to maintain and strengthen the Triple Entente. Among his greatest worries were Russian and English flirtations with Germany, which he feared might leave France without dependable support, a prey to blackmail or attack.[34] He was haunted by memories of French weakness during her long isolation after 1871.

[33] Poincaré, II, 281–82.

[34] For instance, Poincaré tried to prevent the adoption of any Anglo-German formula of nonaggression during the Haldane conversations. He feared that it might give ammunition to critics of the Entente, and that it might cause quibbling if France should be forced to declare war on Germany (Poincaré to P. Cambon, March 30, 1912, *D.D.F.*, II, 276; *ibid.*, April 11, 1912, pp. 334–35; P. Cambon to de Fleuriau, April 3, 1912, pp. 301–3). Poincaré was instrumental also in strengthening the Entente through the Grey-Cambon letters (Bertie to Grey, July 30, 1912, G. P. Gooch and Harold Temperley, *British Documents on the Origins of the War 1898–1914* [London, 1926–38], X, Part II, 605–6; this publication will be cited hereafter as *British Docs.*).

In the case of Russia, Poincaré gave voice to his irritation when Sazonov seemed too intimate with Italy, and when a meeting of the Tsar with the Kaiser was announced (Poincaré to Louis, March 23, 1912, *D.D.F.*, II, 251–52; *ibid.*, April 11, 1912, pp. 335–36). Poincaré tried to bind the alliance closer by Franco-Russian naval conversations and by a personal trip to St. Petersburg in August. On the Georges Louis affair, see *infra,* chapter iii.

To avoid any rifts in the Entente he was sometimes carried beyond the bounds of prudence. One such instance occurred just after the first Balkan War. At that time Poincaré reversed his usual policy and urged Russia not to hang back in the Balkan crisis.[35] Some critics have regarded his attitude as proof of his bellicosity. According to their theory Poincaré had finally come to realize the potential strength of the Balkan League and desired to keep its friendship in preparation for the coming European war.[36] As a matter of fact, Poincaré did fear that Austrian ascendancy might crowd out Entente influence in the Balkans.[37] But this was not his only reason for attempting to stiffen Russia's Balkan policy. Poincaré feared also that Austria was about to execute a coup against Serbia which would catch the Russians napping. Should Russia refuse to accept the *fait accompli,* the European war would be set off with the Entente powers several jumps behind their enemies.[38]

Except for this incident, Poincaré consistently tried to restrain Russia's Balkan ambitions during 1912.[39] The exception was significant. Poincaré resented the idea that Russia might drag France into a war originating in the Balkans. But by ceasing to restrain his ally this one time he showed that the French government would accept such a war if necessary. Better the cataclysm, Poincaré thought, than a weakening of the

[35] Izvolsky to Sazonov, December 18, 1912, *Iswolski,* II, 396–99.

[36] For example, Sidney Bradshaw Fay, *The Origins of the World War* (New York, 1930), I, 442.

[37] Poincaré to Louis, November 2, 1912, *D.D.F.,* IV, 333; Poincaré to P. Cambon, December 13, 1912, *D.D.F.,* V, 86.

[38] Poincaré to P. Cambon, December 3, 1912, *D.D.F.,* IV, 632; Poincaré circular, December 12, 1912, *D.D.F.,* V, 63–65; Izvolsky to Sazonov, December 11, 1912, *Iswolski,* II, 383–84. Cf. Gooch, *Before the War,* II, 193.

[39] Note, for example, his distrust of the Serb-Bulgar treaty. He tried for several months to secure details of its provisions. When finally enlightened at St. Petersburg, he was incensed at its warlike character (Poincaré memorandum, August 1912, *D.D.F.,* III, 340–41). His mind was seldom free from suspicion about Russian policy; he instructed Ambassador Louis to keep in close touch with Sazonov in order to know what Russia was doing (Poincaré to Louis, April 11, 1912, *D.D.F.,* II, 334).

Russian alliance. Like Ambassador Louis in St. Petersburg, he believed that France could not desert Russia even if the latter should precipitate a crisis, for "that would mean definitely assuring the domination of Germany in Europe."[40] Poincaré ended his year in power with a ringing public affirmation that Russia could depend on France.[41]

Poincaré's national policy of 1912 was a threat to European concord. He worked for peace so long as it did not clash with his version of French prestige and security.[42] At the same time he seriously doubted that peace could be long preserved, and this doubt was the weak link in his pacific efforts. His fears for the future were largely justified, especially in view of the disquieting reports which he received from the military attaché in Berlin.[43] But his blunt and unyielding methods did nothing to diminish tension in Europe. He aimed to prepare France materially and spiritually, at home and abroad, for the threatening crisis. In so doing he dulled the distaste for war among his own people and contributed to the growth of suspicion across the Rhine. Perhaps no policy could have prevented war in the anarchical Europe of that period. At any rate Poincaré's policy was one of those least likely to avert it.[44]

[40] Louis to Poincaré, April 10, 1912, *D.D.F.*, II, 326–27.

[41] *Senate Debates,* December 21, 1912, p. 339.

[42] In October 1912, for example, he labored strenuously to avert war in the Balkans. "At this stage," Gooch has said, "no statesman in Europe was working harder to keep the peace" (*Before the War,* II, 180). Even Kiderlen-Wächter praised Poincaré for this (*G.P.,* XXXIII, 200). While Poincaré sincerely desired a pacific solution, he hoped that it might be turned into a diplomatic success for the Entente (cf. Ernst Christian Helmreich, *The Diplomacy of the Balkan Wars 1912–1913* [Cambridge, Mass., 1938], p. 149).

[43] Colonel Pellé, the military attaché, wrote at length of German projects for increasing the army. Only the military party desired war, he said, but the German public was irritated against France as a result of the Agadir episode and the rise of French national feeling. In his opinion a majority still desired peace, but it would require only a slight spark to change this. See his reports of January 1, 1912, *D.D.F.,* II, 455–56; February 3, 1912, *ibid.,* I, 594–98; April 7, 1912, *ibid.,* II, 286–91; May 20, 1912, *ibid.,* III, 57–62.

[44] Poincaré hoped to frighten Germany into keeping the peace. He told

A large proportion of the French people approved Poincaré in his conduct of affairs.[45] His cabinet had begun its task backed by the nation's sympathy and hope; at the end of 1912 he possessed its confidence as well. Although most Frenchmen knew little of what was going on behind the diplomatic scenes, they could understand the patriotic fervor of Poincaré's public addresses. His belief in the strength of France was contagious; his firmness at the Quai d'Orsay seemed to show that the opinions of France once more carried weight in the councils of Europe. When 1913 arrived, Raymond Poincaré was generally regarded as his country's strongest statesman.

a journalist in January 1912: "I have one firm conviction . . . . that every time we have desired to show ourselves conciliatory toward Germany she has abused our good will; and on the other hand every time that we have shown ourselves firm toward her, she has given way. Germany does not understand the language of right and wrong; she only understands strenuous measures." (Stéphane Lauzanne, *Great Men and Great Days* [New York, 1921], p. 48.)

[45] It is impossible to determine just what percentage of the French people backed Poincaré's cabinet, since there was no general election during 1912. The next election, two years later, showed a slight majority for Left-wing candidates. In 1912, however, his following was probably larger. The Chamber gave him strong votes of confidence throughout, and vocal opinion was overwhelmingly favorable. One cannot read the newspapers and periodicals of the time without concluding that support of the cabinet was genuine and widespread. The reports of foreign ambassadors in Paris revealed their belief that the Poincaré government rested on the patriotic emotion of the inarticulate masses as well (Bertie to Grey, February 19, 1913, *British Docs.*, Vol. X, Part II, pp. 674–75; Lancken to Bethmann, February 14, 1912, *G.P.*, XXIX, 452–54). Massiani (*loc. cit.,* p. 857) compared Poincaré's popularity to that of General Boulanger. Cf. also Auguste Gérard, *Mémoires* (Paris, 1926), pp. 452–53. On the other hand, see Fay, *Origins of the World War*, I, 315; Fay has declared that Poincaré followed "an aggressive and dangerous policy, which was not a reflection of the wishes of the great majority of the truly peace-loving French people from 1912 to 1914, and which they would not have approved, had they been fully aware of it . . . ." This may be true; nevertheless, Poincaré did have popular approval, even if it was based on ignorance.

CHAPTER III

THE ELECTION OF 1913

THE POINCARÉ CANDIDACY

No presidential election in the history of the Third Republic can compare with that of January 17, 1913, in the amount of sustained public interest which it aroused. It marked the climax of the strong-presidency agitation which had been gradually coming into the open for many years. As Fallières' septennate neared its end, the discussion began to take on a practical character rather than an academic one. It had been harmless enough to theorize about what might happen if an outstanding personality should enter the Elysée; now, it appeared, there might be a chance to try it out. And coinciding with the spread of this theory was the rise of Poincaré in public esteem. The junction of the man and the idea seemed almost inevitable.

Poincaré has never adequately explained why he decided to run for the presidency. He was already premier, which gave him active control of the government. Prospects were excellent for many more months in power, for his prestige, both at home and abroad, had reached a level seldom equaled since 1870. The honor of becoming France's chief magistrate doubtless had its attraction; yet Poincaré was not a man to love mere pomp and show when he could be directing affairs.[1] He could have expected "retirement" to the Elysée in due course, after his active political career was over; for the presidency was generally re-

---

[1] It is possible, of course, that Madame Poincaré's ambition to become *la présidente* may have influenced her husband's decision.

garded as a position which climaxed and concluded a man's official life.[2]

Poincaré would not have exchanged the reality for the appearance of power in 1913 if he had expected it to mean the usual "premature burial." One can hardly doubt that he was impressed by the swelling current of agitation for real leadership at the Elysée. In his memoirs he has avoided mention of this campaign for presidential revival, although in 1920 he admitted his familiarity with it and branded the idea as illusory.[3] His textbook on French government, published early in 1913, revealed nothing but a thoroughly orthodox conception of the presidency.[4] Recalling the period of his election, he has written: "I felt no liking for a role whose necessity I recognized and whose greatness I admired, but which, carrying no legal responsibility, inevitably left little initiative and independence to him who exercised it. . . . . As for me, I was scarcely tempted to place seven years of my life under the sway of protocol."[5]

Yet no politician of Poincaré's astuteness could have ignored the talk of reviving the presidency. During January 1913 proponents of the theory made no secret of the fact that they rested their hopes on his candidacy. In spite of his reticence,

[2] His widow many years later provided her explanation of Poincaré's candidacy. She asserted that her husband was urged by men of all parties to accept the presidency in order to forestall Clemenceau, who desired the office. "On a beaucoup insisté," stated Madame Poincaré, "pour éviter ce danger au pays" (letter to the author, October 14, 1938). Poincaré himself has also hinted that Clemenceau aspired to the Elysée in 1913 (Poincaré, III, 37). It is strange that not even Clemenceau's worst enemies accused him of such an ambition at the time. Georges Mandel, who was one of the Tiger's chief aides, has flatly denied it (interview, October 29, 1938). Madame Poincaré's story appears to be a product of the Poincaré-Clemenceau feud during and after the war. After all, when Clemenceau did become an avowed candidate for the presidency in 1920, Poincaré remained deaf to the pleas of his friends that he try for re-election in order to "prevent this danger to the country."

[3] Poincaré in *Le Temps,* August 9, 1920.

[4] *How France Is Governed,* written shortly before his election.

[5] Poincaré, III, 34, 36.

they had reason to support him. They recalled his Commercy speech of 1896, which was a classic statement of the case against legislative encroachment.[6] His own party came out publicly in 1912 for a president who would use all his prerogatives.[7] Poincaré must have felt that the time was ripe for a capable man to shift the balance of French politics toward the Elysée.

Poincaré's name was first publicly linked with the presidency in September 1912. His intimate friend, Gabriel Hanotaux, the eminent historian, was the author of this initial suggestion. Writing in Le Figaro, Hanotaux lent his voice to those who were sponsoring a revival of presidential influence. He asked no new powers for the office, for he considered them extensive enough already. All that was needed was a worthy president to exercise them; and, according to Hanotaux, circumstances had never been more favorable for the election of such a man. Hanotaux mentioned several possible candidates but showed obvious partiality for Poincaré.[8]

During several weeks electoral preparations continued to simmer quietly. The premier gave no indication that he wished to become master of the Elysée, although persons unfriendly to Poincaré have asserted that he aimed at the presidency all through 1912.[9] Already in April Poincaré had approached his friend Léon Bourgeois and had suggested that the latter be-

[6] Jules Roche, loc. cit., p. 398.

[7] Le Matin, January 1, 1913.

[8] Le Figaro, September 27, 1912.

[9] Poincaré has implied in his memoirs that he gave no thought to the presidency during 1912, even though Léon Bourgeois had mentioned the possibility to him as early as April (Poincaré, II, 72). On the other hand, his enemies have charged that he played politics for several months in order to gain the Elysée and that he took power in January 1912 simply to prepare for the forthcoming presidential election (Joseph Caillaux, "Les responsables," Les Documents Politiques, Diplomatiques, et Financiers [March 1926], p. 88; Les carnets de Georges Louis [Paris, 1926], II, 54–55, 246). Likewise the German ambassador reported his belief that the idea was in Poincaré's mind (Schoen to Bethmann-Hollweg, October 13 and November 24, 1912, G.P., XXXIII, 216, 401).

come a candidate. Bourgeois was a Radical senator of great prominence. He had served in several cabinets and had represented France at both Hague peace conferences. Although affiliated with the Radical party, he showed marked sympathy for Moderate principles. In such a question as electoral reform, for example, he differed sharply from the Radicals as a group. His innocence of extreme partisanship and his recognized prestige seemed to indicate him as likely presidential timber. Bourgeois, however, showed no interest in Poincaré's suggestion, pleading ill health. Early in December Poincaré again proposed that Bourgeois seek the office. Bourgeois refused once more, and this time repaid the compliment. "The gravity of the hour," he said, "made it the premier's duty to become a candidate himself." Apparently Bourgeois expected Poincaré to be something more than a figurehead at the Elysée; for he would not have wished to bury an outstanding man in a position of no power if the moment had been really grave. Poincaré subsequently mentioned the insistence of Bourgeois as one of the chief reasons for his entry in the race.[10]

Meanwhile the press was beginning to fill its columns with news and rumors of the approaching election. One of the first articles of note appeared in the conservative weekly *L'Opinion:* "The 'powers' of M. Fallières are about to end. It is the occasion for all specialists to ask themselves exactly what these powers are. Much has been written about this recently. . . . . But so many historical, philosophical and juridical dissertations

[10] Poincaré, II, 72. Bourgeois probably had other reasons for refusing. According to Seignobos, his sponsorship of proportional representation had won him so many enemies in the Senate that he could not hope for election (Seignobos, *La troisième république,* p. 282; cf. Gabriel Hanotaux in *Le Figaro,* September 27, 1912). One writer has quoted Bourgeois as saying some years later that he "didn't give a damn about the presidency" but wanted to become a member of the *Académie Française.* According to this story, Bourgeois and Poincaré agreed on reciprocal support for their respective ambitions (Michel Corday, *L'Envers de la guerre; journal inédit* [Paris, 1932], II, 159).

will change nothing . . . . ; at the Elysée, as elsewhere, the office will be worth what the man is worth."[11] The editor of *L'Opinion* mentioned no names; his colleagues of the daily press also kept their predictions anonymous during the first fortnight in December. On the 15th the *Journal des Débats* carried Bourgeois's announcement that he would not be a candidate and his suggestion of Poincaré and Ribot as leading possibilities. The lid was now off, and names began to fly more freely. Poincaré, Ribot, Dubost, Deschanel, and Delcassé were mentioned most often, while rumors of a Bourgeois candidacy were not finally quashed until December 20.[12]

Radical party organs maintained the silence which customarily surrounded presidential elections. They understood well enough that the current agitation was aimed not only to break up their monopoly on the Elysée but also to weaken their doctrine of legislative superiority. Rather than fight fire with fire, they turned to political maneuvers in the Chamber and the Senate. In the early years of the republic it had been customary for legislators of all republican groups to hold a caucus before presidential elections. By selecting a single candidate on whom to concentrate their votes, they could avoid the danger that the strong monarchist-imperialist bloc might control the election. As time had passed, the monarchist minority had decreased, and so had the need for republican union. The caucuses broke down completely in 1887 and 1894; none was summoned in 1899; and in 1906 the powerful Radical majority used the caucus as a ratifying machine for its candidate.[13]

Although the Radicals had lost much of their political strength between 1906 and 1913, they decided upon another attempt to utilize the atrophied caucus system. Delegates of the various Left groups met on December 17 and agreed "in prin-

[11] *L'Opinion*, V (December 7, 1912), 710.

[12] *Journal des Débats*, December 20, 1912.

[13] *Ibid.*, January 8, 1913; Zévort, *Histoire de la troisième république*, IV, 6.

ciple" that a meeting of all republicans should be called to choose a candidate.[14] Organs of the Center and Right were indignant; they branded it as a scheme to insure the election of a Radical nominee. Their charge seemed to be substantiated when a steering committee of Leftists announced that the Progressists on the Right wing and the Unified Socialists on the Left would be excluded from the proposed caucus.[15] This exclusion policy raised such an outcry that the steering committee was forced to make concessions. The next day it decided to admit the Senate Progressists, and shortly afterward the Unified Socialists and one section of the Chamber Progressists were added to the invitation list.[16] The legislature thereupon adjourned until the eve of the election.

Poincaré chose this moment to take an unprecedented step. On December 26 he allowed a note to be sent to the Havas news agency announcing that he would be a candidate for the presidency of the republic.[17] Only twice before in history had candidacies been openly declared, and in each case the declaration had been made only three or four days before the balloting.[18] Poincaré has explained that the violent campaign carried on against him by the Radicals caused him to accept the combat openly.[19] There was probably a weightier reason, however. The strong-presidency agitation must have made him aware that an open declaration by a successful and prominent states-

[14] *Journal des Débats,* December 18, 1912.

[15] *Ibid.,* December 21, 1912.

[16] *Ibid.,* December 22 and 23, 1912; *Revue Politique et Parlementaire,* LXXV (February 1913), 190. The Progressists admitted were the groups known as *Gauche républicaine* in the Senate and *Union républicaine* in the Chamber.

[17] Alexandre Ribot imitated him on the following day. Poincaré had been encouraging Ribot to run but suddenly announced his own candidacy without having informed Ribot (Benoist, *Souvenirs,* III, 181–82). Poincaré has glossed over this fact in his memoirs (III, 38).

[18] *L'Œuvre,* January 2, 1913, p. 9.

[19] Poincaré, III, 38.

man, supported by the newspapers, might give the election an entirely new character. Certainly it did so; and Poincaré was no callow beginner in politics who would take such a step without weighing the consequences. It was significant that the *Journal des Débats* greeted Poincaré's declaration of candidacy with this remark: "In everyone's opinion, the office of head of the state must be raised. . . . . The presidency of the republic will not be a simple honorific post in the times which are coming."[20]

THE PRESS CAMPAIGN

Poincaré's action was not only a breach of custom in itself but led to a second change in usage—it made possible an open and public campaign. The newspapers welcomed the opportunity. Until this moment they had confined themselves mostly to implications and generalities about the presidency as an office. Now, with two names available that were in obvious favor, they declared that the time for a change had arrived. "The fog is dissipated," wrote Gaston Calmette, editor of *Le Figaro*. "It is certain that M. Raymond Poincaré would be president of the republic tomorrow if the country were consulted."[21]

With the arrival of the new year the election took first place on the front pages of the Paris press. Most journals carried daily feature articles on past elections and prospects in the current campaign, with the obvious purpose of arousing public opinion or at least making the legislators think it was aroused.[22] At the same time there was an intensification in the strong-presidency propaganda. "France would not be displeased," wrote the noted economist Paul Leroy-Beaulieu, "if something were changed in the practice and also in the spirit of our

[20] *Journal des Débats,* December 28, 1912.

[21] *Le Figaro,* December 27, 1912.

[22] See *Le Matin,* January 5, 1913, for quotations from a large number of newspapers.

institutions."[23] The Catholic organ, *La Croix,* criticized President Fallières because, it said, he had allowed his ministers a free hand for seven years.[24] Threats were gratuitously distributed to the legislature: this election would be its last chance; if the members of the National Assembly should fail to heed the country's demands, the flood would carry them away.[25]

The Radicals at last decided that they must fight back openly as well as in the lobbies. Camille Pelletan, one of their leaders, issued a warning in the columns of *Le Matin:*

> Men of party and of action, designed for an active role of governmental direction, have their place marked out in the premiership, where they answer for their acts before the chambers. It would be an absolute violation of the spirit of the constitution to bring them to the Elysée, where they would inevitably be led to usurp an active role without any of the responsibilities which, in a free country, are inseparable from power.[26]

One of the less extreme Radicals, Gaston Doumergue, expressed regret at the noisy campaign which was being carried on. "The election of the president of the republic," he declared, "which ought to be a normal event in the political life of the nation, this time will have broken the equilibrium of its life by party and individual intrigues, and by the calculations of all sorts which are made regarding it." Doumergue believed that the strong-presidency agitation of preceding months had a hidden purpose. "In exalting the role of the president of the republic," he charged, "it is the legislature which they wish to diminish, it is the country which they are trying to despoil insensibly of its sovereignty."[27] The official party organ, *Le Radical,* was more

---

[23] Paul Leroy-Beaulieu, "L'élection présidentielle," *L'Economiste Français,* January 4, 1913, p. 2.

[24] *La Croix,* January 3, 1913.

[25] *L'Echo de Paris,* January 4, 1913; *La République Française,* January 6 and 7, 1913. Deputies could expect nothing less than constitutional revision limiting their powers, according to these journals.

[26] *Le Matin,* January 5, 1913.

[27] *La Grande Revue,* LXXVII (January 10, 1913), 192–93.

reserved; it merely declared that the president was already strong enough, and cast a few aspersions at the memory of MacMahon.[28] Nevertheless, implied fears of a possible dictatorship could be discerned, especially in the remarks of Radical deputies.[29]

Pelletan's article in particular was the signal for a tempest from the Center and Right dailies. The latter greeted with scorn the rumor that the Radicals might select as their candidate Jules Pams, the innocuous minister of agriculture.[30] They accused the Leftists of cowardice for refusing to make a public nomination.[31] They chorused that their demand for a worthy president actually mirrored the opinion of the nation.[32]

When the journalists asserted that they were merely echoing the average Frenchman's desire for leadership, they may have been partly sincere. Beyond any doubt, popular interest in the election did reach an unusual height. Even small provincial towns saw students putting up posters, "Have your deputy vote for Poincaré!" or "for Pams!"[33] L'Excelsior conducted a straw vote among its readers in which Poincaré received 20,000 ballots, or five times the total of his nearest competitor.[34] On the day before the election Le Matin told of crowds massed before its office from five o'clock in the afternoon to midnight chanting "Poin-ca-ré!"[35] One writer declared dramatically: "facing

[28] Le Radical, January 1, 2, 10, 1913.

[29] Gabriel Hanotaux in Le Figaro, January 15, 1913.

[30] Journal des Débats, January 5, 1913.

[31] Ibid., January 8, 1913.

[32] Ibid., January 16, 1913; Le Temps, January 10, 1913; La Croix, January 2, 1913; La République Française, January 11, 1913; Le Correspondant, CCL (January 10, 1913), 206.

[33] Adam de Villiers, Poincaré, p. 5.

[34] L'Excelsior, January 16, 1913. A taxi driver asked one journalist, "It is Poincaré who will be elected, Monsieur?" "Probably." "That would be certain, if it were we who voted . . . ." ("Film," "La vie qui passe," Revue Hebdomadaire, February 1, 1913, p. 119).

[35] Le Matin, January 17, 1913.

danger, as in times of ancient threats, the Gauls desire to choose their leader."[36]

But there were other facts which suggested that the journalists hoped to exert pressure on the legislators by pretending to speak for the country. Late in December 1912 *Le Correspondant* complained: "It is a sign of the times that the public expresses absolutely no interest. No name is imposed; it desires no one."[37] Two weeks later a senator wrote that he would vote for Poincaré because the "quasi-unanimity" of public opinion had designated him; yet he added, "The affair will pass off without noise, almost without éclat, amid amused curiosity or polite indifference."[38] An inquiring reporter who asked opinions in the street found that Poincaré's name was most often mentioned; but he encountered many Parisians who did not even know the candidates. One citizen's blank reaction was: "Alors? le Président de la République est donc mort?"[39]

THE DU PATY DE CLAM AFFAIR

Barely a week before the election a minor incident came near wrecking Poincaré's presidential hopes. This was an order by War Minister Millerand reinstating one Lieutenant-Colonel du Paty de Clam as a reserve officer in the French army. Du Paty de Clam had been retired from active service in 1900, and his

[36] Alfred Capus in *Le Figaro,* December 30, 1912.

[37] *Le Correspondant,* CCXLIX (December 25, 1912), 1243.

[38] "Un sénateur," in *L'Opinion,* VI (January 11, 1913), 33.

[39] *L'Opinion,* VI (January 11, 1913), 34. The campaign was followed with special interest in Russia and England. Newspapers there openly expressed a desire to see Poincaré successful. They felt that his election would bind the Triple Entente more closely together and that a strong hand at the Elysée would increase the stability of the French government. One London periodical, the *Saturday Review,* outdid most Paris magazines in its insistence that "the genuine importance of the Presidential office must be accentuated at all costs," and in demanding that Poincaré be named (CXV [January 11, 1913], 38). Only the liberal *Daily News* was frankly hostile to Poincaré. Russian newspapers were quoted in the *Journal des Débats,* January 11, 1913.

name stricken from the rolls, for his prominent part in the condemnation of Alfred Dreyfus some years earlier. To all good Dreyfusards any favor granted to such a man was a provocation.

The Chambers were on vacation when the order was published on January 9, but a group of Left-wing legislators who had stayed in Paris gathered at the Palais-Bourbon to cry out against what they called treason to the republic. Although the Dreyfus affair had lost some of its poignancy by 1913, it had left scars which were still sensitive. With the presidential election barely a week away it was embarrassing for old hatreds to begin spinning about Poincaré's head. The press which supported him immediately accused the Left of utilizing the incident for political purposes in order to overthrow his cabinet on the eve of the balloting.[40]

Poincaré was conscious of his dilemma. Millerand had issued the reinstatement order on his own authority, without consulting the premier. Nevertheless the principle of cabinet solidarity seemed to imply that if Millerand were forced to resign, the whole ministry ought to follow him. A cabinet collapse at this moment would greatly weaken Poincaré's chance of becoming president. On the other hand, if he should decide to approve and defend Millerand's act, he would invite the suspicion of the Dreyfusards and the Left wing in general. If he should choose the third possible solution—disavow Millerand and force the latter to resign—the Center and Right would doubtless condemn him for weakness and for excessive personal ambition.

It was the third line of conduct which Poincaré chose to follow. He called three special sessions of the cabinet in two days but could not bring himself to abandon the war minister until the last meeting.[41] Certain Right-wing newspapers imme-

---

[40] *Le Temps*, January 12, 1913; *Journal des Débats*, January 12, 1913.
[41] Poincaré, III, 45; *Le Temps*, January 13 and 14, 1913.

diately lashed out at Poincaré for "running after votes."[42] One asserted bitterly: "His own friends will vote for him, but will not defend him. He has sacrificed his companion at arms to a personal ambition."[43] The Poincarist press in general received the decision sullenly, but they were not ready to abandon him as a presidential candidate. Of the three paths that had been open before Poincaré the one which he selected probably cost him the smallest number of votes.[44]

THE REPUBLICAN CAUCUS

The du Paty de Clam squall had barely subsided when the legislature reconvened on January 14. Paul Deschanel and Antonin Dubost were re-elected to preside over the Chamber and the Senate, respectively. Each hoped for promotion to the Elysée within a week and therefore seized the opportunity to make a campaign speech from the rostrum. Deschanel's address

[42] *La Croix,* January 14 and 15, 1913; *L'Eclair,* January 13, 1913.

[43] *L'Autorité,* quoted in Fernand Gouttenoire de Toury, *Poincaré a-t-il voulu la guerre?* (Paris, 1920), p. 119.

[44] The du Paty de Clam incident remains something of a mystery. Millerand explained at the time that he considered the order a purely administrative, nonpolitical act. Poincaré disagreed sharply, and complained that he should have been notified beforehand (Poincaré, III, 42). Millerand also asserted that he was merely carrying out a promise made by his predecessor in 1911. This was the case; but Millerand failed to explain why he waited an entire year to reinstate du Paty and then chose such an embarrassing moment for it (cf. Gaston Doumergue in *La Grande Revue,* LXXVII [January 25, 1913], 419–21). At least one other minister, Steeg, knew late in December that the order was impending; but Steeg had said nothing to Poincaré, on the ground that it was not his affair (*Le Matin,* January 14, 1913; *Le Temps,* January 15, 1913). The most obvious explanation would be that Millerand wished to "torpedo" Poincaré's presidential campaign. But this fails to hold water, for Millerand was an old personal friend of the premier, continued to support him thereafter, and was one of the chief architects of Poincaré's success on January 17. It is possible that Millerand aimed to help the premier by rallying extreme Right votes (cf. Payen, *Poincaré,* p. 390). Certainly Right-wing journals applauded the order; and the rumor spread that Poincaré himself had engineered the whole affair to gain Right votes (*Le Gaulois,* January 11, 1913; *Le Figaro,* January 13, 1913).

of acceptance was climaxed by the statement that "Personal power has cost France too dear—(*Lively and repeated applause at the Left, extreme Left and Center*)—for us to be tempted to try it again."[45] Likewise in the Senate, Dubost made transparent remarks about the danger of one-man government.[46] Even Poincaré could recognize that these were veiled thrusts at his candidacy.[47] Ever since he had thrown his hat into the ring, the Radicals had been hinting that they feared eventual dictatorship. From all appearances, the electoral issue had come to be the question of increased presidential authority, with Poincaré regarded as the symbol of a change. This issue seemed all the more clear-cut when the Radicals chose as their candidate a virtual nonentity—"the amiable M. Pams, who could not by any stretch of the imagination be conceived to represent anything but cigarette paper."[48]

The time had now arrived for the republican caucus sponsored by the Left-wing groups. Although the Moderates continued to grumble about attempts to manipulate the election, most of them agreed to come. The Socialists, however, refused to attend, and named their own candidate.[49] Only 748 invitations were issued and 652 legislators actually attended, while at Versailles there would be a total of 897 eligible to cast ballots. Thus almost one-third of the National Assembly was absent from the caucus—a fact which could be of great importance.

[45] *Chamber Debates,* January 14, 1913, p. 5.

[46] *Senate Debates,* January 14, 1913, p. 4.

[47] He complained that he was "almost denounced as a future dictator" (Poincaré, III, 50–51).

[48] Lawrence Jerrold, "President Poincaré," *Contemporary Review,* CIII (February 1913), 181. Pams was a wealthy manufacturer of cigarette paper.

[49] *Le Temps,* January 15, 1913. The Socialist strategy was to attack both Radicals and Moderates indiscriminately. Their organ, *L'Humanité,* condemned "a presidency which would be simply a non-hereditary monarchy." As for the Radical ideal of "King Log," it scoffed: "I would prefer a dummy with a phonograph in its belly." *L'Humanité* concluded in favor of suppression of the presidency (January 9, 1913).

On January 15 the 652 met to select their nominee. While the vote was proceeding copies of an anonymous letter on official Chamber stationery began to circulate about the hall. This letter attacked Poincaré as an ally of the reactionaries, "corrupter of the French and foreign press, chief of neo-Boulangism."[50] So naïve a piece of propaganda had no effect except to increase bad blood. The first ballot found no one with a majority:[51]

	VOTES
Poincaré	180
Pams	174
Dubost	107
Deschanel	83
Ribot	52
Dupuy	22
Scattering	14

Although the caucus was an amorphous body without organization or chairman, everyone seemed to agree that a second vote should be taken. Maneuvers flew thick and fast during the brief interim. Dubost withdrew in favor of Pams, but his Senate group met and voted unanimously in favor of swinging to Poincaré.[52] Deschanel and Ribot both withdrew without conditions. A large group of deputies congregated in the main hall; noisy attacks on Poincaré and "seven years of Right ministries" were heard, with just as much noise from his defenders; but confusion was too great to reach any decision.[53]

[50] *Le Temps,* January 16, 1913; *Journal des Débats,* January 16, 1913.

[51] Gaston Jèze, "La présidence de la république," *Revue du Droit Public et de la Science Politique,* XXX (January 1913), 110; *Revue Politique et Parlementaire,* LXXV (February 1913), 397.

[52] *Le Temps,* January 17, 1913. According to one report, Dubost told his followers that Poincaré's candidacy represented dictatorship and could not be supported (*Le Figaro,* January 16, 1913).

[53] *Le Temps,* January 17, 1913. In *Le Matin* of January 16 Stéphane Lauzanne quoted Poincaré as declaring after the first ballot that he was determined to run at Versailles, no matter who should win in the caucus. Yet Poincaré proceeded to go through the motions of two more ballots as though their outcome were vital. Lauzanne's article was never denied.

Withdrawals had apparently left only two candidates in the race. Scattering votes, however, again prevented a majority, although the lead now shifted to Pams:

	VOTES
Pams	283
Poincaré	272
Ribot	23
Deschanel	22
Scattering	18

Here was a situation which embarrassed both sides. Following a precedent set in 1887, a third vote was arranged for the next day. Political maneuvers were redoubled; rumors flew of dark-horse candidates; Poincaré once more appealed to Léon Bourgeois without success.[54] Thus the tension during the final ballot was no more relaxed than on the previous day. The results were as follows:

	VOTES
Pams	323
Poincaré	309
Ribot	11
Delcassé	2
Deschanel	1

In 1887 a third indecisive ballot had resulted in simple adjournment to Versailles. But this time, in the din of the caucus room, someone discovered that Pams lacked but a single vote of an absolute majority. A disorderly meeting dominated by Radicals at last decided to send a delegation to Poincaré inviting his withdrawal on the basis of "republican discipline." This delegation included Combes, Clemenceau, Monis, Caillaux, Augagneur, and several others. Its composition showed clearly that the Radicals were simply trying to bluff Poincaré out of the way. Some of them, however, may have believed sincerely

[54] *Le Temps,* January 17, 1913; *Le Matin,* January 17, 1913; Poincaré, III, 51.

that Pams's vote was close enough to a majority to justify his selection.[55]

Arriving at Poincaré's office, the delegates made Clemenceau their spokesman. Clemenceau brusquely proposed that Poincaré withdraw in the name of the republican majority, since he could be elected the next day only by the votes of the extreme Right. Poincaré politely declined to become *le guillotiné par persuasion*. He observed that Pams was a member of his own cabinet, so that there could be no political difference involved in the contest. After several vain suggestions as to compromise candidates, the interview broke up in a rather charged atmosphere. Clemenceau flung at reporters who were hovering about the door: "What do you want? News of my health? It is excellent!"[56] The disappointed delegation returned to the Senate building, where it was awaited by some two hundred parliamentarians, mostly Radicals. This rump meeting proceeded to endorse Pams as the only republican nominee.[57]

Poincaré's excuses for maintaining his candidacy in spite of the caucus results were none too sound. In his defense it may be said that some republican deputies and senators were not present at the caucus, that his own total was not far short

---

[55] Cf. Jerrold (*loc. cit.*, p. 181), who wrote: "I suppose that in the game of politics no such amazing move has ever been played before. It was too extraordinary a one not to have been at least partly honest. M. Clemenceau honestly marched out as the champion of the Republic against Heaven knows what dark schemes for establishing 'personal power'."

[56] *Le Temps,* January 18, 1913. On this remarkable incident, see Poincaré, III, 53–54, and Jèze, *loc. cit.*, pp. 119–22. Monis proposed during the interview that both Pams and Poincaré withdraw, with the latter to choose a conciliation candidate; but neither Clemenceau nor Poincaré would agree. Poincaré objected that he had already tried to bring in Bourgeois for this purpose.

[57] Jèze, *loc. cit.*, p. 120; *Le Temps,* January 18, 1913; Poincaré, III, 56. An eruption occurred during this session when Clemenceau misconstrued a remark made by one of Poincaré's supporters. After rumors of a duel and an exchange of fiery notes, the whole affair was written off as a misunderstanding.

of Pams's, and that the Radicals were far from sincere in their
use of the caucus. But Poincaré was playing politics too. For
one thing he went solemnly through the motions of the caucus,
evidently expecting to become the sole republican candidate if
he should gain a majority. Yet in a note issued to the press that
night he declared that the vote had been meant to bind no one.[58]
He contended in the same note that discipline should have been
invoked after the first ballot if at all. But he failed to mention
that the first ballot produced a five-way split, while in the third
Pams lacked a single vote of having a clear majority. Finally
he argued that there could be no issue save one of personalities
between two members of the same cabinet. This begged the
real question; for the split in republican ranks meant that the
Right-wing extremists might hold the balance and determine
the victor. Poincaré had promised when he became premier in
1912 that he would act only with a true republican majority
back of his cabinet. He had thereby repudiated any support
which might be lukewarm toward the principles of the Revolution. But now he was faced by the necessity of accepting
royalist and clerical votes if he expected to gain the presidency.[59] Evidently Poincaré placed his desire for office higher
than the extremely rigid and uncompromising republicanism of
which he so often spoke.

JANUARY 17

Election day dawned in an atmosphere of uncertainty. Official Paris moved to Versailles early. Cards for admission to the
National Assembly had been exhausted a week before; 1,600
soldiers surrounded the palace, and more were held in reserve
to handle the expected crowds.[60] The time for maneuvers had

---

[58] *Le Temps*, January 18, 1913; Jèze, *loc. cit.*, p. 121.

[59] The correspondent of *The Times* was almost alone in observing this
flaw in Poincaré's argument (January 17, 1913).

[60] *Le Temps*, January 11 and 12, 1913.

passed; but "if Poincaré is elected," warned someone in Clemenceau's entourage, "we shall be back here in three months."[61]

The first ballot gave the following results:

	VOTES
Poincaré	429
Pams	327
Vaillant (Soc.)	63
Deschanel	18
Ribot	16
Scattering	14

Poincaré therefore barely lacked a majority; he had received 120 more votes than at the caucus, most of them coming from monarchists and ultraclerical republicans. Dubost, presiding, suggested that a recess might be called before the second ballot; this produced great disorder, for the Poincarists felt victory within their grasp and opposed granting the Radicals a respite to pull wires. Dubost was therefore forced to proceed at once to the second vote. Its result was conclusive:

	VOTES
Poincaré	483
Pams	296
Vaillant	69
Scattering	11

The announcement of Poincaré's total was greeted by "prolonged applause at the Left, Center, and Right, and acclamations.—Noise at the extreme Left and on some benches at the Right." The official report continued:

The President: M. Raymond Poincaré having obtained the absolute majority of votes . . . .

Voice at the Left: With the Right! (*Yes! yes! at the Right.*)

M. Brager de la Ville-Moysan [a Right-wing Senator]: Well, yes, we have elected him in spite of you!

The President: . . . . I proclaim him president of the French republic (*interruptions from some benches at the Left—protests and applause*) for seven years from the day when the mandate of the president

[61] B.-E. Gueydan, *Les rois de la république* (Paris, 1925), I, 235.

in office ends. (*Long applause—cries: "Long live the republic!"—a large part of the Assembly rises and acclaims the name of the president-elect.*)

M. *Brizon* [a Socialist deputy] : Down with the dictator! (*Exclamations and laughter from a large number of benches.*)

The President: The session of the National Assembly is closed . . . .[62]

Such was the commotion in which Poincaré reached his goal. His own feelings, as he described them years later, were not much quieter:

I had some trouble in hiding my emotion. I felt that the presidential irresponsibility was great with moral responsibility, and I was so dismayed by the burden which was going to weigh on my shoulders that all sentiment of satisfaction froze in me. I was completely dominated by the fear of being inferior to the new task which had devolved upon me.[63]

Poincaré's return to Paris was in the nature of a triumphal entry, with thousands of demonstrators massed at the station. It was in sharp contrast to earlier elections, when the president-elect had been ignored or else met by a hostile crowd.[64] Whether this interest was spontaneous or whipped up by the newspapers, it was certainly a novel experience for the Third Republic.

For the Paris press, the election was almost a personal success, and they did not hesitate to claim it as such.[65] Their victory chorus had a double theme: first, the triumph of public opinion; second, the significance of the election for the presidency itself. The people had chosen, ran the refrain. They had chosen not only a man but an idea. "The president of the republic must not be . . . . a sort of Asiatic divinity." "Let M. Poincaré do his duty, all his duty as head of the State . . . ." "The day of January 17, 1913, will mark not only the date of

[62] *Annales de l'assemblée nationale,* 1913, p. 6.

[63] Poincaré, III, 60.

[64] *Journal des Débats,* January 18, 1913.

[65] *Le Temps,* January 19, 1913; *Revue Politique et Parlementaire,* LXXV (February 1913), 189.

a death, but also that of a rebirth." *"Quelque chose finit, quelque chose commence. ..."*[66] Even Professor Gaston Jèze, a prominent French authority on constitutional law, made a cautious prediction:

The presidential election of January 17, 1913, apparently must mark an interesting date in the political history of France and of the presidency of the republic, both by the choice which has been made and by the intentions manifested by the new president-elect. From both points of view, there is something of a change. It may be, however, that the force of events will decide otherwise.[67]

Among the Left-wing organs *Le Radical* expressed a colorless confidence that Poincaré would uphold republican ideals.[68] Jaurès, the Socialist spokesman, was still more reserved: "We await M. Poincaré at work, without hostile prejudice, but with absolute independence."[69] Beneath this apparent unanimity, some observers did not fail to see signs of trouble. "Will it be a presidency of seven years or of seven months?" asked Ernest Judet in the conservative journal, *L'Eclair.* "Black clouds are gathering on all sides, both abroad and at home."[70] But Judet's

[66] *Le Temps,* January 19, 1913; *La Croix,* January 20, 1913; *La République Française,* January 18, 1913; Jacques Piou in *La Croix,* January 20, 1913.

[67] *Revue du Droit Public,* XXX (January 1913), 13.

[68] *Le Radical,* January 18, 1913.

[69] *L'Humanité,* January 18, 1913.

[70] *L'Eclair,* January 18, 1913. Judet described his newspaper as "absolutely independent." His editorial sympathies leaned toward clericalism and nationalism during this prewar period, but unlike most journalists of that stamp he was critical of Poincaré.

Certain British journalists also feared that the abnormal struggle of the past month might react against Poincaré. *The Times's* correspondent wrote (January 18, 1913): "There has been a good deal of political bitterness excited by this election, and it is feared that it means the beginning of a period of perilous agitation and discord in the political life of France." He predicted that Poincaré would try to be a "strong" president, but that the Radicals might make his efforts futile. Lawrence Jerrold (*Contemporary Review,* CIII, 179, 182) also doubted the advisability of all the congratulations which Poincaré was receiving: "The danger of the French political situation at the present moment is the tendency of some journalistic oracles

warning was lost in the tumult of rejoicing and predictions of a "renaissance."

THE ROLE OF RUSSIAN GOLD

The charge has sometimes been made that Poincaré's election was bought with Russian gold, used to bribe the Paris press.[71] It is a fact that the Russian government renewed its subsidies to the French newspapers late in 1912, after a lapse of several years. It is likewise certain that the important dailies carried on a pro-Poincaré campaign on a scale hitherto unknown during presidential elections. It is necessary to determine whether or not these two circumstances were interrelated.

Ambassador Izvolsky had been asking his government for a press fund ever since 1911, in order to keep French opinion favorable toward Russia. Not until October 1912 did St. Petersburg agree to appropriate 300,000 francs for the purpose. Izvolsky tried to give his superiors the impression that Premier Poincaré had approved his request for money. He carefully refrained, however, from making a positive statement

---

to make out that M. Poincaré really is at last the heaven-sent King Stork. . . . . There is no danger whatever that M. Poincaré will be really King Stork."

In general, however, the foreign press viewed Poincaré's victory as marking the end of presidential "effacement." *Le Temps* rightly observed (January 19, 1913): "If we did not know that this election . . . . marks, for many reasons, an important date in our history, the reading of foreign newspapers would inform us of it." According to the London *Saturday Review* (CXV [January 25, 1913], 104): "M. Poincaré intends to exercise as active a supervision as President of the Republic as he did as President of the Council. The actual constitution of the Ministry is a subordinate question as long as it does the work which the President of the Republic imposes upon it . . . ." On the Continent Italians alone expressed the hope that Poincaré was being "kicked upstairs" away from actual control. In every other capital it was believed that he would take his power with him to the Elysée.

[71] Harry Elmer Barnes, *The Genesis of the World War* (New York, 1929), pp. 117–18; William L. Langer in *The New Republic*, XLII (April 15, 1925), Supplement, p. 14.

that he had received such approval from the premier.[72] He had asked Poincaré's opinion but had apparently received a rather noncommittal answer.[73] The bribery campaign did not originate with the French cabinet but with the Russians themselves.

Kokovtsov, the Russian prime minister, was skeptical about the advantages of Izvolsky's plan. He sent a personal agent to interview Poincaré, declaring that the money would be used if Poincaré judged it "indispensable."[74] Poincaré informed the agent that the whole idea was Izvolsky's, that he could only advise very careful distribution of the money.[75] Because Kokovtsov was depending entirely on Poincaré's opinion, the latter really opened the way for the expenditure of the bribery fund when he failed to answer with a firm "No." Poincaré has excused himself by recalling that the appropriation had already been made, so that he could only try to delay and control its

[72] Izvolsky to Sazonov, October 25, 1912, in *"L'abominable vénalité de la presse," d'après les documents des archives russes* (Paris, 1931), pp. 327–29. (This collection of Russian documents was published by the communist editors of *L'Humanité*. Its title was borrowed from a dispatch of Artur Rafalovich, the Russian financial agent in Paris. For the sake of convenience, it will be cited hereafter as *Rafalovich*.) Izvolsky wrote: "I have reason to think that M. Poincaré considers it desirable that we have recourse to this method [bribery] . . . . From my interview with M. Poincaré I became convinced that he was ready to lend us his assistance in the present affair and to indicate to us the most suitable plan for distributing the subsidies. The person of Lenoir is apparently well known to him and he would probably have suggested to us [*il nous aurait probablement fait ressortir*] that his collaboration would be desirable. . . . . He was most grateful that I had discussed the present question confidentially with him, and added that he would himself have approached me to ask that I undertake nothing without a prior agreement with him." The use of the conditional verb, along with such phrases as "I have reason to think," "I became convinced," and "apparently," seems to indicate that Izvolsky was trying to twist Poincaré's words to suit his own purposes. This interpretation has been given by Poincaré in his memoirs.

[73] Poincaré, III, 98.

[74] Kokovtsov to Poincaré, October 30, 1912, *Rafalovich*, pp. 332–33.

[75] Poincaré, III, 99, 106–7; Kokovtsov to Sazonov, December 3, 1912 (Old Style), *Rafalovich*, p. 351.

use.[76] But he gave Kokovtsov's agent the impression that he considered the press fund a desirable thing to have on hand.[77]

Poincaré left it to Klotz, his minister of finance, and Lenoir, a somewhat mysterious publicity agent, to collaborate in handling the funds. This pair demanded and secured full control of distributing the money.[78] Before long this French control became so obvious that the Russian government complained to Izvolsky; it feared that thousands of rubles were being spent for the benefit of a French political faction rather than for Russian interests.[79] Izvolsky, much aggrieved, admitted that Klotz and Lenoir had acquired full charge of passing out the funds. But he pointed out that, *in connection with the presidential election*, certain newspapers had been spreading the idea that French foreign policy was becoming too subservient to Russia. In Izvolsky's opinion Klotz knew where the money should go to check this press campaign, and so the latter's control of the purse strings was justified.[80] In other words, the way to defend Russian interests was to suppress criticism of the Poincaré cabinet. And this criticism had begun, according to Izvolsky, with the aim of keeping Poincaré out of the Elysée. In a roundabout manner the "Poincaré-for-president" campaign thus became a secondary and incidental object of the Russian press subsidy.[81]

Poincaré has declared that he knew nothing of how the

[76] Poincaré, III, 106–7.

[77] Davidov to Kokovtsov, November 11, 1912, *Rafalovich*, p. 336.

[78] Rafalovich to Davidov, December 11, 1912, *ibid.*, pp. 345–46.

[79] Kokovtsov to Sazonov, December 16, 1912, *Iswolski*, II, 391–94; Rafalovich to Izvolsky, December 24, 1912, *ibid.*, pp. 404–5.

[80] Izvolsky to Sazonov, February 14, 1913, *Iswolski*, III, 63–65.

[81] Most of the Russian gold was eventually spent for such incidental purposes. Accounting later for the use of the first 100,000 francs, Financial Adviser Rafalovich reported that they were "used especially from the parliamentary point of view and for internal politics. They have served to prevent attacks and unfavorable interpretations" (Rafalovich to N——, November 6, 1913, *Rafalovich*, pp. 393–94).

funds were used in 1912 and 1913.[82] It seems unlikely that Klotz, his own minister of finance, would have kept him in the dark. This point is of no great importance, however, in view of the fact that only 25,000 francs were spent before the presidential election. Even though the money went to journals with "parliamentary and political importance," it was far too meager to have any appreciable effect. If further proof is needed there is the fact that all the money went to organs of the Radicals, among whom Poincaré gained very few votes.[83] His real support came from the "great press"—Center or Right newspapers of wide circulation. They needed no subsidy to sponsor his campaign. It is a mistake to assume that Poincaré's election was bought with Russian gold.

THE ALLEGED CONSPIRACY OF REACTION

Poincaré has been repeatedly accused of selling himself to the religious reactionaries in order to gain election to the presidency.[84] His enemies have observed, correctly, that he received the votes of most anti-republican legislators and of those who wished to broaden the privileges of the Catholic Church. The critics have also recalled that during 1912 Poincaré had loudly refused any support for his cabinet except that of irreproachable republicans. The charge is based on sufficient circumstantial evidence to bear investigating.

The question involves the delicate subject of Poincaré's marriage. No sooner had his candidacy become imminent than rumors began to circulate about his wife. They were always

---

[82] Poincaré, III, 103.

[83] Rafalovich to N———, November 6, 1913, *Rafalovich*, p. 394.

[84] Victor Margueritte, *Les criminels* (Paris, 1925), p. 157; Gustave Dupin, *M. Poincaré et la guerre de 1914* (Paris, 1935), p. 42; Edward von Schoen, *The Memoirs of an Ambassador* (London, 1922), p. 160; Roger Mennevée, "La réaction maîtresse des destinées de la France," *Les Documents Politiques . . . . ,* October 1933, p. 500.

elusive, never appearing in print except in the form of veiled hints. The least impertinent and most important rumor had to do with the fact that Madame Poincaré had been twice married and once divorced before she married Poincaré. Furthermore, her third marriage had been a civil and not a religious ceremony.

In a Catholic country such facts had their significance. The Catholics had become resigned to accepting anticlericals as presidents, but the question of civil marriage was more serious. Leftists saw their opening and suggested audibly that no true Catholic could vote for Poincaré.[85] The latter therefore called in Albert de Mun, leader of the Catholics in the Chamber, M. Simond, editor of the conservative *Echo de Paris,* and Arthur Meyer, editor of the royalist *Gaulois.* He informed them that he had resorted to civil marriage because Madame Poincaré was not sure whether or not her divorced husband was still living. The three men considered this explanation satisfactory to good Catholics; their influence prevented any of the clericals from abandoning Poincaré in the election which followed.[86]

Three months after the presidential election, the Poincarés went through the ritual of a church marriage. All the witnesses swore absolute secrecy, and kept their word so well that no one learned of it until after the war. When the news leaked out, it furnished anti-Poincarists with what seemed to be a damning piece of evidence: Poincaré, a firm republican, had reached the Elysée with the aid of clerical votes; soon after, he had secretly gone through a religious ceremony; ergo, there must have

---

[85] The daily *L'Eclair* carried on a contest entitled, "Who will be *la présidente?*" It denied (January 3, 1913) that the question lacked importance: "It touches the very depths of the parliamentary election of the head of the state." The implication was obvious. For the effect of the slander on Poincaré, see Benoist, *Souvenirs,* III, 183.

[86] The story finally came to light in 1936 when Payen (*Poincaré,* p. 389) published his semiofficial study of Poincaré's career up to 1913. One of Poincaré's bitterest critics had revived the controversy in 1934 by printing the official *état-civil* of Madame Poincaré (Roger Mennevée, "Le mariage de M. Poincaré," *Les Documents Politiques* ... , October 1934, p. 510).

been a mutual agreement. But this argument, too, has been answered. Just after the election of 1913 Madame Poincaré received evidence of her first husband's death. The single obstacle to a church marriage was thereby removed.[87]

For the accusations that Poincaré bought clerical votes by promising to restore diplomatic relations with the Vatican, by sponsoring the return of the religious congregations to France, or by adopting a general policy of blind reaction, absolutely no proof has been advanced. His political principles remained what they had always been, rigidly nationalist and ultrapatriotic. This alone had been enough to win him the support of the Right, without any necessity for plots and promises. His anticlericalism was no obstacle, for every other candidate was just as bad from the Catholic point of view.

Although Poincaré was not involved in any reactionary "conspiracy," he did place himself in an embarrassing position by accepting Rightist votes. These men hoped for, if they did not actually expect, some repayment. They could remind him of past services when exerting pressure at the Elysée. Poincaré must have realized this, especially in view of a letter which de Mun wrote to him just before the election. De Mun demanded frankly that the Radicals be kept out of power for seven years:

> Tomorrow, master of the supreme power, armed with all the prerogatives which it permits, can you ever allow the destinies of the country to fall back into their hands . . . . ? Is not this preservation of the national interest the foundation of the patriotic pact which unites us, in spite of all dissent? . . . . If you are elected, as I hope, a magnificent task awaits you. You can be the savior of the country by snatching it from the hands that are rending it.[88]

De Mun obviously hoped that Poincaré would become a quasidictator in certain circumstances. This does not prove that

[87] Payen, *Poincaré,* pp. 406–7.

[88] *Ibid.,* p. 389. Cf. de Mun's article in *L'Echo de Paris,* January 18, 1913.

Poincaré adopted the doctrines of those men whose votes he accepted. The fact remains, however, that he spoke no word which would tend to destroy their illusions. Evidently his ambition had become stronger than his frankness. Men like de Mun felt justified, therefore, in pinning their faith on Poincaré. And their attitude gave substance to the suspicions of the Left—suspicions which proved to be stumbling blocks when Poincaré entered the Elysée.

CHAPTER IV

THE ERA OF MODERATE CABINETS

"NEITHER BIRD NOR MOUSE"

President-elect Poincaré had to wait a month and a day before his inauguration. His position during the period was somewhat anomalous. In his own phrase, he was neither bird nor mouse. Should he continue to function as premier, or should he begin at once to demean himself as an irresponsible president? No precedent could be found, for never before had a premier's term been cut short by elevation to the Elysée. There was no constitutional reason why the Poincaré ministry should not have continued in power until the day of the inauguration. Nevertheless, he decided to resign at once; for a cabinet crisis during the interim would have made his accession to the presidency most awkward.

The outgoing ministry left office because of an excess of confidence, so to speak. It was to be expected, therefore, that its successor would resemble it in membership and policies. It was natural, too, that President Fallières should consult with Poincaré before he selected Aristide Briand as the new premier. But custom indicated that Poincaré and Fallières should stop

---

[1] In a number of instances during the Third Republic presidents had used their influence to bring men into the cabinet. Thus Faure put pressure on Hanotaux to accept the portfolio of foreign affairs (Gabriel Hanotaux, "Jules Méline," *Revue des Deux Mondes*, January 15, 1926, p. 449); and Grévy likewise urged Goblet in 1886 (René Goblet, "Souvenirs de ma vie politique," *Revue Politique et Parlementaire*, CXLI [October 10, 1929], 10). Conversely, presidents had at times maneuvered to exclude certain politicians from ministerial posts (Joseph van Tichelen, *Le président de la république et le problème de l'état* [Liège, 1939], p. 337). But such interference was definitely the exception rather than the rule, even during Grévy's term.

there, leaving the actual construction of the cabinet to Briand.[1] It is true, of course, that presidents-elect were rare birds whose habits were not regulated by any well-established usage. In the eyes of the public, however, Poincaré was more than a president-elect; he was already regarded as the heir apparent and the de facto head of the state instead of Fallières.[2] His resignation of the premiership seemed to suggest that he chose to identify himself with the presidency henceforth. Therefore his immediate attitude was likely to be taken as a foretaste of the seven years to come.

Poincaré's acts showed at once his disregard of custom. He kept in touch with every move in the formation of the cabinet, consulting with Briand several times between January 19 and 21.[3] When Briand had difficulty in finding a foreign minister, Poincaré influenced Charles Jonnart to accept this portfolio. Jonnart was a colorless figure without experience in foreign affairs; he announced that he had accepted only because Poincaré promised his "close collaboration" until inauguration day and his advice thereafter. This collaboration, according to *Le Matin,* would take the form of daily conferences.[4] There was nothing remotely unconstitutional about all this; Briand and Jonnart had a perfect right to seek advice from any citizen. But the conduct of the president-elect did suggest the arrival

[2] *Le Correspondant,* CCL (January 25, 1913), 408.

[3] *Le Temps,* January 20–22, 1913; *Le Matin,* January 21, 1913.

[4] *Le Matin,* January 21 and 22, 1913; *Le Temps,* January 22, 1913; Gaston Jèze, "La présidence de la république," *Revue du Droit Public,* XXX (February 1913), 123–24. Anti-Poincarists charged then and later that the president intended Jonnart to be a straw man. They called him "M. Poincaré's phonograph," and even asserted that Poincaré wrote the letters which Jonnart signed during the pre-inaugural period (Judet, *Louis,* pp. 207, 212). Georges Suarez, on the other hand, believes that it was Briand who chose Jonnart and used him as a straw man (Georges Suarez, *Briand, sa vie, son œuvre* [Paris, 1938–39], II, 406). Although Jonnart was not a strong and independent statesman, it is not so certain that he was chosen for ulterior motives. After all, the Moderates had very few men available with experience at the Quai d'Orsay.

of a new spirit. It meant, too, that Jonnart would be inoculated with the Poincaré viewpoint in foreign policy.

Poincaré never admitted, either at the time or subsequently, that he wished to broaden the presidency. In his memoirs he has gone to the other extreme, steadily minimizing the extent of his activity during the pre-inaugural month. He has barely mentioned his part in the formation of the Briand cabinet and his relations with Jonnart. He has indignantly denied the false story that he presided at ministerial councils during this period.[5] At the same time he has neglected to mention certain informal sessions of the cabinet which he did attend.[6] Moreover, the ministers must have realized that Jonnart was really presenting Poincaré's ideas on foreign policy in council. In his later recollections Poincaré wrote: "I was more and more engrossed with receptions, dinners, ceremonies of all sorts, in which I saw with dismay the introduction to my new destiny."[7] This was undoubtedly the case. But there were other indications during the interim period which led close observers to predict a more active presidency henceforth.[8]

Poincaré's enemies of the Left suspected that he had authoritarian dreams, but they could scrape together little proof. Not until after the war did evidence appear which seemed to furnish some justification for their fears of 1913. This was the correspondence of Alexander Izvolsky, published by the Soviet government. In a dispatch of January 29, 1913, the Russian ambassador reported: "I have just had a long conversation with Poincaré, who told me that in his capacity as president of the republic, he would be fully able to exert direct influence upon the foreign policy of France . . . ."[9]

---

[5] Poincaré, III, 70–74, 115.

[6] Jèze, *Revue du Droit Public,* XXX, 124.

[7] Poincaré, III, 85.

[8] Jèze, *Revue du Droit Public,* XXX, 125; *L'Opinion,* VI (January 25, 1913), 99.

[9] Izvolsky to Sazonov, January 29, 1913, *Livre noir,* II, 14–15.

When this dispatch came to the attention of Poincaré, he immediately accused Izvolsky of exaggeration and untruth in reporting his words.[10] Izvolsky was dead by this time; but his Austrian colleague, Szécsen, unwittingly came to his aid. The publication of the Austrian diplomatic documents revealed that Ambassador Szécsen had written to Vienna in words very much like those of Izvolsky:

> Unlike his predecessors, who occupied themselves only with the representative duties of the presidency, M. Poincaré will strive to exert a decided personal influence on the external and internal policy of this country. Several weeks ago, when I spoke to him confidentially of the possibility of his election and expressed my regret that in case of his call to the presidential chair I could no longer remain in direct business communication with him, he said: "Don't worry about that, I will see to it that a man takes my place who will carry out my policy. It will be as though I were still at the Quai d'Orsay."[11]

Unless two ambassadors misunderstood him in the same way, it would seem that Poincaré planned to break with past practice. He had in mind no dictatorship of any kind, but only a strengthening of presidential influence.

Poincaré must have been encouraged to enter upon such a path by the apparent pressure of public opinion.[12] The editors

[10] Poincaré, III, 94–95.

[11] Szécsen dispatch, January 19, 1913, *Austrian Docs.,* V, 493–94.

[12] Poincaré's remarkable popularity during this interim period was indicated in a dispatch of the Belgian ambassador: "M. Poincaré is the daily object of manifestations of sympathy; he is offered banquet upon banquet; his praise is sung in ditties at the street-corners; and in all the *cafés-concerts* and cinemas the appearance of his picture and the mention of his name bring applause . . . ." (Guillaume to Davignon, February 14, 1913, *Die Belgischen Dokumente zur Vorgeschichte des Weltkrieges 1885–1914,* 1 Ergänzungsband, p. 267—this will be cited hereafter as *Belgian Docs.*). His enemies retaliated by selling a song of their own in the streets:

> J'suis le président sans manières
> Qui veut devenir populaire.
> Dès aujourd'hui, je l'dis sans hésiter,
> Je n'veux plus être un machine à signer.
> Ça va paraître étrange
> Il va falloir que tout change . . . .

> *L'Humanité,* February 3, 1913

of the "great press," who claimed the credit for his victory, made it plain that they expected him to govern as well as reign. Even the extreme Right did not hesitate to demand a quid pro quo for its support. The royalist *Action Française* called his election "an imperative mandate . . . . to apply, *at last,* the constitution."[13] *Le Gaulois* urged him: "Re-establish the principle of authority, re-establish it to your own advantage, be acclaimed. The country will get the habit and will not lose it again."[14] The clerical leader, Albert de Mun, called on Poincaré to exert all his influence in council meetings and to ignore "party fluctuations" in the selection of ministers.[15]

The anti-constitutional flavor of suggestions like that of de Mun aroused the hostility of the Left. "Let him receive the applause and the enthusiasm with a certain mistrust," warned Jaurès.[16] *Le Radical* demanded that Poincaré reply to the "insulting hope" placed in him by the conservatives.[17] Senator Doumergue asserted his belief that the extreme Right's "burning sympathy" for Poincaré was merely an attempt to sow discord among good republicans.[18] Nor were the Radicals much encouraged by the list of Briand's ministers, for it included no one who had voted against Poincaré at Versailles.

Poincaré was doubtless aware of these warnings, but he was more likely to be influenced by the opinions of those who had elected him. The continual talk about presidential revival in the "great press" created a psychological atmosphere which he could not entirely escape. Enveloped in this atmosphere, Poincaré prepared to take up his new task.

---

[13] *L'Action Française,* January 23, 1913.

[14] *Le Gaulois,* January 27, 1913. The Right-wing Senator Jénouvrier maintained openly that "we were really the masters of the election . . . ." (*Le Gaulois,* February 3, 1913). Cf. also *La Croix,* January 20, 24, and 27, 1913.

[15] *L'Echo de Paris,* January 18, 1913.

[16] *L'Humanité,* February 17, 1913.

[17] *Le Radical,* January 21 and 29, 1913.

[18] *La Grande Revue,* February 25, 1913, p. 863.

THE INAUGURATION

Poincaré's popularity reached a peak on February 18, the day of his accession to the presidency. Despite bitter cold weather, Parisians turned out in large numbers to view the ceremony at the Hôtel de Ville. This drew the mockery of Jaurès: "Since Louis XVI, it appears, no such reception had been given to the head of the state—it is true that this did Louis no good."[19] But jibes were few and plaudits many. Paul Leroy-Beaulieu, professor at the Collège de France, called his inaugural "a sort of apotheosis," and perorated: "In the forty-two years that the republic has existed in France, such a burst of confidence and hope around the head of the government has never been seen . . . ."[20] The French diplomat, Auguste Gérard, recalled later that "his entry into the Elysée took place in the most powerful surge of popularity that this country had known since the great days of . . . . Gambetta."[21] The only dissent was expressed by the royalist journal L'Action Française, which called the crowd "lukewarm."[22]

The French equivalent of an inaugural address was the president's message to the Chambers on February 20. After pledging himself to defend the constitution, Poincaré launched into more interesting statements:

. . . . The reduction of the executive power is the wish of neither the chambers nor the country . . . . During all my magistracy, I will see, in accord with the responsible ministers, that the government of the republic maintains intact, under the control of parliament, the authority which it must have.

[19] L'Humanité, February 18, 1913.

[20] Leroy-Beaulieu, "La nouvelle présidence," L'Economiste Française, February 22, 1913, p. 257. Similar statements appeared in: Le Correspondant, CCL (February 25, 1913), 320; Journal des Débats, February 20, 1913; Le Temps, February 20, 1913; Le Figaro, February 17, 1913; Le Gaulois, February 19, 1913. See Bertie to Grey, February 19, 1913, British Docs., X, Part II, pp. 674–75.

[21] Gérard, Mémoires, p. 453.

[22] L'Action Française, February 19, 1913. Editor Charles Maurras some-

He mentioned the need for certain domestic reforms, including the introduction of proportional representation, and then continued: "It is possible for a people to be effectively pacific only on condition that they are always ready for war. A diminished France, a France exposed through her own fault to challenges or humiliations, would no longer be France." In conclusion, he called for any sacrifice to strengthen the army and navy.[23]

The message left a somewhat sibylline impression. Its wording was such that each listener could discover his own implications. Thus *Le Radical* felt able to praise it without reserve, while Jaurès called it "moderate in tone and rather colorless."[24] The press of the Center and that of the Right preferred to regard the message as a manifesto forecasting a "new era," or as "the complete program of a strong government."[25] Gaston Calmette in the conservative *Figaro* applauded "the affirmations which it contains concerning the active role of a president of the republic . . . ." Another conservative newspaper, *La Libre Parole,* went so far as to urge that Poincaré use the message power freely henceforth, to address the country over the heads of the legislature.[26] A few journals saw nothing very striking in the message but felt that it "left a place for acts."[27]

Although it was full of qualifying phrases, Poincaré's first state paper did carry echoes of the strong-presidency campaign. His promise to maintain the executive power intact could have had no other implication; for it was in no danger of being

what resented Poincaré's success in capturing many potential followers of Maurras' own ultranationalist movement.

[23] *Chamber Debates,* February 20, 1913, pp. 601–2.

[24] *Le Radical,* February 21, 1913; *L'Humanité,* February 21, 1913.

[25] Citations from many secondary journals appeared in *Le Figaro,* February 21, 1913.

[26] *Le Figaro,* February 21, 1913; cf. *L'Intransigeant,* February 22, 1913; *Le Temps,* February 20, 1913; *L'Echo de Paris,* February 21, 1913; *Saturday Review,* CXV (February 22, 1913), 222–23.

[27] *Le Correspondant,* CCL (February 23, 1913), 821; *The Statist* (London), February 22, 1913, pp. 350–51.

further reduced. In addition, his outspoken declarations in favor of electoral reform and military preparedness were unusual for a president to make; they formed what might almost be called a definite presidential platform. It was clearly stated and understood that the constitution would not be violated in carrying out this platform. But for the new president to present himself as the champion of a certain program, promising meanwhile to maintain intact all the prerogatives of the executive, was something which France had not seen since the days of MacMahon and Casimir-Périer.

THE CASE OF GEORGES LOUIS

Three days after Raymond Poincaré entered the Elysée he placed his signature on a decree for the first time. It provided for the recall of Georges Louis, French ambassador to Russia, and his replacement by the Germanophobe Théophile Delcassé. Few of Poincaré's presidential acts have led to more controversy than this, his first.

The replacement of Louis did not come out of a clear sky. Almost a year earlier, Izvolsky and Foreign Minister Sazonov had begun to complain of Louis in their official correspondence. They criticized him somewhat vaguely for inaccuracy in reporting conversations and for hostility toward Sazonov. Izvolsky finally asked Poincaré, then premier, to replace Louis; and the French government agreed in May 1912 to do so.[28] But the ambassador, showing unexpected spirit, at once asked and received permission to visit Paris in order to defend himself. He did this so well that the French cabinet reversed itself and sent him back to his post.

When Poincaré made an official visit to St. Petersburg in August 1912, he discussed the Louis question with Sazonov,

[28] Poincaré, I, 369. Rumors of Louis's replacement appeared in the press at the time, but they were denied. As late as 1920 Poincaré continued to conceal the fact that his government had decided to recall Louis. Instead, Poincaré declared that he had considered the charges against Louis unjustified, and had therefore defended him (Poincaré in *Le Matin*, December 20, 1920).

Prime Minister Kokovtsov, and the Tsar. Sazonov alone confessed to any grievances against the French ambassador, and his were not very well founded. Although Poincaré defended Louis against some of the accusations, he realized that henceforth there could be no real confidence between Sazonov and Louis. He suggested that both Izvolsky and Louis be recalled simultaneously, but this did not please the Russians.[29] The matter was finally dropped, with an understanding that Louis should be replaced "eventually."[30] For a time thereafter, Sazonov made an effort to get along with the ambassador, but by the end of 1912 their relations had again deteriorated.[31]

Thus the idea of Georges Louis's replacement originated with Sazonov and not with Poincaré. The latter did not bind himself to name a new ambassador, but he was aware of the existing friction which prevented smooth co-operation between France and Russia. It was this situation, and not any basic difference of opinion between him and Louis, which made Poincaré ready to recall the ambassador if the opportunity should arise.[32]

On February 17, 1913, the day before Poincaré's inauguration, Foreign Minister Jonnart ordered Louis to return from his post. Jonnart gave as his reason the state of Louis's health; but this was a plain subterfuge.[33] After the war Poincaré of-

[29] Count Kokovtsov, *Out of My Past* (Stanford University Press, 1935), p. 334.

[30] Sazonov to the Tsar, August 4, 1912 (Old Style), *Livre noir*, II, 345.

[31] Kokovtsov, *op. cit.*, p. 360.

[32] Ernest Judet (*Georges Louis*) and F. Gouttenoire de Toury (*Poincaré a-t-il voulu la guerre?*) have argued that Louis was removed because he tried to block the "warlike designs" of the French and Russian governments. Louis's dispatches in the French published documents show no evidence of serious difference of opinion between him and Poincaré. Both men were suspicious of Russian activities; both believed, nevertheless, that France would have to aid Russia in any crisis, in order to avert German domination of Europe (e.g., Louis to Poincaré, April 10, 1912, *D.D.F.*, II, 326–27).

[33] A dispatch from Buchanan, British ambassador to Russia, confirmed Louis's own insistence that his health was quite normal (Buchanan to Grey, February 19, 1913, *British Docs.*, IX, Part II, p. 508).

fered as a second reason the fact that Louis had avoided attendance at social functions important from the diplomatic point of view.[34] Yet he was replaced by Delcassé—a man of bourgeois habits, who avoided Russian night life by retiring regularly at ten o'clock.[35] As a matter of fact there were valid reasons for a change at the St. Petersburg embassy. It was a strange commentary on Poincaré's sincerity that he continued to use the old prewar excuses and even thought up new ones.[36]

More important for present purposes is the question of Poincaré's personal share in the recall of Louis. His contemporaries gave him full credit for the act, and considered it deeply significant: "M. Poincaré's first gesture is singularly eloquent," declared *La Croix*.[37] "There we have an act," wrote the editor of *Le Gaulois* enthusiastically. "It preceded words; its whole significance lies in that fact."[38] *L'Echo de Paris* called it a worthy inauguration of the president's "beneficent activity."[39] Diplomats in Paris and abroad and the press in most European capitals all accepted it as striking evidence that Poincaré would continue to show initiative at the Elysée.[40] Jaurès alone expressed doubt that Poincaré intended this act to mark out the direction of his presidency. None the less, Jaurès warned that if Delcassé's intrigues in Russia should

[34] *Chamber Debates,* July 6, 1922, p. 758.

[35] Porter, *Delcassé,* p. 314. Cf. Czernin dispatch, January 17, 1914, *Austrian Docs.,* VII, 737.

[36] In *Le Matin* for December 20, 1920, Poincaré maintained the old explanation that Louis's poor health led to his recall.

[37] *La Croix,* February 21, 1913.

[38] *Le Gaulois,* February 21, 1913.

[39] *L'Echo de Paris,* February 21, 1913.

[40] European newspapers were quoted in *Le Temps,* February 22, 1913; *Le Figaro,* for February 22, 1913, summarized the reports of its foreign correspondents. Cf. also: Dumaine to Jonnart, February 21, 1913, *D.D.F.,* V, 525–27; Buchanan to Grey, February 19, 1913, *British Docs.,* IX, Part II, p. 506; Buchanan to Nicolson, February 20, 1913, *ibid.,* p. 521; Szécsen dispatch, February 21, 1913, *Austrian Docs.,* V, 786; Guillaume to Davignon, February 21, 1913, *Belgian Docs.,* pp. 271–73.

bring on a crisis the responsibility would rest on Poincaré's head.[41]

It would seem reasonable enough to assume, as contemporaries did, that Poincaré engineered this change; but he has emphatically denied it. According to him, Briand and Jonnart alone conceived the idea of sending Delcassé to Russia; they merely spoke to Poincaré about it, as they spoke to many others. Moreover, they took the decision at the last council session over which Fallières presided, so that Poincaré merely signed the already adopted decree when he reached office.[42]

Poincaré's reasoning bore the marks of his legal training. This was only one of many times when he emphasized the letter and ignored the spirit of circumstances. Technically, every item of his self-defense was true: he acted as a signing-machine, nothing more. But other things lay behind the replacement of Georges Louis.

To begin with, Poincaré knew since his recent journey to St. Petersburg that Sazonov and Louis were at odds. His purpose was to strengthen the Franco-Russian alliance, and he knew that this could not be achieved so long as there was personal friction between the two men. He had agreed in August that Louis should be replaced "eventually." Poincaré alone knew all the details of the affair; he alone had talked with the Russian officials, had conducted the negotiations of the past year. He could hardly expect anyone to believe that he stepped out of contact with the government after January 17 and left the decision to ministers who had just entered office.

As proof that it was Jonnart's act alone, Poincaré has cited a note which he received from Jonnart later, stating his reasons for taking the step.[43] Jonnart declared in this note that until he became foreign minister he had heard nothing but good about Georges Louis. "But," he continued, "upon my arrival at the Quai d'Orsay I was informed that for several months

---

[41] *L'Humanité,* February 21, 1913.

[42] Poincaré, III, 115.   [43] *Ibid.,* pp. 116–18.

our ambassador in Russia had no longer shown the activity which the circumstances required." Perhaps it was the permanent officials at the Quai d'Orsay who so informed him. But such information was far more likely to come from Poincaré, who knew at first hand the implications of the question and who was Jonnart's adviser during the apprenticeship of the latter in foreign affairs. The new cabinet had been chosen to follow the policies of the old; therefore Jonnart would not have undertaken an important change without Poincaré's sanction.[44]

Finally, Poincaré followed an unusual procedure when he gave Delcassé a personal letter addressed to the Tsar. This letter described the appointment as an effort to strengthen the alliance; it also gave Delcassé a special mission to discuss the problem of strategic military railways in Russia.[45] Such use of a personal message made it appear almost as though Delcassé was to be considered a presidential agent, to carry out the policies outlined during Poincaré's 1912 journey to Russia.[46]

There is no clinching proof of primary responsibility for the recall of Georges Louis. The available evidence points

[44] In private conversations at the time, the president was less unwilling to accept responsibility. Ambassador von Schoen quoted Poincaré as saying frankly that he had taken the decision to name Delcassé (Schoen to Bethmann, February 22, 1913, *G.P.*, XXXIX, 160–62). Naturally, Jonnart never admitted that anyone influenced his act (e.g., Bertie to Grey, February 17, 1913, *British Docs.*, IX, Part II, pp. 506–7). Judet, in attempting to prove that Poincaré was responsible for the removal of Louis, has used newspaper evidence. An article in a Russian journal of February 22, 1912, purporting to be an interview with a friend of Delcassé, told how Delcassé refused Jonnart's offer of the Russian post. Poincaré and Briand had to intervene on February 8, using the argument of patriotic duty, to convert Delcassé (Judet, *Louis*, pp. 205–6; cf. *L'Echo de Paris*, February 21, 1913). The authenticity of this story cannot be checked, but it does not contradict any of the facts known to be true. Even if it were false, however, Poincaré could still have exercised his influence through Jonnart.

[45] Poincaré to Nicholas II, March 20, 1913, *D.D.F.*, VI, 62–63.

[46] At his first interview with the Russian minister of war, Delcassé stressed the topics "which the president of the republic had more particularly called to my attention" (Delcassé to Pichon, March 26, 1913, *D.D.F.*, VI, 94).

toward Poincaré, in spite of his denials. During the six weeks preceding Louis's recall, Poincaré had been accused of desiring to make the presidency a controlling force. If he disliked this implication, if he sincerely meant to sink back into the ordinary presidential rut, he would not have permitted his first official act to be such a striking one. Poincaré knew enough about politics to realize what the nomination of Delcassé, coincident with his own inauguration, would mean in the minds of Frenchmen. He must have foreseen also the agitation and anger in Berlin and Vienna, the "lively satisfaction" in Russia and Serbia.[47] To take such a resounding step on the morrow of his inauguration was to draw European attention to the French presidency. So experienced a statesman would not have permitted a coincidence of this kind without having weighed the effects.

In short, Poincaré apparently was not averse to being considered a "different" sort of president. That impression was created by an event which Poincaré could easily have prevented or delayed, in view of his paramount influence at the time. As to how "different" he would be, the succeeding months alone could show; but neither the hopes nor the fears of French political factions were lessened by the recall of Georges Louis.[48]

THE FIRST CABINET CRISIS

The ministry of Aristide Briand, formed on the morrow of the presidential election, was in fact the Poincaré cabinet under a new leader. Delcassé and Pams were almost the only prominent figures who were replaced. This continuity was un-

[47] Dumaine to Jonnart, February 21, 1913, *D.D.F.*, V, 325–27; Girard to Jonnart, February 25, 1913, *ibid.*, pp. 332–33; Descos to Jonnart, February 23 and 25, 1913, *ibid.*, pp. 535, 636–57.

[48] It was whispered about at the time that Delcassé had been sent to Russia by his political rivals (Briand, Poincaré, and others), who wanted to get him out of the Chamber (*Carnets de Louis,* II, 218; Dumaine to Jonnart, February 21, 1913, *D.D.F.*, V, 526; *L'Eclair,* February 21, 1913). This was probably a Paris political canard of the garden variety.

derstandable, for Poincaré had not lost the confidence of the Chambers. Some pretended to believe, however, that its composition was a reward to the Poincaré supporters at Versailles, or that it signified the concentration of all power in a little group which centered around the new president. In the Chamber, the Radical deputy Franklin-Bouillon charged that the ministry had been created by the Right, and added: "No one will contest the fact that here all the 'great electors' of yesterday are recompensed."[49] Jaurès also pointed out that all the ministers had voted for Poincaré at Versailles.[50] The exclusion of Pams may seem to lend plausibility to the Left's suspicions; but Pams had resigned his portfolio of his own accord. No one took the objection very seriously, for the Chamber gave Briand a convincing majority of 324 to 77. There is no reason to suppose that the continuance of the ministers in office was a reward for their support at Versailles. The worst that one can say is that Poincaré, who prided himself on being "president of all the French," accepted a ministry without any Left-wing representatives. He missed a golden opportunity to make a gesture of conciliation.

Still, the fact that the Briand cabinet was unanimously Poincarist (having, in fact, been selected with his aid) left the president more open to attack than might otherwise have been the case. The relationship between ministry and president meant that any onslaught on the cabinet would touch Poincaré as well. The president had increased his vulnerability by his inaugural message, in which he had come out frankly in favor of electoral and military reform. Observers pointed out, therefore, that a vote repudiating the cabinet on one of these two issues might bring a presidential crisis.[51] Poincaré's enemies continually alluded to him as the motive power behind the cabinet. The campaign was led by Clemenceau in his new daily

[49] *Chamber Debates,* January 24, 1913, pp. 38, 40.
[50] *Ibid.,* p. 43.
[51] Gueydan, *Les rois de la république,* I, 259.

L'Homme Libre, which was said to have been founded for this express purpose.[52]

In spite of the rousing vote of confidence given to Briand on his first appearance in the Chamber, and in spite of his arrival in office on the crest of the Poincaré popularity wave, barely six weeks passed before his downfall. Briand was attempting to push through the Senate a bill on proportional representation which had already been adopted by the Chamber. Opposition to the proposed change centered in the upper house, where the Socialists (who sponsored the bill, in strange collaboration with the Right wing) were nonexistent. Even before the debate started, therefore, fears were expressed that Senate obstinacy might bring extraordinary results. The Progressist editor of *La République Française* believed that a hostile vote would cause not only a ministerial crisis but a "national crisis."[53] The Right-wing *Libre Parole,* putting it less delicately, asserted that it would "expose" the president.[54] The disputed question of the Senate's constitutional right to overthrow cabinets was overshadowed by a second question: what effect might its disapproval have on the presidency?

As the debate progressed, Poincaré's supporters remained uneasy. They pointed out that if the Senate and the Chamber should hold to opposite viewpoints on the electoral issue the deadlock might make any cabinet impossible, and might force the president to resign.[55] A British correspondent charged the Radicals with playing politics to reduce the prestige of Poincaré and of his future governments.[56] One editor predicted that a constitutional revolution would follow an adverse Senate vote.[57] But the upper house proceeded imperturbably to defeat Briand on a question of confidence, 161 to 128.

[52] *L'Opinion,* VI (February 22, 1913), 231.

[53] *La République Française,* March 13, 1913.

[54] In *Le Matin,* March 14, 1913.

[55] Charles Benoist in *L'Intransigeant,* March 17, 1913.

[56] *The Times,* March 17, 1913.   [57] *L'Intransigeant,* March 18, 1913.

Briand went at once to the Elysée and submitted his resignation. Poincaré insisted that Briand stay in office, but failed to convince him.[58] There was some ground for the president's apparent attempt to fly in the face of the legislature, for the Senate's right to overthrow governments was still a highly controversial question at that time.[59] It was probably fortunate for Poincaré that Briand proved adamant, for the president's desire to oppose the will of the upper house, by keeping in power a cabinet accused of being his creatures, might have led to a genuine crisis. The episode showed that Poincaré was thoroughly prepared in the early weeks of his incumbency to invoke all the prestige of his office, to run the risk of disaster, rather than sacrifice any of his program. A president in the old tradition would have accepted the resignation mechanically, proceeding to find a new premier as a matter of course.

The Senate vote was generally regarded as an indirect blow at the chief magistrate. As *L'Action Française* put it, "the political honeymoon of the Poincaré presidency is over."[60] Moderate journals were far from moderate when they received the news. Paul Leroy-Beaulieu charged that the upper house resented the great popularity of Poincaré and had chosen this method to take vengeance.[61] He added that Clemenceau was the ringleader of the plot, aiming to create an impasse before which the president would have to resign.[62] The royalists of *Le Gaulois* also blamed the Senate's fear of a popular leader for this scheme to force him out of the Elysée.[63] "A challenge to Poincaré," it was called by a German news correspondent,

[58] Poincaré, III, 155.

[59] Even an eminent scholar like Esmein argued that the Senate had no right to destroy a government (Esmein and Nézard, *Droit Constitutionnel*, II, 262).

[60] *L'Action Française*, March 19, 1913.

[61] *L'Economiste Français*, March 22, 1913, p. 405.

[62] *Ibid.*, March 29, 1913, p. 445.

[63] *Le Gaulois*, March 19, 1913. Cf. *L'Echo de Paris*, March 21, 1913, and *L'Eclair*, March 19, 1913.

who added that the phrase freely used among legislators was "revenge for Versailles."[64]

The president's self-appointed advisers did not stop with recriminations against his foes but suggested lines of action. They spoke of reviving the power of dissolution; for, they declared, the two chambers were now deadlocked on the issue of electoral reform, so that no cabinet could possibly satisfy both houses.[65] The most obvious difficulty, of course, would be to secure the Senate's consent for dissolution. Leroy-Beaulieu asserted that the country would stand behind Poincaré if the senators proved balky; therefore he urged the president to take things into his own hands.[66] Other Right-wing journals gave Poincaré similar encouragement to fight the legislature by a public appeal for support.[67]

The president had enough common sense to ignore this sort of suggestion. If Briand had agreed to stay in office, Poincaré would have accepted the combat with all its implications. Since such was not the case, he turned quietly to choosing a successor who would carry out the same ideas as completely as possible. Many feared that Briand's fall meant the doom of the proposed law for strengthening the army. Poincaré made certain, however, that the new government would sponsor military reform. The crisis had not arisen over a very clear-cut issue, so that he had fairly complete freedom of choice. He chose as premier Louis Barthou, a member of the fallen Briand cabinet. Barthou and Poincaré had been close friends since student days. They had been the "boy wonders" of politics in the 'nineties, and had held their first ministerial portfolios in the same cabinet. Both were Moderates in politics.

[64] *Berliner Tageblatt,* March 19, 1913.

[65] *L'Intransigeant,* March 20, 1913.

[66] *L'Economiste Français,* March 22, 1913, p. 406.

[67] *Le Gaulois,* March 19, 1913; *L'Echo de Paris,* March 20, 1913. De Mun in *L'Echo* declared that Poincaré had failed in his duty to his electors when he permitted Briand to resign.

Barthou's combination, unlike its predecessor, included several men who had voted for Pams at Versailles. Poincaré later pointed with pride to this fact as evidence that he held no grudges.[68] Other factors, however, were more important to him at the time. His intimate friend, Maurice Paléologue, then stationed at the Quai d'Orsay, found him very well satisfied with the Barthou government: "Poincaré assures me that Louis Barthou lacks neither experience, patriotism, nor energy; that I can therefore be fully reassured as to the national policy of the new cabinet."[69] This, of course, meant a continuation of Poincaré's own ideas in foreign affairs and military reform.

The Barthou cabinet was generally regarded as a duplicate of Briand's except that its leadership was weaker.[70] This similarity was used against Barthou in his first appearance before the Chamber. One deputy called the cabinet "a third edition of the Poincaré ministry, revised and rather badly corrected."[71] The Radicals complained that an overthrown government ought not to be replaced by one with identical policies.[72] The target for their most severe attacks, however, was the new minister Joseph Thierry—a Progressist, and therefore a reactionary in the eyes of the Left. The Progressists had been excluded from power ever since the Dreyfus affair; and the sudden elevation of Thierry was considered significant in view of Poincaré's recent election with the aid of the Right.[73] But there was little danger that one man could have much effect on the cabinet's policies; certainly it did not appear in the ministerial declaration, which was a strange fusion of conservatism and liberalism.

[68] Poincaré, III, 137.

[69] Maurice Paléologue, "Comment le service de trois ans fut retabli en 1913," *Revue des Deux Mondes,* May 15, 1935, p. 307.

[70] *L'Intransigeant,* March 23, 1913. Barthou's ministerial declaration stressed the three-year service law above all, and spoke vaguely of compromise on the electoral reform issue.

[71] *Chamber Debates,* March 25, 1913, p. 1500.

[72] *Ibid.,* p. 1493.

[73] Gaston Martin, *Joseph Caillaux* (Paris, 1931), p. 110.

Although the Left brought forward no very solid criticism of Barthou, his vote of confidence was remarkably small. He was given a mere plurality of 225 to 162, with 165 abstentions —the narrowest margin which a cabinet had ever received on its initial test.[74] The Chamber was accustomed to give any new ministry a fair trial before voting against it, so that this case was characterized as a near-repudiation and one that was aimed at Poincaré. It showed, said the newspaper *L'Autorité,* that the Radicals meant to continue their enmity, that the conflict would inevitably grow worse, that government would become impossible.[75]

Barthou's feeble plurality was not fully explicable in any other way. He had straddled rather successfully on the question of electoral reform, and his stand on the military-service law was soon approved by a legislative majority. The vote rested on several issues, but behind them in the minds of deputies lay the question of presidential influence. Both ministry and president had received fair warning to proceed with caution.[76]

THE THREE-YEAR LAW

The principal item in Poincaré's inaugural program was a promise to strengthen the armed forces of France, in order to insure the country against threats or humiliation. Less than

[74] *Le Radical* headlined its report of this vote, "The Defeat of the Cabinet" (March 26, 1913). Jaurès recalled Diderot's story about the plague at Marseilles (*L'Humanité,* March 26, 1913): "The men who were gathering up the corpses piled in the streets, and throwing them into carts, one day carried off a recalcitrant corpse: 'I am not dead,' it said. '——Oh yes,' replied the others, 'you are dead enough.' "

[75] In *Le Matin,* March 26, 1913. *Le Radical* kept reminding Barthou that he had not received a majority of the Chamber's potential vote, and that to govern under such circumstances was unconstitutional (March 27, 1913).

[76] The cabinet's position remained so unstable that Klotz asked the Russian financial representative for more money to buy off the press. It was granted this time only on condition that Russia's interests be supported along with those of the ministry (Kokovtsov to Sazonov, June 4, 1913 [Old Style], *Rafalovich,* p. 382; Izvolsky to Sazonov, July 4, 1913, *ibid.,* p. 386).

six months passed before a new law was placed on the statute books providing that every young Frenchman must spend three years instead of two with the colors. Poincaré's connection with this "three-year law" gave clear evidence that he was no *président fainéant*.

The responsibility for setting off the military increases of 1913 has not been established beyond cavil. Poincaré always insisted that his cabinet never once thought of a change to three-year service during 1912. According to him, it was news of Germany's new military measures early in 1913 which caused Premier Briand to prepare a reply.[77] Publicists of another persuasion have contended that the French government had already decided upon military reform in 1912 and was only awaiting an excuse to bring it forward. The Germans furnished the excuse when they presented an army bill in the Reichstag early in 1913.[78]

This chicken-or-the-egg debate is less important than it might seem. Both governments made their decisions at approximately the same time. Each one acted because of reports which described the chauvinistic and militaristic mood in its rival's capital, and because of the increased tension produced by the Balkan wars. Each government naturally accused the other of starting the race in order to win legislative support for its own measure.

Not all Frenchmen were convinced that the change was necessary. It could not add a single soldier to the army; for every able-bodied man was already included in the reserve, ready for rapid mobilization. Nor would it make them better soldiers; everyone agreed that a two-year period was ample time to train a private in the ways of warfare used in 1913.

---

[77] Poincaré, II, 78.

[78] Georges Michon, *La préparation à la guerre; la loi de trois ans* (Paris, 1935), p. 109; Georges Suarez, *La vie orgueilleuse de Clemenceau* (Paris, 1930), pp. 431–32; Fay, *Origins of the World War*, I, 349; Guillaume to Davignon, February 19, 1913, *Belgian Docs.*, p. 271.

True, it would maintain a larger force constantly under arms, ready to meet an *attaque brusquée,* without mobilization; but that contingency was remote. The proposed three-year law was chiefly a gesture—an answer to Germany's challenge by a counterchallenge. Political leaders like Jean Jaurès fought the bill out of a sincere belief that provocative measures were dangerous to peace. Other deputies, more "realistic," knew that the question of three-year service could wreck many a parliamentary career.

Poincaré knew that strong opposition existed and felt himself duty-bound to overcome it. As premier during 1912 he had always replied to the Germans in their own terms. It would be a sign of fatal weakness, he believed, to change that policy now. From the day he entered the presidency, he became an open protagonist of the three-year law, despite his position above parties and conflicts. His inaugural message did not confine itself to generalities about the army; it lent emphasis and authority to the campaign for a "reply to Germany," which had suddenly burst forth in the Center and Right-wing press several days before.[79] On March 4 Poincaré called a meeting of the superior war council—its first session since a decree of 1912 had placed it under the chairmanship of the president of the republic.[80] The assembled generals were invited by Poincaré to weigh the military situation carefully, and "to listen only to the voice of their conscience."[81] The generals listened,

[79] *Le Temps,* February 16, 1913, and thereafter.

[80] Hostile critics have asserted that Poincaré had this decree adopted early in 1912 in preparation for the time when he would become president (*G.P.,* XXXIX, 156 n.; Max Clauss, *Das Politische Frankreich vor dem Kriege* [Karlsruhe, 1928], p. 28). There is not the slightest proof of this allegation.

[81] Poincaré, III, 148. The impression of contemporaries was that Poincaré had "intervened repeatedly" during this council, had even "shaped its policy" (*Le Matin,* March 5, 1913; *Saturday Review,* CXV [March 8, 1913], 285). This belief was based on no proof, but it shows that people considered Poincaré to be more than a mere moderator. Cf. Izvolsky to Sazonov, March 13, 1913, *Livre noir,* II, 42.

and unanimously demanded three-year service. Their recommendation was adopted by the cabinet and presented as a bill before the chambers.

Protagonists of the reform experienced some anxious moments before it was finally adopted in August. The Socialists and a large majority of the Radicals were bitterly opposed. It was generally believed that dislike of the military project contributed to the fall of Briand in mid-March. When Poincaré selected a successor to Briand, his chief concern was to find someone who would sponsor the three-year law. The president did not stop there; he took an active part in winning support for the bill. On March 15 he called General Joffre and Maurice Paléologue to the Elysée, and asked them to furnish arguments which would help justify the law before the Chamber army commission.[82] In May, when opposition was running high and young conscripts were rioting against the idea of serving an extra year, he created a sensation by calling Clemenceau to the Elysée. Poincaré knew that this appeal to his bitterest enemy would shock the political world. His purpose was to warn the Chamber that if it should overthrow the Barthou cabinet, Poincaré would nominate Clemenceau, ferocious partisan of the military law, and not Caillaux, its chief opponent. The president told friends privately that he would use all his constitutional rights to force through the three-year law. He was even ready to revive the power of dissolution, to call upon the country over the heads of the deputies. And if the Senate should refuse to sanction dissolution, he expected to resign.[83]

Such drastic measures did not prove to be necessary. Poincaré confined himself to public addresses in favor of the bill, the most notable of which he delivered at Toulon in June.[84]

---

[82] Paléologue, *Revue des Deux Mondes*, May 1, 1935, p. 93. Paléologue, a career diplomat, was director of political affairs at the Quai d'Orsay in 1913. Poincaré expected him to justify the army reform on the basis of the European diplomatic situation.

[83] *Ibid.*, May 15, 1935, pp. 318–19.   [84] *Le Temps*, June 10, 1913.

This open appeal for popular support came while the Chamber was in the midst of debating the three-year law; it was a plain attempt to exert pressure on the deputies. When the bill was adopted soon after, Poincaré deserved much of the credit for its success.[85]

The president's part in this campaign was not ignored by his enemies. The Socialists charged that he had brought back the three-year law from Russia during his journey of August 1912.[86] They openly demanded the truth about this rumor in the Chamber and heard it denied by Premier Barthou.[87] The Socialist municipal council of Limoges voted to refuse Poincaré an official reception during his projected visit to their city. "It is no longer possible," they announced, "to consider the present head of the state as being outside of and above parties. M. Poincaré is a *président de combat,* whose presence at Limoges can only inflame the civil dissensions aroused by the military project whose principal author is M. Poincaré."[88]

These provincials of Limoges only stated openly what many were thinking and saying privately. In the campaign for the three-year law, Poincaré was not a moderator over disputing groups, an official who stood above parties. He adopted and worked actively in favor of a measure which was supported by the Center and the Right, and which was opposed by most of the Left. Consciously or unconsciously, he identified himself with certain political groups against others; he became a party president, a chief executive with a program.

Poincaré probably did not realize all the implications of his policy. In his blind sincerity he could see only one possible side. He felt that citizens who held different views were simply mis-

---

[85] Cf. Joseph Noulens, "Le gouvernement français à la veille de la guerre," *Revue des Deux Mondes,* February 1, 1931, p. 609; Schoen to Bethmann, August 8, 1913, *G.P.,* XXXIX, 202–5.

[86] *L'Humanité,* March 27, 1913.

[87] *Chamber Debates,* June 16, 1913, pp. 774–79.

[88] *L'Humanité,* June 4, 1913.

guided and that their views were a menace to the community. Poincaré's speeches and memoirs contained abundant references to himself as "president of all the French." But the stubbornness of his conviction made him identify his own program with what he called "the interests of France." He came to regard the three-year law as a symbol of national strength and unity, not as a party measure. He failed to understand that there might be a distinction between "France" and "the Moderates"; he confidently believed them to be one and the same thing. And simultaneously, of course, he failed to understand the effect which this could have on the presidency. From such a beginning the president of the republic might gradually develop into an official with policies of his own. That, however, was not Poincaré's conscious purpose when he sponsored the three-year law.

THE PRESIDENT AND THE PUBLIC

The cabinet crisis of March 1913, culminating in the near-defeat of Barthou on his first vote of confidence, had warned Poincaré that presidential irresponsibility might not protect him against all attacks. His safest procedure would have been to retire behind the walls of the Elysée, leaving the parties to dispute freely among themselves. This he refused to do. During the ensuing months he emerged from his "prison" repeatedly to deliver manifestoes in favor of the three-year law. Nor did he stop when the military reform had been adopted. The summer and autumn of 1913 brought a remarkable series of presidential journeys throughout France—journeys whose undisguised object, in the eyes of many, was to enhance Poincaré's personal prestige.[89]

Whether or not that was his real purpose, it was certainly the result of his travels. At every stop he was greeted by volleys of acclamations: along with "Vive Poincaré!" went cries

[89] Albert Guérard, *Beyond Hatred* (New York, 1925), pp. 50–51.

of "Long live the army!" and "Long live the three years!" Earlier presidents had made official visits too; but, as *Le Matin* observed after he returned from Le Havre in July, "There is no doubt that M. Poincaré inaugurated a new concept of presidential journeys yesterday."[90] For when Poincaré attended a public ceremony he was not regarded as a mere silk-hatted layer of cornerstones. Instead, he symbolized active leadership toward a goal of national strength.

The climax came in September, when the president arranged to spend his vacation traveling in southwestern France. "Poincaré is the victim of his popularity," wrote *Le Matin* when it learned of the plan.[91] The trip was to be made by automobile—a considerable venture in those days—ostensibly to build up interest in the newborn practice of touring. Clemenceau and Jaurès thought they divined hidden purposes, however. They believed that the journey was really a political enterprise, in preparation for the legislative elections of April 1914. It was, they said, an attempt to aid Moderate candidates in the old Radical stronghold of the Southwest.[92]

The experiment in *tourisme* developed into a veritable triumphal procession. Some trouble had been anticipated at Limoges and Toulouse, where the Socialist municipal councils had refused to prepare ceremonies of welcome.[93] Other organizations, however, substituted for the city councils, and the public appeared to be no less enthusiastic there than in other towns. At Limoges the newspapers reported a continual series of acclamations from the crowd. *Le Figaro* considered it significant that the cries most often heard were "Vive Poincaré!" and "Vive l'armée!"[94]

---

[90] *Le Matin*, July 24, 1913.

[91] *Ibid.*, July 31, 1913.

[92] *L'Homme Libre*, September 13, 1913; *L'Humanité*, September 15, 1913.

[93] *Journal des Débats*, September 10, 1913; *Revue Politique et Parlementaire*, LXXVIII (November 1913), 183.

[94] *Le Figaro*, September 9, 1913.

The Moderate and the Right-wing press, whose reporters flocked after the presidential procession, filled their front pages with long daily articles. These were always in the same vein: they told of ardent receptions, frequent speeches, and repeated references by Poincaré and the crowd to his Lorraine origin. The *Journal des Débats* approved what it described as the country's desire to show its support "by the acclamations which greet the words, the acts and the person of the president . . . . everywhere. And it is thus that a 'tourist trip' serves other interests besides those for which it was undertaken . . . ."[95] As the journey reached its culmination at Bordeaux the same journal asserted that popular approval of the new president was now too obvious and too intense to be denied.[96] Minister of the Interior Klotz called the trip "a popular ratification of the act of Versailles."[97]

In his public statements during September Poincaré never departed from a strictly constitutional and conservative attitude. He realized that his travels were viewed with suspicion by many, and so he was careful to call attention to the non-party character of his office.[98] When one village mayor expressed his hope that the new president's septennate would have far-reaching effects upon France, Poincaré hastened to reply: "The executive does not possess the same freedom as the legislature. Charged with enforcing the laws, he must respect them; I regret very much, therefore, that I must reply in only a word to the gracious speech which has just been addressed to me."[99] He made it clear that no one could expect anticonstitutional or dictatorial conduct from him.

At the same time, this sincere insistence left him full freedom to use whatever powers the constitution contained. He

[95] *Journal des Débats,* September 11, 1913.

[96] *Ibid.,* September 21, 1913.

[97] *Le Figaro,* September 23, 1913.

[98] *Journal des Débats,* September 10, 1913, *et seq.*

[99] *Le Figaro,* September 11, 1913.

knew very well that most of these powers could be exercised only if he had the country's strong support. It is reasonable to assume that he viewed his September trip as something more than an advertisement for the tourist industry. An increase in his own popularity was certain to build up sentiment in favor of the Moderate program, which constituted for him the health and safety of France. It could easily be described as France's rebuke to the Radicals for their hostility toward the president. Whether intentionally or not, Poincaré made a great deal of political hay during September, and at a time when the horizon bore signs of storm.

THE PRESIDENT AND THE RADICALS

Strong Poincaré supporters openly admitted their belief that the president had felt attacks coming and had adroitly called on the country. The results pleased them greatly; they boasted that opposition had disappeared, and jeered that the Radicals had been forced to swallow their wrath in the face of this strikingly revealed popularity.[100] There was probably some truth in this, for Left-wing politicians were not insensitive to manifestations of public opinion. But an incident soon occurred to show that the breach between Poincaré and the Radicals was both wide and deep.

On October 16 the Radical party convened at Pau for its annual congress. In the course of a poorly attended session on the second day, an obscure deputy named Bouyssou arose and complained that the people were beginning to cry "Vive Poincaré!" more often than "Vive la République!" He then presented the following motion:

[100] *La République Française,* September 20, 1913; *L'Opinion,* VI (September 20, 1913), 356. The monarchist Léon Daudet, however, warned Poincaré that his enemies would make him pay for these acclamations (*L'Action Française,* September 21, 1913): "Let M. Poincaré make no mistake . . . . He has never been more seriously threatened."

The congress calls to the attention of the . . . . Socialist-Radical party all the . . . . indications of a personal policy which may decrease the authority of parliamentary institutions, and which favor the return of . . . . reaction . . . .[101]

This motion, translated into direct language, meant that its author pretended to fear dictatorship. It was adopted unanimously by the few delegates who were present.

The Moderate press was highly indignant at this action, which violated the tradition that the irresponsible president should not be mentioned in public dispute. Many Radicals realized that they had made a tactical error. The next day they adopted a second motion affirming their "constitutional loyalty" and declaring that they "placed the personality of the president of the republic above party disputes." The congress had now adopted two opposing motions, one of which had to be wiped from the records. Bouyssou, author of the first declaration, retreated enough to explain that he did not blame Poincaré personally but objected to the public demonstrations which always accompanied the president's trips and to what he called a "national bluff." After some desultory discussion, both motions were thrown out and the whole question was left unsettled. The subsequent election of Joseph Caillaux as chairman of the party's executive committee was regarded as a substantial repudiation of the attack on the president. Caillaux had disapproved of the Bouyssou motion, so that his defeat of the extremists' candidate had some significance.[102] A few days

---

[101] *Le Figaro,* October 19, 1913.

[102] The official account of this incident was contained in the party's publication, *Treizième congrès du parti républicain radical et radical-socialiste tenu à Pau le 16, 17, 18, et 19 octobre 1913* (Paris, 1913), pp. 51–52, 297–306. The Radical interpretation appeared in *La Grande Revue,* LXXXII (November 10, 1913), 192–93, and in *Le Radical,* October 19, 1913. They accused the Moderate press of disfiguring the affair and using it for political purposes, which was probably true. The Moderate version may be found in *Le Figaro,* October 19, 1913; *Journal des Débats,* October 19 and 20, 1913; *L'Opinion,* October 25, 1913, p. 513; and Poincaré, III, 355. See also *Revue Politique et*

later the Radicals attempted to retrieve their mistake when the party's Paris unit voted its confidence in Poincaré's "republican loyalty."[103] The Pau incident accomplished nothing except to cast a brief ray of light on Radical hostility toward the president. That party's enmity had been accentuated rather than reduced by Poincaré's popular appeal. After his first six months in office, he was as far as ever from his declared wish to be "president of all the French." Poincaré denied that the crowd's enthusiasm was addressed to him as an individual, and maintained that it sprang from the people's joy in "affirming their democratic convictions, their love of liberty, their confidence in the destinies of France."[104] The Moderates in general ridiculed any fears of personal power. The crowd simply liked a bit of personality and activity, wrote the prominent author-journalist, Alfred Capus:

There was something disagreeable in the concept of an almost anonymous head of the state, immured in the constitution like a queen bee in her cell of wax; like her, fertilized once for all in the nuptial flight of Versailles, then immobilized forever and having only to produce ministers and decrees ad infinitum![105]

But however much Poincaré might scoff at the exaggerated fears of the Radicals, he could not overcome those fears as long as he maintained his unusual activity. It was inevitable that some suspicious republicans should recall Louis-Napoleon's triumphal journeys about France between 1849 and 1851. Even those Radicals who knew that Poincaré was no Louis-Napoleon objected to the use of his prestige for political purposes. Six and one-half years remained of Poincaré's term at the Elysée. With the Left wing almost solidly against him, those years promised to become increasingly difficult for the president.

Parlementaire, LXXVIII (November 1913), 377; Izvolsky to Sazonov, October 23, 1913, *Livre noir,* II, 163–64; Clauss, *op. cit.,* p. 90.

[103] *Journal des Débats,* October 31, 1913.
[104] *Le Figaro,* October 27, 1913.
[105] *Ibid.,* October 20, 1913.

FOREIGN POLICY IN 1913

A number of revisionist historians, in their effort to saddle Poincaré with a share of war responsibility, have contended that he retained control of French foreign policy even after entering the Elysée. As one of them put it, "M. Poincaré. . . . prolonged himself at the Quai d'Orsay through successors of his choice."[106] It has even been suggested that he was more powerful as president than as premier.[107]

It is true that the constitution of 1875 left the presidential prerogative broadest in the field of foreign affairs. All treaties were signed by him, and in most cases no further ratification was necessary. Foreign diplomats were accredited to him, and he had the right to confer with them at will. The only notable instances of presidential activity between 1877 and 1913 had occurred in questions of foreign policy.[108] The reason for this is clear. In dealing with other governments, the head of the state could carry more prestige than the head of a party cabinet. But presidents had never tried to outline policies or guide the daily conduct of foreign affairs. They had played host to traveling sovereigns, and had repaid these formal visits. They had conversed with ambassadors from time to time, usually confining themselves to banalities. At rare intervals they had acted on their own initiative, sometimes even in disregard of the foreign minister. Usually, however, their intervention occurred only in time of stress, and then at the request of the

---

[106] Alfred Pevet, *Les responsables de la guerre* (Paris, 1921), p. 344. Other writers who have held to this theory include Victor Margueritte, *Les criminels* (Paris, 1925), p. 156; Alfred Fabre-Luce, *La victoire* (Paris, 1924), p. 168; Joseph Dessaint, *Les enseignements de la guerre* (Paris, 1916), p. 63; and Georges Louis, *Carnets*, II, 154. Professor Fay (*Origins of the World War*, I, 315), has reached a somewhat similar conclusion.

[107] Count Michael Karolyi, *Fighting the World* (London, 1924), p. 75; *Carnets de Georges Louis*, II, 161.

[108] Grévy in the Schnaebelé affair; Carnot in the creation of the Franco-Russian entente.

cabinet. Most presidents had been as inactive in external as in domestic affairs.

During most of 1913 the Quai d'Orsay was occupied by men who approved the foreign policy of the late Poincaré ministry. Both Charles Jonnart and Stephen Pichon, who held office from February until December, were sincere nationalists. Like Poincaré in 1912, their guiding principles were the maintenance of peace with honor, the solidification of the Triple Entente, and deep distrust of Germany. They also desired to solve the Balkan tangle while keeping the friendship of as many Balkan states as possible.[109]

This continuity of purpose did not necessarily mean that Poincaré was the operator who manipulated the strings of puppet foreign ministers. It meant, rather, that he insisted upon the selection of men whose ideas were like his own. At Versailles immediately after his election he promised to maintain a national policy; he did this by seeing that "correct" men were placed at the Quai d'Orsay. Such persons were likely to consult Poincaré and to follow his advice. In this sense, the president kept some power in his hands; but it existed only so long as the minister was willing to accept his counsel. The fact that both Jonnart and Pichon were rather feeble reeds, unlikely to carry on an independent policy, is therefore significant.

Any attempt at precise measurement of the president's influence is hopeless. No one can tell whether Poincaré provided the impetus for Jonnart's and Pichon's acts or whether he merely approved after the fact. His activity was largely of the hidden variety, carried on through private conversations which were seldom recorded at the time. Here and there a remark in published memoirs or documents has briefly illumined the presi-

---

[109] Poincaré himself has observed that Pichon's foreign policy did not differ from his own (Poincaré, III, 217). For years Pichon had been the henchman of Clemenceau, but he broke away from *"le patron's"* influence in 1913 to vote for Poincaré. During the war Pichon returned to the fold. Never a strong and independent character, he was often the butt of the Tiger's sarcasm.

dent's hand among the shadows of his office. Such references appear frequently enough to justify the belief that Poincaré really did stay in active contact with foreign affairs, although without exceeding his constitutional prerogatives.

In addition to exercising this indirect control the new president evidently expected to take some active part in diplomacy. Izvolsky reported that Poincaré wished to continue his personal conversations with the ambassador, just as he had done in the past.[110] Poincaré has protested that Izvolsky twisted his "banal formula of politeness," which gave the latter access to the Elysée.[111] But he has been unable to explain away two similar dispatches written by the Austrian and German envoys. Szécsen reported that he had been invited to pay frequent calls at the presidential palace, where he would be cordially received for confidential talks about questions of diplomacy.[112] Von Schoen, the German ambassador, was actually startled at Poincaré's frank suggestion that he visit the Elysée often for personal interviews. Von Schoen regarded this proposal as a breach of tradition, and foresaw that it might cause embarrassment.[113] He realized that past presidents had rarely gone beyond formalities in the absence of a responsible minister.

The focus of French diplomacy during 1913 was southeastern Europe. This was the period of the second and third Balkan wars, which threatened the peace and the national interests of every great power. Most of the disputes which grew

---

[110] Izvolsky to Sazonov, January 30, 1913, *Livre noir*, II, 19–20.

[111] Poincaré, III, 96.

[112] Szécsen dispatch, March 1, 1913, *Austrian Docs.*, V, 853.

[113] Schoen to Bethmann, February 22, 1913, *G.P.*, XXXIX, 156–62. Von Schoen reported to Berlin that he would be extremely wary in acting upon Poincaré's invitation, considering French ideas of constitutionality and the character of the president. He promised to use it sparingly, and only for acts of courtesy. Apparently the ambassador was more concerned about presidential tradition than Poincaré was. This conversation, incidentally, took place during an official visit which Poincaré made to the German embassy; no other president had set foot inside those doors since the war of 1870.

out of the Balkan wars had to be met during Pichon's term at the Quai d'Orsay. Every step that the minister took was approved by Poincaré; but whether or not the president helped to formulate French policy cannot be determined.

One thing is certain, however: Poincaré was more than a silent observer of Pichon's activity. He gave active aid to the foreign minister in his diplomacy. An example in point was the Scutari incident. The powers had decided to reserve this town for their foster child, the new state of Albania. But Montenegrin troops had occupied Scutari, and refused to evacuate it. There followed a long dispute among the powers over a proposal to force the Montenegrins out by means of a naval demonstration. In the course of this negotiation Poincaré was always consulted before the Triple Entente made a decision.[114] Not only Pichon, but Poincaré as well, warned the Austrian ambassador that hasty action at Scutari might bring on a European war.[115] When he recalled this incident in his memoirs Poincaré told of Pichon's warning but failed to mention his own conversation with Ambassador Szécsen.[116]

[114] Poincaré, III, 169–78; Izvolsky to Sazonov, April 2, 1913, *Iswolski*, III, 114; Grey to Bertie, April 2, 1913, *British Docs.*, IX, Part II, 639–40; Izvolsky to Sazonov, April 9, 1913, *Livre noir*, II, 67–68; Pichon to P. Cambon, April 25, 1913, *D.D.F.*, VI, 432.

[115] Szécsen dispatch, May 8, 1913, *Austrian Docs.*, VI, 390–91.

[116] Poincaré, III, 166. Petty omissions such as this one are difficult to explain in a ten-volume work which contains so many minor details. They occur frequently, and may mean nothing at all. But they do leave the impression that Poincaré wished to conceal any evidence of his personal activity, however harmless it may have been. There were other occasions when Poincaré showed great care in keeping his diplomatic activity secret. When Austria proposed to publish a Red Book on Balkan affairs, the president requested that his name be omitted from one of Szécsen's reports of April 30, 1913. At that time he had insisted to Szécsen that Scutari go to Albania (*Austrian Docs.*, VI, 301). His request for the omission in 1914 was based on the fact that he was president when he made the statement to Szécsen (Somssich dispatch, March 14, 1914, *Austrian Docs.*, VII, 968). He probably realized that the Left would object to such evidence of presidential intervention in diplomacy.

The attempt to re-define Balkan boundaries also caused sparks to fly during the summer of 1913. Most serious was the problem of Albania's southern frontier, where the claims of the new state clashed with those of Greece. Italy and Austria favored a strong Albania, but the French government gave its support to Greece.[117] The controversy dragged on for several months, to the rising annoyance of the Italians. They blamed Poincaré for this French intransigeance, asserting that Pichon would have made no trouble had it not been for the president's interference.[118]

A second dispute soon complicated the Albanian question. Greece also laid claim to the Aegean islands, former Turkish possessions which had been seized by Italy in the war of 1911–12. Here again the French gave their support to the Greeks; and again Rome laid the blame at Poincaré's door.[119] A dispatch from the Austrian ambassador at London, Count Mensdorff, lent some color to their theory. Mensdorff described a conversation with Poincaré and Pichon in which the president spoke out more openly than the foreign minister in favor of Greek demands.[120] As the French continued to resist all compromise throughout the summer, the exasperated Austrians and

[117] This support was not based on pure generosity. Both Poincaré and Pichon pointed out to the Greek ambassador that they expected Greek friendship as a quid pro quo (Pichon to Delcassé, August 18, 1913, *D.D.F.,* VIII, 47–48).

[118] The Austrian ambassador in Rome reported: "San Giuliano sees in this attitude the hand of Poincaré, whose influence Pichon cannot entirely avoid against his own better judgment" (Mérey dispatch, May 21, 1913, *Austrian Docs.,* VI, 483). This Italian belief was also mentioned in Mérey's telegram of May 9, 1913 (*ibid.,* p. 401), and in von Flotow's dispatch of May 10, 1913 (*G.P.,* XXXIV, 815). Von Jagow thought that the Cambon brothers rather than Poincaré were responsible for the French efforts in favor of Greece (Jagow to Tschirsky, May 30, 1913, *G.P.,* XXXIV, 879). According to the French documents, however, Paris was more intransigeant than Paul Cambon (P. Cambon to Pichon, June 13, 1913, *D.D.F.,* VII, 118–19; Pichon's annotation to a dispatch from Rome, July 29, 1913, *ibid.,* VII, 540).

[119] Mérey dispatch, August 6, 1913, *Austrian Docs.,* VII, 66.

[120] Mensdorff dispatch, June 25, 1913, *Austrian Docs.,* VI, 725–26.

Italians began to speak of the Greek claims as "the Poincaré project."[121]

This suspicion rested on little except prejudice. The Italians had regarded Poincaré with a jaundiced eye ever since he had injured their feelings in the "Carthage" and "Manouba" incidents of 1912.[122] Most of the accusations brought against the president in connection with the Balkan boundary disputes originated in Rome, where the accusers knew little about the formulation of policy in Paris. By a process of wishful thinking, they attributed everything evil to the man they disliked. At the same time, the Austro-Italian complaints showed that European statesmen did not dismiss Poincaré as a prisoner of protocol, without any control over the French government. They regarded him as an essential cog in policy-making: and as a result, their ambassadors could not ignore the Elysée. Szécsen's opinion in June 1913 may have been mistaken, but it indicated the new importance which diplomatic circles attached to the presidency:

In my reports I have often mentioned that M. Poincaré exercises direct influence over M. Pichon in foreign policy. Especially the Cambon brothers in London and Berlin are very little concerned with the views of M. Pichon, who scarcely dares to give them instructions, so that both these ambassadors make their own policies on their own responsibility but at the same time stay in constant touch with the Elysée . . . .[123]

Other indications have appeared here and there to show

[121] Berchtold to the ambassadors in Rome and London, August 7, 1913, *Austrian Docs.*, VII, 73. Cf. note of Sir F. Bertie, August 7, 1913, *D.D.F.*, VII, 605.

[122] These incidents occurred in January 1912, during the Italo-Turk war in Tripoli. The Italians stopped two French ships bound for Tunis, alleging that they carried military supplies and soldiers destined for the Turkish army. Poincaré, who had just become premier, insisted that both ships be released. The Hague Court awarded damages to the French government soon after. Although the Italians were proved to be in the wrong, they resented the harsh, intransigeant manner which Poincaré adopted in this affair.

[123] Szécsen dispatch, June 13, 1913, *Austrian Docs.*, VI, 644–45.

that Poincaré kept his finger on the pulse of diplomacy, although they are insufficient to permit a detailed study of his activity. Certainly few men in France knew so much about the course of European events. For example, when King Albert of the Belgians visited Berlin late in 1913 he came away much agitated by the Kaiser's bellicosity. The report which Albert wrote was entrusted to only half a dozen men in Paris; Poincaré was one of that number.[124] Another source of information was Maurice Paléologue, then a high official at the Quai d'Orsay. The president often called him in for private discussions.[125] Pichon always talked with Poincaré before he took any step, not only in Balkan affairs but on every important question. Even when the president was vacationing in the country Pichon kept in contact with him by letter.[126] Once, during a temporary absence of the foreign minister from Paris, the permanent officials at the Quai d'Orsay came to the Elysée for directions. The president gave them orders without hesitation, apparently on his own responsibility.[127]

Included among Poincaré's contacts were his frequent conversations with ambassadors and with foreign statesmen visiting Paris. Interviews of this sort were common to all French presidents, but on more than one occasion Poincaré seems to have discussed current affairs with remarkable frankness.[128]

[124] Paléologue, *Revue des Deux Mondes,* May 15, 1933, p. 334; J. Cambon to Pichon, November 24, 1913, *D.D.F.,* VIII, 660.

[125] Paléologue, *loc. cit.,* pp. 308–9.

[126] Poincaré, III, 267. Cf. also pp. 220, 224–27; Pichon to Delcassé, June 28, 1913, *D.D.F.,* VII, 242; Izvolsky to Sazonov, July 25, 1913, *Livre noir,* II, 111–12; Kokovtsov to the Tsar, November 19, 1913 (Old Style), *ibid.,* II, 392.

[127] Paléologue memorandum, May 4, 1913, *D.D.F.,* VI, 544–45.

[128] Poincaré's memoirs barely mention most of these conversations. The following items furnish fuller details: Tschirsky to Bethmann, June 5, 1913, *G.P.,* XXXV, 15; Schoen to Bethmann, July 5, 1913, *ibid.,* p. 127; Radowitz dispatch, September 30, 1913, *ibid.,* XXXVI, 374; Szécsen dispatch, July 13, 1913, *Austrian Docs.,* VIII, 902; same, November 22 and 25, *ibid.,* VII, 583–84, 586; von Mittag dispatch, November 11, 1913, *ibid.,* VII, 553; Fürsten-

Prime Minister Kokovtsov of Russia, who arrived in November to borrow money for strategic railways, gave the president much credit for the successful negotiation of the loan.[129]

Secrecy continues to veil the discussions which took place in ministerial councils. In one case, however, a brief written record of such a meeting has been preserved. This was a special session of six ministers at the Elysée, convoked to study certain aspects of the German Berlin-to-Bagdad railway.[130] Poincaré intervened twice to insist that Germany accept certain French demands before any further negotiations should take place. This bit of evidence suggests that he did not act as a mere presiding officer but took an active part in the council.[131]

There was one formal duty attached to the French presidency which Poincaré utilized to advantage. As ceremonial head of the republic, presidents sometimes made state journeys abroad in order to affirm existing alliances or to prepare the ground for new ones. Poincaré made two such journeys during his first year in office, the most important taking him to London in June 1913.

berg dispatch, November 15, 1913, *ibid.*, VIII, 564; Pichon to Delcassé, May 21, 1913, *D.D.F.*, VI, 674–75; same to same, August 18, 1913, *ibid.*, VIII, 47–48; Sazonov to the Tsar, October 24, 1913 (Old Style), *Livre noir*, II, 361.

[129] Kokovtsov to the Tsar, November 19, 1913 (Old Style), *Livre noir*, II, 408–9; Kokovtsov, *Out of My Past*, p. 381.

[130] November 6, 1913, *D.D.F.*, VIII, 558–60.

[131] On the other hand, M. Charles Dumont, minister of finance in the Barthou cabinet, furnished the author with the following sketch (letter to the author, October 26, 1938): "Never during the course of the Barthou ministry, in the year 1913, did the president try to infringe in the smallest degree upon the full responsibility and the full liberty of the ministers. In the course of the council's deliberations, as well as in his private conversations, he put at the service of the ministers his magnificent culture, his extraordinary memory, all his intelligent foresight. After a deliberation in his presence, after a conversation anywhere on a particular subject, no aspects of a question any longer remained in the shadow. President Poincaré did not weigh upon the opinion of the ministers and the government. He clarified it."

It was Poincaré who took the initiative for this trip to Britain. Rumor had it that the president acted for personal as well as diplomatic reasons.[132] Otherwise, some Frenchmen complained, Poincaré would have respected custom by awaiting a visit to Paris by King George; for President Fallières' state journey of 1908 had not yet been repaid. This sort of talk doubtless sprang from personal hostility toward Poincaré. His fundamental purpose was to emphasize Anglo-French co-operation, and in that aim the Paris press gave him its full approval. "When we recall the practical effects of his stay in Russia last year," wrote *Le Temps,* "we have the right to expect no less of his sojourn in England."[133] *Le Temps* did not mention the fact that in 1912 Poincaré had been a responsible minister, while in 1913 he was "the prisoner of the Elysée."

The journey proved to be a brilliant success. The enthusiasm of the London crowds strengthened popular sentiment for the Entente on both sides of the Channel. Poincaré's task was to converse with royalty while Foreign Minister Pichon transacted business; but the president did not confine himself to such formalities. He took part in a Pichon-Cambon-Grey discussion of Balkan affairs, during which agreements were reached on the Albanian boundary question and on the desirability of localizing any new Balkan war.[134] He also talked with a number of prominent political and military figures as well as with members of the royal family.[135] Doubtless most of these interviews were mere exchanges of civilities. The evidence is nevertheless sufficient to show that Poincaré participated in

[132] Schoen to Bethmann, April 16 and June 25, 1913, *G.P.,* XXXIX, 128–30. It was said that Queen Mary would never pay a visit to Madame Poincaré, a divorcée, unless forced to do so in repayment.

[133] *Le Temps,* June 26, 1913.

[134] Poincaré, II, 253; Pichon circular, June 30, 1913, *D.D.F.,* VII, 252–53; Grey to Buchanan, June 27, 1913, *British Docs.,* Vol. IX, Part II, p. 871. "Visit has given great satisfaction here," Grey added.

[135] Paléologue, *Revue des Deux Mondes,* May 15, 1935, p. 322.

discussions of policy, while his British counterpart, King George, was not invited.

Poincaré later wrote in his memoirs: "Obviously it was France which London acclaimed, and I was only a symbol, most formally attired and cravatted in white."[136] Press and private opinion showed that he was far too modest. *The Times* called it the most important state visit of recent years and added that London's tumultuous welcome was a tribute to the man as well as to the official representative.[137] In the view of the *Daily Chronicle,* the visit was first of all a personal success for the president and, secondly, a demonstration of Entente cordiality.[138] A Paris daily added: "Nothing can better prove the personal influence that a man can exercise, even in the present republican system, when he has the courage to free himself from the tyranny of groups and political coteries."[139] Pichon told Paléologue after the journey, "The president was admirable. He astonished everyone by the extent of his knowledge, the precision of his words, and the vivacity of his wit. It is a great success for him and for France."[140]

The lone dissenting voice was that of Ambassador von Schoen, who thought that the newspapers were trying to cover up the disappointing diplomatic results of the visit. Von Schoen believed, however, that Poincaré had succeeded in his second purpose, which was to increase his personal prestige in France, with the aid of the press.[141] Von Schoen's judgment here was warped, for he exaggerated Poincaré's personal aims. None the less the president's willingness to assume the spotlight did have its effect. With some justice Europe continued to regard him as an active diplomatic representative of France.

---

[136] Poincaré, III, 242.   [137] *The Times,* June 24, 26, and 28, 1913.

[138] In *Le Matin,* June 27, 1913.   [139] *L'Intransigeant,* June 26, 1913.

[140] Paléologue, *Revue des Deux Mondes,* May 15, 1935, p. 322.

[141] Schoen to Bethmann, June 28, 1913, *G.P.,* XXXIX, 131–32. Von Schoen even thought that Poincaré may have arranged to return just before the running of the Grand Prix in order to add éclat to his welcome.

Poincaré's second state journey to foreign parts occurred in October, when he passed three days in Spain. He later bewailed his status there as "prisoner of a retinue and serf of two associated protocols"; but he had time to accompany Pichon in a long political discussion with the Spanish king and prime minister.[142] Nor was this conversation confined to mere platitudes. Alfonso was rash enough to propose a plan for absorbing Portugal, and tried to win Poincaré's support for the scheme.[143] So far as the Spanish public was concerned, the president's reception was remarkably barren of enthusiasm.[144] To his own fellow citizens, however, his popularity was still at its height. Proof of this was the extraordinary ovation which greeted him on his return from Spain to Marseilles.[145]

One may conclude that Poincaré was no shadow president during his first year in office so far as the conduct of foreign affairs was concerned. During that period, however, his political allies were at the Quai d'Orsay. The arrival of an opposing faction in power was likely to bring a certain change in his position.

THE END OF THE MODERATES

The Barthou ministry entered office in the face of storm warnings. As early as August 1913 some observers predicted that it would be overthrown soon after the legislature reconvened three months later.[146] Poincaré's subtle appeal to the

---

[142] Poincaré, III, 291, 295.

[143] Albert Pingaud, *Histoire diplomatique de la France pendant la grande guerre* (Paris, 1938), I, 64. The author of this work had access to the documents at the Quai d'Orsay.

[144] *Vossische Zeitung* was quoted (*Le Figaro,* October 9, 1913) as saying that the reception in Madrid was "glacial." The French press explained this lack of enthusiasm as due to bad weather and an excess of protocol.

[145] *L'Intransigeant,* October 13, 1913.

[146] Schoen to Bethmann, August 8, 1913, *G.P.,* XXXIX, 204. Von Schoen believed that the Radicals were actually aiming at Poincaré when they threatened the cabinet, and that their suspicion of the president was justified by the latter's conduct. The ambassador predicted, however, that Poincaré would

country in his September trip to southwestern France strengthened both his own position and that of the cabinet which represented his views. But it did not destroy the opposition; the Pau congress gave evidence of that.

Late in November the Chamber began debate on a bond issue to finance the three-year service law and other projects. Barthou insisted that the bonds be tax-exempt. Poincaré, who foresaw danger ahead, urged him not to make this a question of confidence. But Barthou refused to take heed—thus showing, incidentally, that a president could not always impose his advice even on a friendly minister.[147] Poincaré's fears proved well founded; the opposition seized its chance and repudiated the cabinet on December 2. The session ended in disorder, with the Socialist Vaillant crying, "Down with the three years!" and the deputies disputing as to whether or not the military law was really the question at issue.[148]

This second crisis within a year proved far more severe than the first. It was generally believed that the Chamber had aimed at Poincaré in its vote of nonconfidence, so that his task was made doubly difficult.[149] His choice of a new premier could not fail to arouse the animosity of at least one political group. The nomination of another Moderate would have lent color to the suspicion that Poincaré wished to pursue a personal policy at the Elysée. On the other hand, the victorious opposition was led by Caillaux, and his appointment to the premiership would have alienated the president's allies.[150]

even accept a Caillaux ministry if that should prove necessary to assure the Left wing of his firm republicanism.

[147] Poincaré, III, 337.   [148] *Chamber Debates,* December 2, 1913, p. 674.

[149] Schoen to Bethmann, December 4, 1913, *G.P.,* XXXIX, 233–36; Izvolsky to Sazonov, December 4, 1913, *Livre noir,* II, 195; *La Liberté,* December 4, 1913; *Le Gaulois,* December 3, 1913; *L'Humanité,* December 4, 1913.

[150] Izvolsky expected Poincaré to set up a transitional cabinet, aimed to last until the eve of the general elections in 1914, when he would again appoint someone like Barthou or Millerand. The Russian envoy admitted that if Caillaux were not named, it would be a breach of established custom in France (Izvolsky to Sazonov, December 3, 1913, *Livre noir,* II, 191).

Though the Moderates scoffed at Caillaux's hopes of reaching office, they were obviously nervous. They began to talk of dissolving the Chamber—that procedure always suspect to republicans since MacMahon. A prominent Moderate deputy, Joseph Reinach, contended that dissolution was the only way out, that with a general election only four months away a new cabinet could achieve nothing in the interim, and that the time had come for a return to "constitutional truth."[151] The *Journal des Débats* agreed that dissolution was generally approved but thought that a ministry should first be named and repudiated, in order to prove that a Radical government was impossible.[152]

Poincaré was aware of this pressure but was unwilling to take any step which might have been interpreted as an act of desperation.[153] Therefore he continued to call politicians to the Elysée in a steady stream, seeking a viable solution. Caillaux was among them; but he emerged without a mandate, since Poincaré declared himself resolved to maintain the three-year law.[154]

The Moderate senator Alexandre Ribot was finally offered the premiership. He attempted to organize a cabinet, but was forced to admit failure when no Radical would agree to take part. A second Moderate, Jean Dupuy, ran into the same stone wall.[155] The political allies of Ribot and Dupuy began to be both angry and worried; they characterized the Radicals' stubbornness as "a sort of *coup d'état* against the legislature

---

[151] *Le Figaro*, December 4, 1913; *La République Française*, December 4, 1913.

[152] *Journal des Débats*, December 5, 1913.

[153] Poincaré, III, 343.

[154] *Ibid.*, p. 341. It was rumored that Caillaux had arrived confidently with a list of ministers all prepared, and that in his disappointment he had threatened: "If M. Poincaré pays no attention to our decisions, we will make life impossible for him and his cabinets" (*La Liberté*, December 6, 1913).

[155] According to Auguste Gérard, Poincaré caused the failure of Ribot and Dupuy by attempting to dictate their choice of ministers so that their task became impossible (Gérard, *Mémoires*, p. 529). There is no other evidence to support this assertion.

and against the constitution."[156] The deadlock was complete; the crisis was becoming appallingly long; the country was restless. Even the president's confidence seems to have been shaken; he assertedly told Ribot that he would resign if hindered from carrying out what he regarded as his duty.[157]

As a last resort Poincaré called in Gaston Doumergue, a Radical senator with Moderate tendencies, who had voted in favor of the military law. Here was a possibility that the three-year service might be saved by the very party which opposed it. Doumergue quickly succeeded in forming a cabinet which differed widely from the governments of 1913. Not a single minister carried over; every man was from a party which was unquestionably Left. "Republican concentration" (which was really government by the Moderates) had disappeared.

These same Moderates, who had placed Poincaré in office and had supported him, were furious. The editors of *Le Figaro* affected not to believe the news: "As long as we have not read this list in the *Officiel* .... it must be affirmed that such a ministry is impossible, not viable, nonexistent. If it were not a fable, it would be a challenge. Therefore let us retain a faint hope."[158] Another conservative journal declared that "it is not a cabinet; it is a clique .... The whole opinion of the country will be stupefied and anxious."[159] *L'Echo de Paris* called it "this ministry of discord, humiliation, and ruin, born of an abominable plot against the national will and the most sacred interests of the country."[160] Furthermore, some observers believed that Minister of Finance Caillaux would be the real leader of the government, "with Doumergue as umbrella."[161]

---

[156] *Journal des Débats,* December 7, 1913.
[157] *Carnets de Georges Louis,* II, 96.
[158] *Le Figaro,* December 9, 1913; cf. *Le Gaulois,* December 7 and 8, 1913.
[159] *Journal des Débats,* December 9, 1913.
[160] *L'Echo de Paris,* December 9, 1913.
[161] Gueydan, *Les rois de la république,* II, 299.

Because of this, Moderates cried out that Poincaré had been duped, or had forgotten his obligations to his supporters; they called on the legislature to destroy the new government. The president was not repudiated by his friends, however. Men like Gaston Calmette of *Le Figaro* proclaimed their confidence that Poincaré, Briand, and Barthou would save France from ruin at the hands of the Radicals.[162]

Without question it was a bitter pill for the president to swallow. Clemenceau wrote with glee: "I am told that the Elysée thermometer marked a polar temperature at the reception of the ministers . . . ."[163] Baron von Schoen believed that the new cabinet meant the end of Poincaré's national policy. For the first time, observed the German ambassador, the president had been granted little influence in the choice of ministers. Only two of his personal friends were included: Doumergue as premier and Albert Lebrun in a minor post. Moreover, it seemed that Doumergue's leadership might be purely nominal as long as Caillaux was in the government.[164]

Poincaré undoubtedly felt some pique at being forced to replace his allies by a group of men who had voted against him at Versailles.[165] Yet the president's position might have been worse, even though the Moderate ship had foundered. He had saved something from the wreckage, and that something—the military-service law—was of first importance to him. A majority of the new ministers had bolted their party to vote for three-year service; therefore Doumergue's promise to maintain the law was likely to be kept. Moreover, the general elections were not far off. In view of the president's popularity so strikingly manifested on his recent travels, perhaps the opposition to him in the Chamber would be repudiated when the country went to the polls. Until then little progress could be made

[162] *Le Figaro*, December 10, 1913; cf. *Le Gaulois*, December 9, 1913.

[163] *L'Homme Libre*, December 11, 1913.

[164] Schoen to Bethmann, December 10, 1913, *G.P.*, XXXIX, 237-40.

[165] Poincaré, III, 345.

anyway; the key measure of the national program was safe; better things could be hoped for in the near future. Poincaré considered it regrettable, of course, that the Radicals were to control the administrative machine just before the election, for they could thus exert a certain amount of pressure. But there were other ways to maneuver and electioneer. Besides, Doumergue was personally friendly and would see that the president received due consideration. Especially in foreign affairs, where Doumergue was without experience, Poincaré might make his influence felt to offset that of Caillaux.[166] The Radical victory did not necessarily mean that Poincaré was ready to withdraw into the obscurity of a Loubet or a Fallières. A battle had been lost; but the campaign had just begun.

[166] According to the *Carnets de Georges Louis* (II, 93–94), Poincaré admitted that he had chosen Doumergue because of the latter's ignorance of foreign affairs. This is doubtful; Poincaré simply wanted a Radical with Moderate leanings.

CHAPTER V

THE ERA OF LEFT-WING CABINETS

POLITICS AND INTRIGUE IN 1914

The selection of Gaston Doumergue as premier introduced a new period in the history of Poincaré's septennate. During the preceding ten months, cabinet and president had seen eye to eye. From December 1913 to the outbreak of war, Radicals held a majority of the ministerial portfolios. This was likely to have an adverse effect upon Poincaré's political influence and freedom of action.

Doumergue's ministerial declaration did not forecast any very fundamental changes. It was justly described as vague and banal, designed only to keep the cabinet in office until the elections of 1914. It contained one veiled rebuke to Poincaré's Right-wing supporters when it promised "the defense and development of republican institutions, openly or insidiously attacked for some time . . . ." Doumergue added a public repudiation of all support which did not come from the Left.[1] This statement was a slap at the two preceding cabinets and at Poincaré, all of whom had accepted votes from the clerical and antirepublican Right.

Doumergue did his best to spare the president, but Left-wing publicists were not so generous. They criticized Poincaré for his refusal to make Caillaux premier, and warned him not to suppose that he had a mission to save France. "Your duty is much simpler," declared the Socialist leader Marcel

[1] *Chamber Debates,* December 11, 1913, pp. 696, 708.

Sembat. "You are at the window of the Elysée to deliver round trip tickets to the Place Beauvau."[2]

Sour looks were cast at Poincaré from all sides. His Moderate friends resented their fall from power; many of them had honestly believed that the presidential election of 1913 would mean seven years of famine for the Radicals. They swallowed their disappointment and turned their wrath upon the new cabinet. So severely did the conservative press treat Doumergue that the German chargé d'affaires was moved to report the campaign to Berlin. The chargé suspected, although without proof, that certain articles were inspired by the Elysée.[3] Clemenceau openly accused the president of plotting against the ministry.[4] Although Poincaré may have approved the violent anti-Doumergue campaign, there is no reason to believe that he inspired it. No intervention was needed to set off the Moderate journalists. The president could give his silent blessing to his supporters while viewing their activity from afar.

Outwardly at least, Poincaré's relations with the new ministry might have been much worse. He could not fight them openly; constitution and tradition forebade it. By backstage influence and intrigue, however, he could seriously embarrass the government; and some critics have charged him with doing so. Among other things, the president is supposed to have exceeded his constitutional rights by playing politics in preparation for the forthcoming general elections. Late in 1913 a group of legislators met to form a new campaign group called the "Fédération des gauches." Its avowed policies were those of the Moderates. Its leaders were men like Briand, Barthou, and Millerand, all of whom had been instrumental in securing Poincaré's election to the presidency. Its major aim, as re-

[2] *L'Humanité,* December 10, 1913; cf. Jaurès in *L'Humanité,* December 7 and 9, 1913. The ministry of the interior (frequently combined with the premiership) was located at the Place Beauvau.

[3] Radowitz to Bethmann, December 12, 1913, *G.P.,* XXXIX, 240–41.

[4] *L'Homme Libre,* February 9, 1914.

vealed during the ensuing months, was to secure a Chamber pledged to defend the three-year law. Political observers naturally regarded the new party as a Poincaré organization, designed to carry out the policies which he had been supporting for a year.[5]

If Poincaré really helped to establish the Fédération des gauches, he left no evidence of his activity. He did, however, confer frequently with politicians and especially with those who were his staunch supporters; he must have been acquainted with their plans. He was prudent, doing nothing which would publicly reveal any connection with the new group. Yet he needed to do nothing; everyone knew that the Fédération and Poincaré stood for identical principles. It was this state of affairs which led Clemenceau to believe that the president was conspiring against the cabinet.[6]

Poincaré has also drawn censure for his supposed part in the Caillaux-Calmette affair. Soon after the Radical ministry came to power, editor Gaston Calmette of *Le Figaro* began a series of daily attacks on Caillaux. He threatened to publish certain letters which were supposed to impugn Caillaux's honesty and moral character. The affair ended in tragedy when Caillaux's second wife, fearing the publication of private correspondence, shot and killed Calmette.

The charge has repeatedly been made that Calmette's editorials stemmed from the Elysée, whose occupant wanted the

---

[5] *Le Figaro*, December 27, 1913; *Le Matin*, January 14, 1914. In the opinion of Ambassador von Schoen, the new organization meant not only a battle between Moderates and Radicals, "but also a more or less open decision for or against M. Poincaré and his personal policy. For the president himself, this is actually a question of existence; for if his friends fail to displace the men now in power, he will become their slave to a degree which, in the long run, will be incompatible with his independent character and his interpretation of his task." (Schoen to Bethmann, December 31, 1913, *G.P.*, XXXIX, 245–46.)

[6] Poincaré grew extremely irritated at Clemenceau's attacks, and spoke to the premier about methods of curbing this talk of conspiracy (Poincaré, IV, 74).

political scalps of his enemies in the cabinet.[7] There is absolutely no evidence to support this theory, but it is true that the president was indirectly involved in the affair. Calmette was a close acquaintance of Poincaré and would not have undertaken his scurrilous campaign in the face of active presidential disapproval. Caillaux knew this, and finally went to the Elysée to demand that the president intervene. The request came too late; Madame Caillaux was already on her way to the editor's office. Several days after the assassination Poincaré spoke with distaste of the *Figaro* editorials, and declared that he would have stopped them if Caillaux had left him time to restrain Calmette.[8] The fact remains that he failed to exert pressure of his own accord when it would have been of some use.

Caillaux later came to believe that the real author of the *Figaro* editorials was not Calmette but ex-Premier Louis Barthou. That Barthou was directly involved is almost certain. In his possession was the so-called "Fabre document" which linked Caillaux with a financial scandal of 1911 and which he read aloud in the Chamber immediately after the assassination. But Barthou's complicity did not necessarily implicate the president. In fact Poincaré censured Barthou severely for his use of the Fabre document.[9] The president's real responsibility was negative in character; it consisted in his refusal to influence his friends against the campaign of abuse. Much as he may have deplored the *Figaro* articles from the moral standpoint, he

---

[7] Poincaré, IV, 91; VIII, 61; *Carnets de Georges Louis,* II, 145; Schoen to Bethmann, December 31, 1913, *G.P.,* XXIX, 245.

[8] *Journal d'Alexandre Ribot et correspondances inédites 1914–1922* (Paris, 1936), p. 7. In his memoirs Poincaré has excused his nonintervention on the ground that no attempt to restrain Calmette was likely to succeed (Poincaré, IV, 33). This statement does not square with Ribot's account of a conversation with Poincaré: "He reproaches Caillaux for not having left him time to act upon Calmette, which he would have done successfully."

[9] Ribot, *Journal,* p. 6. Georges Suarez has asserted that both Barthou and Briand tried to restrain Calmette in March 1914 (Suarez, *Briand,* II, 476).

found them politically agreeable.[10] Perhaps, by a process of rationalization, he believed that any interference would bring his office down into the realm of party conflicts. As a matter of fact it was his failure to intervene which brought that very result. The Radicals' impression that he was intriguing against the cabinet was only strengthened by the Calmette affair.

During the early months of 1914, the president was much less in the public eye than he had been until that time. The conservatives, somewhat disillusioned by his "capitulation" to the Radicals in December, had lost much of their enthusiasm. Poincaré may have deliberately avoided publicity as an answer to the "personal power" accusations of 1913. He went quietly about his official duties: "My interviews with M. Doumergue and with some of the ministers, rather rare visits from political men, sessions of the council, the reading of parliamentary minutes—this is all that attaches me to public life."[11] The series of provincial excursions that had marked the previous year became rare during the winter season. With the arrival of spring they were resumed; but the attitude of the press showed that they had lost much of their news value. The speeches which he made were inevitably couched in vague and innocuous terms. It almost seemed that he had begun to dodge the public spotlight.

The plain fact was that Poincaré's popularity, at its peak in February 1913 and again in September, was slipping away. The Belgian ambassador reported that people had begun to find the president too lavish in his speeches, that they were criticizing what they called his appeals to popularity and his anti-traditional habit of including Madame Poincaré on most of

[10] In private conversations Poincaré spoke of Caillaux in terms as bitter as those used by *Le Figaro*. He made such statements to a journalist whom he believed to be anti-Caillaux but who was actually on good terms with the minister and reported the criticisms to him (interview with M. Caillaux, October 17, 1938). Cf. also Guillaume to Davignon, March 10, 1914, *Belgian Docs.*, p. 305.

[11] Poincaré, IV, 27.

his itineraries. His own followers were disgruntled, added the ambassador, since Doumergue's accession to power: "He has not given what was expected of him; confidence is disappearing."[12] Others likewise noted this decline in prestige. Ambassador Gérard, friendly to Poincaré, and Georges Louis, hostile to him, both observed it.[13] Izvolsky had to admit in January that, contrary to all expectations, Doumergue was growing stronger and would probably control the elections at the expense of Poincaré and the Moderates.[14] A month later Izvolsky predicted a sharp personal struggle between the new Chamber and the president. The ambassador believed that Poincaré would resist but that his defeat was likely.[15]

Poincaré realized that he was the object of bitter hostility. The neoroyalist *Action Française* society, which had feared all through 1913 that Poincaré's republican nationalism would destroy its own "integral nationalism," now scoffed freely at "the failure of the Poincaré experiment."[16] Clemenceau continued his daily jibes: "The style is tending toward Louis XVI furniture and Louis XIV presidents. Something tells me that we are going to need a Saint-Simon." Or again: "I endure the 'Poincaré experiment,' I do not participate in it."[17] Not only was Poincaré aware of these attacks but he knew that his

[12] Guillaume to Davignon, March 10, 1914, *Belgian Docs.*, pp. 305-7.

[13] Gérard, *Mémoires*, p. 529; *Carnets de Georges Louis*, II, 94. Cf. *Les Carnets de Gallieni* (Paris, 1932), p. 18. Gallieni remarked on the "very cold" reception given to Poincaré at the Concours Agricole in February 1914, and contrasted it with the events of February 1913.

[14] Izvolsky to Sazonov, January 30, 1914, *Die Internationalen Beziehungen im Zeitalter des Imperialismus; Dokumente aus den Archiven der Zarischen und der Provisorischen Regierung* (Berlin, 1931–   ), I, 129-30. (This series will be cited hereafter as *Russian Docs.*)

[15] Izvolsky to Sazonov, March 12, 1914, *Russian Docs.*, I, 434.

[16] *L'Action Française*, March 12, 1914. This royalist journal continually accused Poincaré of such things as "impulsive pusillanimity" and laughed at *"les bonnes poires"* who had placed confidence in him (*ibid.*, January 1, 2, 14, and March 16, 1914).

[17] *L'Homme Libre*, March 2 and 12, 1914.

friends were no longer defending him as they once had done. Just before the elections, therefore, he took a villa on the Mediterranean for a month, partly for recreation and partly to emphasize his avoidance of the electoral struggle.[18] He probably felt that a temporary retirement would be discreet and would shelter him from suspicions of personal interference. The defense of Moderate principles could be left in the capable hands of the Fédération des gauches.

While the president was vacationing in the South, his friend Gabriel Hanotaux published an article in *Le Figaro* which attracted considerable attention. Hanotaux had been one of the leaders of the Poincaré-for-president campaign in 1912. He had vigorously maintained that no new powers were necessary for the president, and that a strong man could raise the office to a high level of influence. He had gone so far as to imply that the chief magistrate of France was a potential Louis XIV.[19] Yet Hanotaux completely reversed himself in April 1914 and plumped for thorough constitutional revision. "A presidency of the American type, surrounded by carefully elaborated means of control, is not so appalling," he wrote. "After fifty years of free activity, the republic can very well endure a president of another sort than a *président soliveau*."[20]

Many years later, M. Hanotaux explained his change of mind as follows:

. . . . The nuance between the two articles is connected with the events of the time:

At the time of the first article, calm of spirits, and moderation in constitutions.

But, at the time of the second article, general situation aggravated, perspectives of great external complications, three-year service, etc. I desired for *execution* the strengthening of the *executive*. . . . .[21]

[18] Izvolsky to Sazonov, April 9, 1914, *Russian Docs.*, II, 200.

[19] *Le Figaro*, September 27, 1912.

[20] *Ibid.*, April 10, 1914.

[21] Gabriel Hanotaux to the author, February 25, 1938.

Hanotaux's explanation was doubtless sincere as far as it went; but it disregarded certain factors. For one thing European tension was not much more severe in the spring of 1914 than it had been in 1912, at the time of the Balkan wars. Furthermore, a president with the potential strength of a Louis XIV should have been able to meet the most serious situation without the aid of a constitutional amendment. Hanotaux failed to mention the effect of Poincaré's first fourteen months at the Elysée on his theory of the presidency. He must have been disillusioned by the "Poincaré experiment," for already it seemed to disprove the idea that a strong man could revive the office of chief magistrate.

Some observers believed that Poincaré shared this disappointment after a year at the Elysée. Clemenceau immediately assumed that the president had inspired Hanotaux's article, in an attempt to set off a movement for constitutional revision.[22] This assumption was strengthened by the fact that Hanotaux and Poincaré were vacationing at the time in the same Mediterranean village. When questioned after many years about the president's influence on his article, Hanotaux replied: "We doubtless talked about it with President Poincaré; but common sense was enough."[23] If common sense was really enough, then Poincaré ought to have agreed that a constitutional amendment was necessary. Yet his memoirs give an opposite impression. Poincaré has recalled that during a conversation with Theodore Roosevelt in June 1914 the latter suggested an American-type presidency for France. According to his own account Poincaré was shocked by this "foolish idea," which he proceeded to extirpate from Roosevelt's mind.[24] Evidently the president lacked either common sense or frankness. The fairest conclusion seems to be that Hanotaux's proposal of an increase in the president's constitutional powers was his own, resulting

[22] L'Homme Libre, May 8, 1914.
[23] Hanotaux letter, February 25, 1938.
[24] Poincaré, IV, 154 (June 5, 1914).

from the failure of his "strong-man-at-the-Elysée" hopes of 1912. And Poincaré raised no objection to the Hanotaux article, although he was doubtless aware that it would be viewed as a reflection of his own theories. If he expected to revive the office when he became president, that expectation must have lost part of its force by April 1914.

THE ELECTIONS OF 1914

No matter how far the president might withdraw from the scene of the legislative elections, he could not pretend to be indifferent to their results. From them would issue the Chamber with which he must work during most of his term. The character of this Chamber would determine the type of ministries that he could expect. A conservative majority would permit him to co-operate intimately with the government; a Radical victory would greatly hamper his influence.

Poincaré's political friends of the Fédération des gauches carried on a vigorous campaign. Briand, Barthou, and Millerand made frequent speeches in favor of their "national" policy, concentrating on the integral maintenance of the three-year law and on the need for a system of proportional representation. They received able support from the Moderate press, which publicized their platform, editorialized in their favor, and continually "exposed" the Radical cabinet's political maneuvers.

Generally regarded as the chief question at issue was the military-service law. That issue was somewhat clouded, however, by a division of opinion among the Radicals. A majority in the party were outspoken opponents of three-year service; but quite a number hesitated to commit themselves definitely during the electoral campaign. The Moderate press naturally exploited the Radicals' tendency to hedge.

The French electoral system provided for a second ballot in districts where no candidate received a majority. Every party could therefore make extravagant claims after the first vote in April 1914, for about half the seats were left undecided. The

Moderates attempted to compile popular vote totals showing that France favored the military law.[25] But their figures could not hide remarkable gains for the Socialists and losses for the Right groups. Socialist candidates, all thoroughgoing enemies of three-year service, received almost 300,000 more votes than in the previous election.[26] Meanwhile the Radicals could point with pride to the fact that every one of Doumergue's ministers, not excepting Caillaux, was re-elected on the first ballot.[27]

At the run-off election two weeks later the Left-wing success became still more pronounced. Radicals and Socialists pooled their strength in most districts, for they were linked by a common hatred of the military law. Some conservatives still strove to make out a victory for themselves and for the three-year law by totaling popular votes and by juggling the party lists. But they were whistling to keep up their courage. No one could ignore the fact that the Socialists alone had made an important gain—rising from 67 to 102 deputies—and that the Radicals had held their own. Left-wing representatives now controlled at least half the seats.[28] An impartial analysis of professions of faith, however, indicated that a slight majority favored retention of the three-year law.[29]

The Moderates and reactionaries were justifiably pessimistic. The *Journal des Débats* believed that the extreme Left "will not be mistress, but . . . . will be powerful." It held that

[25] *Le Matin,* April 27–29, 1914; *Journal des Débats,* April 28 and 29, 1914.

[26] *L'Humanité,* April 28, 1914; *Le Matin,* April 28 and May 3, 1914.

[27] Caillaux had resigned from the cabinet after the assassination of Calmette.

[28] P. O. La Chesnais, "Les élections: statistique des résultats," *La Grande Revue,* LXXXV (May 25, 1914), 255.

[29] According to the best analysis, about 325 of the 602 deputies had declared in favor, while the remainder desired immediate or gradual return to two-year service (Georges Lachapelle, *Elections législatives des 26 avril et 10 mai 1914* [Paris, 1914], pp. 252–56. The Russian military attaché was informed that only 310 deputies would support the law (Ignatiev report, June 11, 1914, *Russian Docs.,* III, 201).

the Left could still be kept out of office if the other deputies were wise enough to unite.[30] The editor of the royalist *Gaulois* was less hopeful, declaring: "Never has a Chamber promised to be more menacing for our interests, for our beliefs, for our faith in the nation . . . ."[31] A British weekly mournfully admitted that "the wave of patriotic emotion which carried M. Poincaré to the Premiership and then to the Presidency is beginning to ebb a little . . . ."[32] Izvolsky characterized the election as primarily a success for the "extreme left revolutionaries."[33]

Poincaré did not escape recrimination from his defeated allies. Even after the indecisive first ballot, Ribot wrote to his wife that "there is much irritation against the president of the republic, who goes walking at Menton and affects indifference to the struggle of parties."[34] When the "monstrous" results of the second ballot arrived, Arthur Meyer of *Le Gaulois* could not confine his wrath: "Oh! our hopes of the congress of Versailles! What an awakening! What a disenchantment!" Meyer went so far as to compare Poincaré to Pontius Pilate.[35]

This criticism did not ease the difficult situation which faced the president on his return to Paris. The election had given no one an unquestioned mandate, but it was certain that Poincaré's enemies had gained strength. Doumergue was expected to resign shortly; but Poincaré was likely to invite trouble if he should try to place his friends back in power. Izvolsky believed that Poincaré could restore the Moderates, in view of the near-balance between Right and Left in the Chamber; but he doubted that the president would have enough courage, after having once failed his supporters in December.[36]

---

[30] *Journal des Débats,* May 11, 1914.   [31] *Le Gaulois,* May 11, 1914.

[32] *Saturday Review,* CXVII (May 16, 1914), 627.

[33] Izvolsky to Sazonov, May 21, 1914, *Russian Docs.,* III, 47–48.

[34] Ribot, *Journal,* p. 2. Cf. *La Libre Parole,* May 1, 1914.

[35] *Le Gaulois,* May 11 and 12, 1914.

[36] Izvolsky to Sazonov, May 21, 1914, *Russian Docs.,* III, 47–48.

The confidence of those supporters was somewhat shaken since the "mistake" of Doumergue's accession; but they knew that the Elysée was their last hope, and they began to exert increasing pressure on its occupant. Arthur Meyer interrupted his complaints to declare that the president had one more chance to prove himself. There must be a choice, asserted Meyer, between the Socialists and the nation: "I cannot believe that you reserve for her [France] a supreme disappointment."[87] Another prominent royalist argued that a conservative majority existed "without knowing itself," that it was the president's duty to indicate this amorphous majority, and that intervention in such a crisis would not be unconstitutional.[88] The academician Alfred Capus, always dramatic, announced that "there is no Frenchman who, since yesterday, does not look anxiously toward the Elysée. Anxiously, but also with the most complete confidence in the patriotism and the high judgment of the head of the state."[89] *Le Correspondant* still grumbled at the president's weakness in the December crisis but believed that he could act if he so desired. "Govern boldly!" it urged in the words of Bossuet.[40] As for the Radicals, their policy was one of silent but watchful waiting. Camille Pelletan, however, did issue a warning against any effort to restore the Moderates to power. Such a cabinet would be a challenge to the nation, he said, and "would not live for forty-eight hours, under whatever pseudonym it were hidden."[41]

This shower of journalistic advice fell upon the Elysée without visible effect. Poincaré gave no public indication of what he would do when the imminent crisis arrived.[42] Pri-

---

[87] *Le Gaulois*, May 12 and 15, 1914.

[88] Count d'Haussonville in *Le Figaro*, May 12, 1914.

[89] *Le Figaro*, May 21, 1914.

[40] *Le Correspondant*, CCLV (May 25, 1914), 824–25.

[41] *Le Matin*, May 19, 1914.

[42] Ambassador von Schoen predicted that Poincaré would ignore these exhortations of "moral duty" to his electors. Von Schoen believed that the

vately he expressed distaste for *Le Gaulois's* provocation and declared that people were too upset over the result of the elections. He told Ribot that he would not expose himself unless a national question, touching upon foreign policy, should make it his duty.[48] The shining example of such a national question was, of course, the military-service law.

Two weeks after the elections, Poincaré finally put an end to his long abstention from public appearances. In a notable speech delivered at Lyon on May 24 he outlined his conception of the presidential office in greater detail than at any other time during his septennate. His choice of moment for this extensive exposé, more than a year after his election, doubtless resulted from the Right-wing demands upon him in view of the approaching crisis. He said:

. . . . I am pleased to hear you say that, faithful to constitutional truth, you place the duties and the person of the president of the republic above parties. If, in the exercise of his magistracy, he can incur no responsibility, parliamentary or political, then he must remain a stranger to the inevitable divisions of a free democracy: he must be and must remain . . . . the president of all the French; he must fulfill, with scrupulous loyalty and with constant care for great national interests, the role of arbiter and counselor which the republican constitution assigns to him.

France, having undergone the sad experience of personal power and not wishing to try it again, intends . . . . to control . . . . the daily activity of responsible cabinets.

These words were designed to calm the fears of the Radicals. But, Poincaré continued:

At the same time, ... [France] desires that all duties in the state . . . . be conscientiously fulfilled by those to whom they were confided, and she expects the president of the republic, like all other citizens, to acquit himself integrally and without default of the duties incumbent upon him . . . .

---

president would remain strictly constitutional, even if it meant the sacrifice of his "personal work," the three-year law (Schoen to Bethmann, May 23, 1914, *G.P.*, XXXIX, 256–58).   [48] Ribot, *Journal*, p. 6.

Because he is charged with representing the whole nation, the president of the republic must seek to raise himself above particular interests . . . . He must free himself from the contingent and the ephemeral to affirm in his mind the idea of permanent necessities; he must . . . . try to consider [all questions] exclusively from the French point of view.[44]

This address gave the journalists an unrestricted opportunity to trade interpretations. Clemenceau scoffed that Poincaré had been talking again about "the metaphysics of his office," adding: "He pronounced some of those ritualistic words which, because they have no definite meaning, generally meet the approval of everyone."[45] Clemenceau's sarcasm was truer than he knew. Each party emphasized the phrases which it found pleasing and ignored the rest. Radicals and Socialists praised the first half of the speech, which upheld presidential irresponsibility and condemned personal power; they saw it as a firm reply to the reactionaries.[46] Moderates skimmed over this portion and fell greedily upon the second part. Le Matin reported that the final paragraphs were pronounced with "an intentional insistence"; it concluded that Poincaré would depart from his "strict neutrality" in certain cases.[47] Le Figaro pointed out that, in view of circumstances at the time, "to speak of the rights and duties of the president of the republic is to show in the clearest and most forceful fashion the intention to act. Opinion and the political world so understand it . . . ."[48] The Journal des Débats interpreted the phrases about "permanent necessities" and "the French point of view" as having reference to the three-year law.[49] In this it was correct.

[44] Poincaré, IV, 130–31; Journal des Débats, May 25, 1914.

[45] L'Homme Libre, June 1, 1914.

[46] Le Radical, May 25 and 26, 1914; L'Humanité, May 26, 1914.

[47] Le Matin, May 25, 1914.

[48] Le Figaro, May 26, 1914.

[49] Journal des Débats, May 26, 1914; cf. Le Matin and Le Gaulois, May 25, 1914.

Many commentators confessed that they were perplexed by the contradictions of the speech. "It is at the same time perfect and insignificant, irreproachable and colorless," wrote one of them.[50] Encouraged by certain statements, they lost confidence again when they looked at other sections.[51] *Le Gaulois* finally concluded that "M. Poincaré's intentions will be known only by their passage into reality. After words, acts. Let us await the acts."[52]

Poincaré probably was aware that he swung a double-edged sword at Lyon. On the one hand, he wished to rebuke Right-wing extremists like Meyer, who asked him to exceed constitutional limits. On the other hand, he warned the Radicals and Socialists that he would fight any attempt to infringe upon France's armed strength, even though he were to fall in its defense. He continued to regard the three-year law, a controversial measure, as something above controversy. The Lyon speech gave convincing proof that Poincaré could not possibly be the traditional type of president. His horror of any sort of coup d'état or antirepublicanism was completely sincere. Yet he was a man of action and of strong convictions: he was simply unable to divest himself of those convictions when he entered the Elysée. Rather than see them go down to defeat, he was prepared to resist with every weapon which lay at hand.

If any doubts remained as to his attitude toward the military law, they were dispelled by a speech delivered at Rennes on the first of June. The president asserted bluntly that there could be no question of reducing France's military strength.[53] In view of the circumstances, this was a risky attitude for an impartial arbiter who stood above parties; for it was still a disputed point whether the country had returned a majority for

[50] *La Libre Parole,* May 29, 1914.

[51] *Le Gaulois* and *La République Française,* May 25, 1914; *La Libre Parole,* May 26, 1914.

[52] *Le Gaulois,* May 26, 1914.   [53] Poincaré, IV, 143.

or against the three-year law. The speech drew a sharp reply from Jaurès, who wrote: "This brutal declaration of the president, at the moment when it occurred, is frankly unconstitutional . . . ."[54] Poincaré's position would certainly become impossible if the Chamber should vote to repeal the three-year law. On the other hand, his open statement might rally a few waverers to its support. The issue was frankly joined; the president had identified himself with a party, even while denying that he had done so.

THE JUNE CRISIS

On the day after Poincaré's speech at Rennes, the Doumergue cabinet resigned without even awaiting the first session of the new legislature. For the third time, the president faced a ministerial crisis. This one proved by far the worst of the three; it was perhaps the most difficult in the history of the Third Republic.

Hastening back to Paris, the president first tried to bring Doumergue to reconsider. When he failed to shake the ex-premier's resolution, Poincaré began the long and tedious series of conferences which would determine his choice. The political spotlight of France was upon him. For a week there had been rumors of an imminent presidential crisis; one journalist compared Poincaré's position with that of Louis XVI on the day after the Bastille fell.[55]

The task of forming a ministry was first confided to René Viviani. Viviani belonged to the Socialist-Republican party, a small group which stood between the Radicals and the Socialists. He had voted against the three-year law but was not one of its most outspoken opponents; therefore he was willing to meet Poincaré's condition that it be faithfully enforced.[56] After two days of effort Viviani succeeded in organizing a viable

[54] *L'Humanité,* June 2, 1914.
[55] *Carnets de Georges Louis,* II, 110; Gueydan, *op. cit.,* II, 176.
[56] Poincaré, IV, 148.

cabinet, but on the morning of June 6 it collapsed like a house of cards. Two Radical ministers, Justin Godart and Georges Ponsot, disapproved of the ministerial declaration because it promised a future modification of the military law "if a change in external circumstances permits." They branded this phrase as derogatory to the pride of France, whose actions were thus made to depend upon those of other nations.[57]

Behind this sudden withdrawal of Godart and Ponsot lay the old Left-wing suspicion that France had become a servant of Russian ambitions. It was revived when Paléologue, now French ambassador to St. Petersburg, arrived in Paris on June 5.[58] Paléologue had returned for other reasons, but on learning of the cabinet crisis he immediately let it be known that he would not return to Russia if the three-year law were sacrificed.[59] Journalists got hold of the story and suggested that there must be some sort of secret Franco-Russian bargain which guaranteed the maintenance of the military law. They quoted from St. Petersburg newspapers, whose attitude lent color to their theory.[60] Paléologue denied the allegation, explaining that his position in the face of Russian opinion would simply become impossible if France should abandon preparedness. But he could not placate the Leftists, who were now convinced that France had sold out her independence to Russia.

Paléologue's indiscreet remarks were a source of sharp embarrassment to Poincaré. They caused the collapse of Viviani's

[57] *Le Matin*, June 7, 1914. Ambassador von Schoen was informed that the real cause of the collapse was Poincaré's interference in the selection of ministers. According to von Schoen the president had demanded that the Moderate Dupuy be included, thus toning down the Radical color of the cabinet and arousing the anger of the Left (Schoen to Bethmann, June 15, 1914, *G.P.*, XXXIX, 266–70; cf. *L'Humanité*, June 9 and 10, 1914). Clemenceau also mentioned this pressure to bring in Dupuy, although he did not believe that it caused the cabinet's breakup (*L'Homme Libre*, June 7, 1914).

[58] Delcassé had resigned as ambassador in December 1913.

[59] Maurice Paléologue, "La Russie des tsars pendant la grande guerre," *Revue des Deux Mondes*, January 15, 1921, p. 228.

[60] In *Le Matin*, June 11 and 12, 1914.

embryo cabinet and, in addition, they embittered the feud between the Radicals and the president. Any suspicion of Russia inevitably reflected on Poincaré, chief protagonist of the alliance. His enemies had alleged in 1913 that the army increase was a direct outgrowth of his first journey to St. Petersburg. When Paléologue implied that the French government was obligated to maintain the three-year law, it seemed natural to conclude that Poincaré must have made a binding promise to Russia.[61] The resultant criticism adversely affected both the president and the Franco-Russian alliance. Izvolsky, who recognized this fact, spoke with contempt of Paléologue's "babbling."[62]

Meanwhile the search for a government had been resumed. On June 7 Poincaré offered power successively to Deschanel, Delcassé, Etienne Clémentel, Jean Dupuy, and Paul-Louis Peytral, and five times met refusals.[63] None of these men save Peytral was an orthodox representative of the newly victorious Left. Faced by an ever darker horizon, the president turned again to Doumergue for advice. Doumergue suggested that only three possibilities remained: Viviani again, Léon Bourgeois, or Alexandre Ribot. Poincaré seized the opportunity to name a Moderate on the advice of a Radical, who could therefore shoulder the responsibility.[64] Ribot accepted the president's offer in order to save him from an embarrassing situation.[65] Immediately the Left, which had been glorying in its

---

[61] A conservative deputy, Major Driant, had revived Leftist suspicions by writing on May 21: "If the three-year law is *really* threatened, the president of the republic has the imperious duty of intervening personally. He went to Petersburg and to London. He *knows* . . . . that our alliances and our ententes hold only if this law remains untouchable . . . ." (*La Libre Parole,* May 21, 1914).

[62] Izvolsky to Sazonov, June 18, 1914, *Russian Docs.,* III, 267.

[63] Poincaré, IV, 132–35; *Le Matin,* June 8, 1914.

[64] Poincaré asked Doumergue to propose Ribot in order to protect himself. His memoirs naturally do not mention this; but Doumergue told Ribot of the maneuver at the time (Ribot, *Journal,* p. 10).   [65] *Ibid.,* p. 9.

new strength and its prospects of power, chorused its disillusionment and anger. The Elysée had finally shown its hand, said their press; control was to be given openly to reaction.[66] Their wrath was intensified when Ribot announced his list of ministers, for it included not a single representative of the powerful Left parties.[67] The Radical deputies met at once and voted 109 to 4 to refuse confidence; they predicted that the cabinet would not live a single day.[68]

The diplomatic corps in Paris observed the tumult and foresaw worse things to come. Ambassador von Schoen predicted a war on the cabinet and on the president, who was accused of violating constitutional principles; he believed that an era of bitter struggle and scandal was about to begin.[69] The Russian military attaché feared that the crisis could be solved only by dissolution and new elections under pressure. The attaché doubted, however, that Poincaré possessed enough courage to dissolve the Chamber, for the president's so-called negligence during the recent elections had destroyed confidence in him.[70] Thus Poincaré was a target for attacks by the Right as well as the Left. He subsequently pointed to this fact as proof of his impartiality.[71] But he failed to mention the fact that Right and Left did not criticize him simultaneously. The conservatives stopped their abuse as soon as their wishes had been met by the nomination of Ribot. When he took this step, the president won the renewed confidence of his old supporters, even while earning the redoubled hatred of the Left.

[66] Many quoted in *L'Homme Libre,* June 9, 1914.

[67] The president did not keep hands off in the selection of ministers. He exerted pressure on Joseph Noulens in an effort to bring the latter into the new cabinet (Ribot, *Journal,* p. 13). He also intervened to hasten the end of the crisis, urging that the ministry present itself at once without further discussion of policy (*ibid.,* pp. 14–16).

[68] *Le Matin,* June 11, 1914; *L'Homme Libre,* June 10, 1914.

[69] Schoen to Bethmann, June 10, 1914, *G.P.,* XXXIX, 263–65.

[70] Ignatiev report, June 11, 1914, *Russian Docs.,* III, 201.

[71] Poincaré, IV, 120, 125.

Ribot and his little band of Moderates must have had forebodings of trouble when they entered the Chamber on June 12. At any rate, it came. The ministerial declaration was repeatedly interrupted by disorder and by outbursts against the military law. Ribot's assertion that the cabinet was composed of "firm republicans" drew sarcastic comments. His program, except for his stand on the three-year law, was surprisingly liberal; he understood the trend of the recent election, and took account of it. The Left admitted that this was the case but refused to believe that a Moderate would really apply such a program. Certain of victory, they repudiated the ministry 306 to 262—a striking corroboration of Leftist claims that they would control 305 votes.[72]

It was, as one journal declared, "a crisis without precedent." The most unpopular cabinets were customarily allowed a few days or weeks of life at least. Only during the MacMahon crisis of 1887 had a government been overthrown on its very first appearance. The repudiation of Ribot was a smashing blow in the teeth of the Moderates.

It was a blow at Poincaré above all, and both sides admitted the fact. Many deputies received the result with cries of "To Versailles!"[73] Crowds thronged the boulevards that evening, and shouts of "Long live Poincaré! Down with Jaurès!" mingled with the "Internationale."[74] *L'Humanité* again revived the old phrase used by MacMahon's enemies, *se soumettre ou se démettre.*[75] In Paris and in the provinces, Radical newspapers gloated: "M. Ribot—perhaps also a person placed higher than he—now knows the cost of trying to brave . . . . the opinion of the country . . . ."[76] Even Izvolsky criticized Poincaré's at-

[72] *Chamber Debates*, June 12, 1914, pp. 144–63.

[73] *Le Figaro*, June 13, 1914; *L'Homme Libre*, June 13, 1914. This did not appear in the official record.

[74] *Le Matin*, June 13, 1914.

[75] *L'Humanité*, June 13, 1914.

[76] In *Le Matin*, June 13, 1914.

tempt to set up a Ribot government in the face of the recent election results.[77]

A few die-hard Moderates continued to declare their faith in the leader at the Elysée and even to urge dissolution. *Le Figaro* called Poincaré the only hope, *"un suprême recours."* "We can be sure," it added, "that this tenacious and patriotic Lorrainer will brave the most unjust campaigns and the most abject attacks rather than fail in the duty which his office imposes."[78] But these were voices crying in a political wilderness. Poincaré knew well enough that his choice lay between a Left representative and resignation. He chose the former, in the mildest possible form. He called Viviani once more, insisted anew on maintenance of the military law as his single condition, and saw a ministry formed within six hours—a speed record for the Third Republic.[79] The Viviani cabinet was drawn from all the Left parties except the Socialist; it promised that the three-year law would be enforced until conditions should permit a change. Without delay, the government was approved by a 342 to 139 vote. The crisis, fourteen days long, was over.

It was over, and Poincaré was still president. His prestige, however, had suffered severely. Much of his popularity had disappeared, and his resignation was freely discussed.[80] The Russian military attaché added that Poincaré had lost his hold upon his former friends, those who had depended upon his strength in times of crisis.[81] Sportsmanlike Radicals reproached him for allowing the "butchery" of an intelligent and generous

---

[77] Izvolsky to Sazonov, June 13, 1914, *Russian Docs.*, III, 210–11.

[78] *Le Figaro*, June 14, 1914. Many papers were quoted in *Le Matin*, June 13, 1914, *Journal des Débats*, June 14, 1914, *L'Homme Libre*, June 13, 1914, and *La Libre Parole*, June 13, 1914.

[79] *Le Matin*, June 14, 1914.

[80] Izvolsky to Sazonov, June 18, 1914, *Russian Docs.*, III, 265–67.

[81] Ignatiev report, June 18, 1914, *Russian Docs.*, III, 265.

man like Ribot.[82] Paul Cambon, a friend and political ally of Poincaré, agreed that Ribot had "sacrificed himself to protect the president of the republic."[83] Conservatives complained sourly, "One can only say that Viviani's cabinet is the worst possible with the exception of a Caillaux or a Combes."[84]

Strangely enough, it was the Radical *Dépêche de Toulouse* which came to Poincaré's defense. It praised him for refusing to fight back and for thus ending all danger of a personal conflict. The Chamber's vote against Ribot was merely an "indication" to the Elysée: "but this very indication is so clear and definite that for four years at least, M. Poincaré will no longer have to fear the threat of a presidential crisis . . . . Henceforth he has the obligatory virtue, which is . . . . the surest and easiest means of winning the rewards owed to virtue."[85]

The Radicals could well afford to be generous in this tongue-in-cheek way. They had placed the president in a position where, it seemed, only the "obligatory virtue" would prevent him from being crushed. Facing him were four years of Left-wing ministries which were likely to keep him in the traditional constitutional shadow. But at least he had not been driven out of office; the three-year law was guaranteed for the time being; Viviani was personally if not politically friendly, and would protect the president. Nevertheless his prospects for a share in the control of the government were not brilliant. Whether or not he would have been willing to serve out his full term under such conditions is a question that need not be answered. For twelve days later Franz Ferdinand was assassinated at Sarajevo and an era dawned in which the old rules had to be altered.

[82] Paul-Boncour in *La Grande Revue,* LXXXV (June 25, 1914), 727.
[83] Ribot, *Journal,* p. 19.
[84] *Le Correspondant,* June 25, 1914, p. 1233.
[85] In *Le Matin,* June 15, 1914.

FOREIGN AFFAIRS IN 1914

During the 1913 era of Moderate cabinets Poincaré had been actively concerned with the conduct of foreign affairs. His opinions had carried weight so long as his allies remained in office. It was reasonable to expect a sharp reduction in his influence when the Radicals came to power; yet the change proved to be almost unnoticeable. The reason for this lay in the character of Doumergue, who became foreign minister at the same time that he took the premiership.

Like Jonnart a year before, Doumergue was a novice in the conduct of diplomatic affairs. Anti-Poincarists have jumped to the conclusion that the president expected to keep the direction of foreign policy.[86] Doumergue admitted privately that he had not desired the portfolio and had accepted it only at "the lively insistence of M. Poincaré."[87] While the president's pressure may have grown out of his desire to find a straw man, it was more probably designed to keep Caillaux out of the Quai d'Orsay. Caillaux's return to the post might have weakened the bonds of the Triple Entente. Doumergue, on the other hand, was not a typical Radical. His views were so strongly tinged with conservatism and nationalism that in later years he became a staunch member of the Right. He was by nature susceptible to the opinions of Poincaré. The course of French diplomacy in 1914 suggests that he sought counsel there rather than from Caillaux, his own party chief. Thus the president kept his electoral promise to maintain unity in French foreign policy.[88]

Poincaré did not confine himself to advising an impressionable foreign minister. Just as in 1913 evidence of his active

---

[86] *Carnets de Georges Louis,* II, 108.

[87] Paléologue, *Revue des Deux Mondes,* May 15, 1935, p. 340. Poincaré did not mention this pressure on Doumergue in his memoirs.

[88] Poincaré has stated that Doumergue came to discuss with him all topics of serious interest (Poincaré, III, 354; IV, 95).

connection with diplomacy filtered through from time to time. European statesmen of several nationalities visited the Elysée to discuss Balkan problems.[89] The president continued his frequent conversations with members of the diplomatic corps in Paris. Izvolsky received from him vigorous assurance of support in the Liman von Sanders affair.[90] When Russia vetoed a loan designed to lure Turkey away from German influence, he reproached Izvolsky severely.[91] He discussed with the Austrian ambassador many phases of the Balkan situation—the fate of the Aegean islands, conditions in Albania, a reported German-Turkish deal in warships. He openly warned Austria against any attempt to build up special influence in the new Albanian state.[92] Szécsen's dispatches, in fact, seemed to attach more importance to Poincaré's opinions than to those of Doumergue. Nor was the German envoy neglected. In January Poincaré became the first French president to dine at the German embassy. After the formalities he took part in a discussion of the Turkish railway question.[93]

Poincaré also continued to aid in the maintenance and strengthening of the Triple Entente. When Delcassé resigned as ambassador to Russia in December 1913, Maurice Paléologue was chosen to succeed him. Paléologue refused the appoint-

[89] Poincaré, III, 346–47, IV, 22–23; Theodor Wolff, *The Eve of 1914* (New York, 1936), p. 170; Karolyi, *Fighting the World*, pp. 77–79; Szécsen dispatch, February 19, 1914, *Austrian Docs.*, VII, 896; Paléologue, *Revue des Deux Mondes*, May 15, 1935, p. 341; Henry Wickham Steed, *Through Thirty Years, 1892–1922* (New York, 1924), I, 388–89; Poincaré to Doumergue, December 22, 1913, *D.D.F.*, VIII, 829–31.

[90] Izvolsky to Sazonov, January 15, 1914, *Russian Docs.*, I, 13. The editors of *Die Grosse Politik* have concluded that Poincaré alone was responsible for France's strong attitude in the Sanders question (*G.P.*, XXXVII, No. 15501 n.).

[91] Izvolsky to Sazonov, January 27, 1914, *Russian Docs.*, I, 118.

[92] Szécsen telegrams, January 27 and February 15, 1914, *Austrian Docs.*, VII, 784, 879.

[93] Schoen to Bethmann, January 21, 1914, *G.P.*, XXXVII, 576–77; Poincaré, IV, 36–37.

ment until Poincaré's insistence won him over.[94] Certain Russian officials disliked Paléologue but accepted him nevertheless because they knew him to be an intimate friend of the president.[95] A second incident some time later involved Anglo-French relations. Britain and Germany suddenly resumed an old negotiation for the eventual division of the Portuguese colonies. Both Poincaré and Doumergue entered immediate protests with the British ambassador, on the ground that Britain had acted without informing France. It was Poincaré who objected most vigorously, insisting that French opinion would be deplorably affected and that the Entente would be harmed.[96]

Again in April 1914, when King George paid a state visit to Paris, the president went beyond mere formalities. The French were eager to promote a closer Anglo-Russian agreement in order to strengthen the weakest link in the Triple Entente. Both Doumergue and Poincaré seized the opportunity of the royal visit to discuss this possibility with Grey. Thus the president did not hesitate to act personally upon the British instead of leaving the business in the hands of Doumergue alone.[97]

[94] Paléologue, *Revue des Deux Mondes,* January 15, 1921, pp. 227–28.

[95] Izvolsky to Sazonov, January 15, 1914, *Russian Docs.,* I, 13. Margerie, a high official at the Quai d'Orsay, was first considered for the St. Petersburg post. Madame Margerie told a Russian diplomat confidentially that Poincaré had engineered Paléologue's nomination in order to keep Margerie in Paris. The president was supposed to fear that a worse cabinet might arrive in power and to desire a trustworthy and able man at the Quai d'Orsay (Sevastopoulo to Sazonov, January 15, 1914, *Russian Docs.,* I, 19). This may have been merely a feminine attempt to save face.

[96] Bertie to Grey, February 11 and 12, 1914, *British Docs.,* Vol. X, Part II, pp. 556–57, 559. Publication of the colonial agreement was finally prevented by a timely German decision against it. The British, impressed by French objections, promised to keep Paris informed of such diplomatic activity in the future. Doumergue attributed to Poincaré a share of the credit for this (Doumergue to Daeschner, March 3, 1914, *D.D.F.,* IX, 502).

[97] Poincaré, IV, 112–13; Grey to Bertie, May 1, 1914, *British Docs.,* Vol. X, Part II, p. 788. The president also undertook to improve Franco-Italian relations. Through a deputy who had connections in Rome, he secured a con-

Such incidents showed that Poincaré was still playing a certain personal role in diplomacy—in agreement with the minister of foreign affairs but not *through* that minister. The complaints of helplessness and isolation which he later wove into his memoirs were only partially justified. Doumergue did not repress the president any more than Jonnart and Pichon had done. Certainly Poincaré was not a free agent; but neither was he a chief magistrate in the Fallières tradition.

THE EVE OF THE CONFLICT

"It is part of the tragedy of the world war that every belligerent can make out a case entirely convincing to itself. For tragedy, in Hegel's words, is the conflict not of right with wrong but of right with right."[98]

Behind this pregnant observation of a noted English scholar lie twenty years of controversy over responsibilities for the war. Dozens of writers have scrutinized the events of the fatal five weeks after Sarajevo. Every detail has been studied so minutely that it would be profitless to begin anew. Yet an effort to isolate the activity of Poincaré during this period is essential. Here one must test the truth of the war-guilt charges which have been heaped upon the president's head.

Extremists have gone so far as to assert that Poincaré actually wanted war and schemed to bring it about.[99] The

fidential report on the causes of Italo-French coolness (Payen, *Poincaré*, p. 405).   [98] Gooch, *Before the War*, Vol. II, p. v.

[99] Gustave Dupin has been the most implacable of these prosecutors. Dupin has given great weight to a *revanchard* statement made by Poincaré in 1920. Writing for the magazine *Revue de l'Université de Paris* (October 1920), the ex-president said: "In my years at school . . . . I saw no other reason for my generation to live than the hope of recovering our lost provinces" (quoted in Dupin, *M. Poincaré et la guerre de 1914*, pp. 101–2). It is true that Poincaré always avoided questions about this article. It is also true, as Dupin has charged, that the October 1920 issue of the *Revue* cannot be found at the Bibliothèque Nationale or at the Sorbonne library. The article was ill advised, as its author doubtless realized. It must be noted, however, that Poincaré was speaking of his opinions as an adolescent, which might have changed, and that he did not specify a recovery of Alsace by war.

published diplomatic documents for 1912–1914 give no support to this theory. Poincaré was admittedly an extreme nationalist, and he never forgot Alsace-Lorraine. But solid proof of a desire for war on his part has never been adduced.

A second factor, however, will bear investigating. Much of the war-guilt controversy has hinged upon the amount of control which the president exercised in July 1914. Poincaré himself has emphasized this side of the question by insisting that his office bound him hand and foot. If this was true, then he could have had no influence over the events just preceding the war. Revisionist historians have dismissed Poincaré's argument as a mere alibi, claiming that the Elysée was the real directing force after 1913.[100] They have pointed to the discrepancy between Poincaré's complaint that he knew little of what was going on and Viviani's postwar statement that Poincaré read all the dispatches emanating from the ministries.[101] They have regarded the president as a criminal who quibbled about constitutional fictions in order to escape responsibility.

René Viviani became foreign minister as well as premier in June 1914. His arrival at the Quai d'Orsay should have meant a change in French foreign policy, for he stood farther to the Left than his three predecessors. It should have meant, too, the end of Poincaré's personal influence. As a matter of fact, neither of those possibilities came to pass. Viviani, like Doumergue and Jonnart, was a novice in foreign affairs. In addition to the fact that he needed guidance, neither his character nor his principles were strong enough to inaugurate a new and firm direction. When Viviani arrived in office he was warned by Paléologue that war was imminent. His immediate reac-

[100] Morhardt has written, for example: "At the moment of the outbreak of the war, M. Raymond Poincaré was the sovereign master of the destinies of France. In the folds of his presidential coat lay, at his choice, peace or war. As we are assured that he said in the council of ministers . . . . he could adopt one or the other at will" (Morhardt, *op. cit.,* pp. 133–34).

[101] Dupin, *Poincaré,* pp. 84–85; Poincaré, IV, 432; *Chamber Debates,* July 5, 1922, p. 717.

tion was characteristically passive: "Well! if it must be so, we will do our duty, all our duty."[102] His socialism did not prevent him from listening to the advice of the president, whom he held in high personal esteem.

The most notable episode of this period was the Poincaré-Viviani journey to St. Petersburg. Plans for the trip had been made several months before, when no one foresaw that it might coincide with a European crisis. Some critics have found fault with the fact that it was not postponed. This criticism is unjust; the crisis was not yet acute when the president left Paris, and a postponement might have created public agitation.[103] A lone voice, that of Jaurès, was raised in protest at the time.[104] Most of Poincaré's enemies saw in the journey not a means of preparing war but a scheme for winning back prestige—an expedient to regain abroad what the Elysée had lost at home.[105]

The trip proved to be one of the most remarkable ever undertaken by a French president. Beyond a doubt Poincaré was the real representative of his government, not only in form but also in fact. Negotiations, interviews, all revolved about him; Viviani disappeared into a gray background, even though his was the responsibility for any decision taken. Viviani's tutelage began on the outward voyage when Poincaré found it advisable to put him "*au courant* with certain questions which he has not yet had time to study thoroughly and on which he will have to

[102] Paléologue, *Revue des Deux Mondes,* January 15, 1921, p. 230. Meanwhile Poincaré called the new minister of war Messimy to the Elysée and warned him that a conflict was imminent. The president adjured Messimy "in sibylline terms" not to touch the three-year law (Adolph Messimy, *Mes souvenirs* [Paris, 1937], pp. 124–25).

[103] The French chargé in St. Petersburg reported a rumor there to the effect that a presidential crisis was inevitable since the fall of Doumergue and that Poincaré's visit would be delayed (Viviani to Doulcet, June 22, 1914, *D.D.F.,* X, 603–4; Doulcet to Viviani, June 24, 1914, *ibid.,* p. 626).

[104] *Chamber Debates,* July 7, 1914, pp. 444–45.

[105] Ernest Judet in *L'Eclair,* July 14, 1914.

confer with M. Sazonov . . . ."[106] But the lessons might have been spared, for from their arrival it was the president whose figure dominated:

> As soon as the presentations are over, the imperial yacht steers for Peterhof.
>
> Seated in the stern, the Tsar and the president immediately enter into conversation, I should perhaps say into a discussion; for it is obvious that they are talking business, firing questions at each other and arguing. As is proper, it is Poincaré who directs the dialogue. Before long, it is he alone who speaks. The Tsar simply acquiesces, but his whole appearance shows his sincere approval . . . .[107]

And so the visit continued, according to Paléologue's somewhat dramatized account. At the first night's banquet, the Tsar listened to Poincaré with close and sympathetic attention. The next day, Tsar and president reviewed all the questions which were preoccupying the chancelleries of Europe. Poincaré spoke briefly with members of the diplomatic corps, not in mere formulas of politeness but in full frankness. At the farewell dinner conversation between the Tsar and the president never ceased.[108]

Paléologue has probably described the presidential visit in overbright colors. But other evidence confirms the fact that Poincaré was the active diplomat. Both the British and the Austrian ambassadors wrote dispatches which showed that the president had consulted widely and had not confined himself to polite phrases.[109] Many years later Poincaré himself virtually admitted that Viviani had played a minor role at St. Petersburg.[110]

It can hardly be denied, therefore, that Poincaré carried

[106] Poincaré, IV, 224.

[107] Maurice Paléologue, *La Russie des tsars pendant la grande guerre* (Paris, n.d.), I, 4.

[108] *Ibid.*, pp. 5–16.

[109] Buchanan to Grey, July 22, 1914, *British Docs.*, XI, 61–62; Szàpàry dispatches, July 21 and 22, 1914, *Austrian Docs.*, VIII, 567–68, 585.

[110] Poincaré, VIII, 191.

on most of the business that was transacted in Russia. He did so in the manner of no other president before him, yet without breaking any constitutional rules. But it does not necessarily follow that he was making the final arrangements for a war. Some revisionists have drawn this conclusion, and so did the German propagandists during the conflict. One wartime pamphleteer declared that "Tsar Nicholas would never have hoisted his feeble body on the war-horse if Tsar Poincaré had not held the stirrups for him."[111] The revisionists have pointed to an interview granted by the Tsar in 1915 wherein he spoke warmly of the "strong words" uttered by the president a year before.[112] They have cited also Paléologue's firmness after the departure of the visitors. Finally they have recalled Poincaré's blunt warning to the Austrian ambassador in St. Petersburg: in the course of their conversation the president said meaningfully that peace might be endangered if an attempt were made to bully Serbia, for Serbia had friends.[113] His warning, however, may have been designed to prevent war by frankness.

This is but feeble evidence of warmongering. Unfortunately for Poincaré, his efforts to absolve himself have been just as weak. Among other things he has offered a letter written by the Tsar in 1916, recalling how they had thought of nothing but peace in 1914.[114] Hardly an impartial witness! Again, he has gone into great detail to prove that Austria delayed her ultimatum to Serbia until he and Viviani had departed from Russia. The Austrians have never attempted to deny this. Their reason for the delay was to prevent an immediate Franco-Russian agreement upon a policy of stiff resistance. They feared that such resistance might turn the Austro-Serb affair into a European war. Poincaré, refusing to believe that Austria could be sincere, has brushed this aside as

[111] Max Beer, *Zar Poincarew; die Schuld am Kriege* (Berlin, 1914), p. 4.
[112] *Le Matin,* August 26, 1915.
[113] Szàpàry dispatch, July 21, 1914, *Austrian Docs.,* VIII, 568.
[114] Poincaré, IV, 281.

a "pitiful explanation."[115] Yet he was always deeply offended whenever critics put his own sincerity in question.

The president would have been wise to admit frankly that he led the dance at St. Petersburg. His attempt at concealment made every bit of contrary evidence doubly damaging. The suspicion immediately arose that a guilty conscience caused him to equivocate. Such a suspicion was not justified. Poincaré had not been a warmonger in the past; he was not likely to turn into one overnight. But he brought the criticism upon himself by his legal-minded refusal to admit anything until forced to do so by cross-examination. What probably happened was this: Poincaré exerted an influence at St. Petersburg which was extraordinary for a president of France; his nationalistic opinions led him to speak firmly, in order to strengthen Russian confidence in the alliance. War did result; but this does not prove that the president worked for such an end. It proves, rather, that Poincaré's policy increased the danger of war to a degree far greater than he realized.

If the diplomatic corps at St. Petersburg saw Poincaré as the real leader of France in July 1914, the people of Paris looked to him in the same way when the crisis came. Austria's ultimatum to Serbia on July 23 suddenly crystallized the danger of war. When the president and the premier touched French soil on July 29 it was evident that the nation turned to Poincaré rather than to the transitory Viviani for guidance. Enormous crowds greeted him at Paris with cries of "Vive Poincaré!" and "Vive l'armée!" *Le Matin* declared enthusiastically: "Never, perhaps, has a chief magistrate heard an ovation so vibrant, so unanimous." The responsible premier might not have existed, so far as the crowd and the newspapers were concerned.[116]

---

[115] Poincaré, IV, 265.

[116] *Le Matin*, July 30, 1914. Cf. Bertie to Grey, August 2, 1914, *British Docs.*, XI, 333; *Journal des Débats* and *L'Eclair*, July 30, 1914; Raymond Recouly, *Les heures tragiques d'avantguerre* (Paris, 1922), p. 73; H. Pearl

One crowded week of frantic negotiations followed before the storm burst. The constitution of 1875 had never met a similar test; Poincaré could find no precedent to follow, even if he desired to do so. According to his own account he stepped back into the Elysian prison where "no one telegraphs to me, no one writes to me, I write to no one . . . . I receive only a brief summary of the diplomatic conversations."[117] His sole contacts, added Poincaré, were with the ministers.

For reasons best known to their author the president's memoirs have dissimulated the truth somewhat. He has endeavored to give the impression that he was powerless, confined within a constitutional cage. Such an impression is false; it fails to show just how much activity was still possible within legal limitations.[118] Immediately upon his arrival in Paris, the president proposed that the council of ministers meet daily henceforth—a suggestion that was accepted.[119] In view of the fact that he presided over this type of meeting,[120] no serious discussions were likely to take place outside his presence. He therefore had plenty of opportunity to express his ideas, even though he could not force their acceptance. In addition to these formal sessions of the council, Viviani and the other ministers appeared at the Elysée at all hours for conferences. Ambassa-

Adam, *Paris Sees It Through; a Diary 1914–1919* (London, 1919), pp. 15–16. Some extremists have attributed bellicose language to Poincaré when he landed at Dunkirk (Corday, *L'Envers,* I, 112). This was probably pure invention.

[117] Poincaré, IV, 432.

[118] Equally false was the extreme-revisionist assertion that Poincaré was in full active command. According to Dupin, "It is notorious that on the evening of the 30th, Viviani had disappeared from circulation" (*Poincaré,* p. 27). In spite of Viviani's ill health, inexperience, and lack of leadership, such a statement was an exaggeration.

[119] Poincaré, IV, 371.

[120] In contrast to the cabinet council, which the president of the republic did not attend.

dors Izvolsky, von Schoen, and Bertie continued to visit the president, and certain private citizens did likewise.[121]

No important decision was taken during this crucial week except after consultation with Poincaré. For example, when news arrived that Russia's war preparations were arousing German anger, Viviani went to the Elysée at 2:00 A.M. on July 30 to discuss the situation. The premier proposed to assure Russia of staunch French support but to suggest that mobilization be avoided. This message was sent, with Poincaré's approval.[122] A more extreme instance was Viviani's telegram to Paul Cambon on August 1, aiming to convince England that France desired peace. This message was actually drawn up by Poincaré.[123] Again, when Izvolsky at last learned that Germany had declared war on Russia, he carried the information to the president rather than to Viviani. It was Poincaré who promised to convoke the council and to inform Izvolsky of its results.[124]

The order withdrawing the French army to a line ten kilometers behind the frontier was another move to which the president was no stranger. Along with Viviani and Minister of War Messimy, he prepared it for submission to the council.[125] At the same time Poincaré began to think of winning new allies. He urged Izvolsky on August 1 to tempt Rumania and Italy

---

[121] Gabriel Hanotaux, "Hommage au Maréchal Joffre," *Revue des Deux Mondes,* January 15, 1931, p. 526; Pierre Barthélemy Gheusi, *La gloire de Gallieni* (Paris, 1938), p. 33.

[122] Poincaré, IV, 385–86; Messimy, *Souvenirs,* p. 84; Izvolsky to Sazonov, July 30, 1914, *Russian Docs.,* V, 201.

[123] *D.D.F.,* XI, 420 n. This message, of course, was in addition to Poincaré's personal letter to King George.

[124] Izvolsky to Sazonov, August 1, 1914, *Russian Docs.,* V, 258–59.

[125] Poincaré, IV, 425–26. The president also supervised its enforcement with a watchful eye (note for the minister of war, August 4, 1914, *D.D.F.,* XI, 532). After the war, neither Poincaré nor Viviani admitted that the president was a father to this measure (R. Poincaré, *Les origines de la guerre* [Paris, 1921], p. 231). The ten-kilometer withdrawal had an obvious diplomatic purpose.

with offers of territory.[126] Apparently he undertook this action on his own initiative; there was no indication that Viviani suggested it to the president.[127]

All these details do not prove, as some writers would wish, that Poincaré was master of the French government during the last week of peace. They simply show that he was able to exert some influence upon the march of events. He was neither a dictator nor a King Log. The question then arises, did his last-minute activity contribute to the outbreak of the war?

Revisionists have sometimes declared that France suddenly adopted a more intransigeant attitude on July 29, the day when Poincaré and Viviani returned to Paris.[128] The published documents fail to reveal any such definite break in the direction of French policy. There may have been a slight sharpening of tone, a greater promptitude of decision, but nothing more.[129] This was understandable enough. The subordinate officials who were in temporary control at Paris naturally maintained a certain reserve, avoiding important decisions until the return of their responsible superiors. Furthermore, Viviani and Poincaré stayed in wireless contact with Paris while aboard ship; thus the broad outlines of French policy were traced by the same men before and after July 29.[130] For instance, Izvolsky secured assurance of full French support and a promise that France would not try to exercise a moderating influence on Russia, even before the travelers returned.[131] In short, the president's

---

[126] Izvolsky to Sazonov, August 1, 1914, *Russian Docs.*, V, 259.

[127] Cf. Sazonov to Poklevski, August 3, 1914, *ibid.*, p. 292.

[128] August Bach, "Frankreichs entschlusz zum Kriege," *Berliner Monatshefte,* XI (August 1933), 758.

[129] Szécsen expected a slight modification as a result of the return of Poincaré and Izvolsky. He did not even mention Viviani (Széczen dispatch, July 27, 1914, *Austrian Docs.,* VIII, 797).

[130] Bienvenu-Martin, "Mon interim de chef de gouvernement," *Revue de France,* August 15, 1933, pp. 643–44.

[131] Izvolsky to Sazonov, July 28, 1914, *Russian Docs.,* V, 138; Ignatiev report, July 28, 1914, *ibid.*, p. 140.

arrival did not generate a current of belligerence in the French governmental machine.

Exponents of Poincaré's war guilt have concentrated their case upon three incidents which occurred during the final week. These were (1) the Russian mobilization, (2) the falsifications of the *Livre Jaune,* and (3) the French mobilization. Question number one was hotly disputed for several years; today it can no longer be denied that Russia was first to issue an order of general mobilization, thus setting Europe's war machinery in motion.[132] If this step made Russia the aggressor, then the defensive Franco-Russian alliance ought not to have gone into operation. But Frenchmen were told at the time that Russia had mobilized only in answer to an Austrian mobilization. They were so informed by the official *Livre Jaune,* whose accuracy they did not doubt. Poincaré used the same explanation in a conversation with the British ambassador.[133] Whether he was sincere or whether he intentionally hid the fact that Russia acted first remains an unsolved problem. Paléologue had telegraphed the mobilization decree from St. Petersburg at once, but his message was delayed almost ten hours in transmission.[134] It finally arrived in Paris *after* the French had learned of Austrian mobilization. Perhaps Poincaré and the ministers honestly drew false conclusions from this circumstance. But at least they had received Paléologue's

[132] Russia's decision to mobilize resulted in part from the encouragement which Poincaré gave during his visit. Sazonov wrote on July 23 that he no longer had any worries about French support but only about the attitude of England (Sazonov to Benckendorff, July 25, 1914, *Russian Docs.,* V, 46–47). The intransigeant attitude of Paléologue throughout the crisis was based upon the declarations exchanged during the presidential visit (Paléologue, *La Russie des tsars,* I, 31).

[133] Bertie to Grey, August 1, 1914, *British Docs.,* XI, 243.

[134] The delay has been explained by the fact that the telegram was sent via Scandinavia in order to avoid its passage through Germany (*D.D.F.,* XI, 357 n.). Reports of Russian mobilization did arrive in Paris earlier from Berlin, but they were regarded as false (Viviani to Paléologue, July 31, 1914, *ibid.,* pp. 360–61).

message in its original form, devoid of any suggestion that Russia acted in reply to Austria.

At this point, the mobilization question merges into that of the falsified *Livre Jaune*. The alteration of dispatches has been proved and admitted. A brazen example was the Paléologue telegram just mentioned; the Paris authorities expanded it by adding a good excuse for Russia's mobilization. Poincaré must have known of the changes at the time. When the Quai d'Orsay sent him copies of the dispatches received, it certainly did not furnish him with doctored versions. Although Poincaré has always refused to admit any complicity, he has continued to defend the falsifications on the ground that they were meant to clarify what was honestly believed to be the truth.[135] This was a rather shaky excuse for taking such liberties. What made the situation worse was the fact that Poincaré continued to cite the *Livre Jaune* as gospel truth even after the war.[136] To use such altered documents and to defend the alterations when they could no longer be denied was to lay his good faith open to question. Dupin has gone too far in writing that "the honesty or dishonesty of the French *Livre* implies before History the honesty or dishonesty of President Poincaré . . . ."[137] At the same time, Poincaré's reputation certainly has not been improved by this sort of trimming.

The criticism which deals with French mobilization is not so well founded. It rests upon the president's decree of August 1, issued three days before war was declared and in the absence of the Chambers.[138] Poincaré's enemies have contended

---

[135] René Gérin, *Les responsabilités de la guerre; quatorze questions par René Gérin—quatorze réponses par Raymond Poincaré* (Paris, 1930), p. 155.

[136] For example, in his *Origines de la guerre*, p. 261. In the same book, Poincaré condemned the Germans for omissions, falsifications, and reversals in the order of telegrams in their White Book (*ibid.*, pp. 246–47, 270).

[137] Dupin, *Poincaré*, p. 132.

[138] *Ibid.*, pp. 64–65; Georges Demartial, *La guerre de 1914, la mobilisation des consciences* (Paris, 1927), pp. 292–94.

that mobilization actually brought France into the war, so that
the president usurped the legislature's legal right to decide
upon war or peace. From the constitutional point of view, this
argument was groundless. No one could deny that the executive possessed full power to decree mobilization. Besides,
Poincaré's signature was covered by the countersignatures of
two ministers. On the other hand, the government's refusal
to convoke the Chambers at once was doubtless meant to place
before the legislators a *fait accompli*. Probably the Chamber
would not have abandoned Russia if it had assembled on
August 1, but there would have been bitter debate and a division of opinion in the crisis. To prevent this dispute the
French government preferred to let Germany declare war
first.[139]

Although Poincaré always maintained that mobilization did
not mean war, he believed as early as August 1 that the conflict was virtually inevitable.[140] He was right. Until that date

[139] Izvolsky to Sazonov, August 1, 1914, *Russian Docs.*, V, 258–60.

[140] Poincaré, *Les origines de la guerre*, pp. 274–75. Cf. Bertie to Grey,
August 1, 1914, *British Docs.*, XI, 243; Izvolsky to Sazonov, August 1, 1914,
Russian Docs., V, 259–60. Every student of war responsibility has devoted a
great deal of effort to proving that mobilization either did or did not mean
war in 1914. During the 1892 negotiations which created the Franco-Russian
alliance, representatives of both governments declared that they regarded
mobilization as equivalent to war. French scholars and apologists have admitted this fact but have argued that only mobilization by the enemy was
considered. French or Russian mobilization, they have maintained, had a
purely defensive purpose, while German mobilization was the first step in
carrying out a plan of aggression (Renouvin, *Les origines immédiates de la
guerre*, p. 262; Gérin, *Les responsabilités de la guerre*, p. 80). Revisionist
historians have replied that general mobilization by either side was fatal to
European peace, for Germany could not fail to mobilize if Russia did so.
Perhaps Poincaré was not entirely hypocritical when he asserted that mobilization did not mean war, but he certainly lacked any real confidence in the
preservation of peace after August 1.

The most telling criticism made by the revisionists has been based on
Poincaré's use of the prior-mobilization argument for many years to fix responsibility upon Austria. When this argument "backfired," he abandoned it
as no longer valid in the case of Russia.

peace might have been preserved if France had exercised strong restraint at St. Petersburg or if Germany had done the same at Vienna. After August 1 the only hope would have been an open repudiation of Russia or of Austria. The alliance system built up during the preceding years had to function or collapse.[141]

One may well doubt whether President Poincaré could have forced the French government to restrain or repudiate Russia even if he had desired to do so. He was by no means all-powerful during the crucial week. But at the same time he was not a mere spectator. His influence was far more important than his own denials would indicate. If he had exerted that influence in a different direction it is conceivable that war might have been avoided. This he did not do, for he regarded the Russian alliance as a lifeline guaranteeing the future safety of his own nation. The crisis of 1914 was the logical culmination of several conflicting national policies, one of which was that followed by France in an intensified form since 1912. The French people were dragged into a war which they did not want, over an incident which did not directly affect their interests. And the chains which bound their government had been forged in part by Raymond Poincaré.

[141] Cf. Bernadotte E. Schmitt, *The Coming of the War 1914* (New York, 1930), II, 228–29.

CHAPTER VI

WARTIME POLITICS

When war comes in the door of a modern state, normal constitutional procedures often fly out of the window. So in August 1914 the entry of France into the conflict sharply modified its government's activity. Until that date Poincaré had functioned as chief magistrate under relatively normal conditions. His first eighteen months in office had fitted into the framework of French history since 1875. But the tornado of war disrupted almost every phase of life in France. New conditions, new needs faced the government of the Third Republic. To meet those needs, the president, like every other high official, was forced to undergo a process of adaptation.

Quick action and centralized responsibility were vital after August 1914. This meant, in all belligerent countries, a shift in the center of gravity from the legislative to the executive branch. The French government followed this trend; but, strange to say, France changed far less than one might have expected in a land of legislative supremacy. After the first five months of the war, the Chambers exercised most of their privileges and remained almost continually in session. They jealously guarded and freely utilized their right of approval and criticism. Not until 1918 was the executive freed slightly by the adoption of a bill which broadened the decree power.

Nevertheless the very existence of war altered the spirit of executive-legislative relations. Only once from 1914 to 1920 did the Chamber dare to overthrow a ministry by an adverse vote. Cabinets did resign of their own accord; but the partial truce in party rivalry, the *union sacrée* which functioned more or less effectively throughout the war, left the president full responsibility for choosing new premiers. In ordinary times the leader of the group which engineered a crisis might expect to be called to power. But so long as the legislature hesitated to provoke such crises Poincaré could select whom he desired to head the government. Thus his most important official prerogative was perceptibly broadened after 1914.

THE VIVIANI MINISTRY (1914–1915)

The first five months of the war of 1914–1918 have been termed a period of quasi dictatorship in France. The legislature adjourned on August 4, leaving the president to take all necessary action by decree. Such decrees, of course, required a ministerial countersignature, so that the president's power increased only in proportion to his influence over the cabinet. The exact extent of that influence cannot be measured. Viviani's Left-wing ministry remained in power, and ought to have been at odds with the Moderate president. But Viviani was not a strong-willed and experienced administrator. He was willing to accept counsel both before and after the outbreak of war from Poincaré, toward whom he was personally friendly. What is more, he turned over the portfolio of foreign affairs to Gaston Doumergue on August 3, keeping for himself only the premiership. Doumergue, most Moderate of the Radicals, was likely to welcome Poincaré's advice in foreign policy, for his one brief passage at the Quai d'Orsay had been marked by sympathetic collaboration with the president.

Poincaré was in intimate contact with the business of government during the first days of the war. Ministers came to the Elysée singly or in small groups for informal sessions. The cabinet or the council of national defense, or sometimes both, met daily under Poincaré's chairmanship.[1] A detailed account of these sessions will probably never be known, for no

---

[1] Poincaré, V, 8, 74; Alexandre Ribot, *Lettres à un ami* (Paris, 1924), pp. 15, 127.

minutes were kept and most of the participants have disappeared. Poincaré himself has been disappointingly reticent. In his memoirs he has mentioned the council meetings in the sketchiest of terms or has buried his descriptions beneath long recitals of the military situation. He has denied any departure from a presiding and summarizing role in which he offered advice freely but did not insist that it be followed. Viviani later confirmed this before the Chamber.[2] But such a role, in time of crisis, left considerable room for expanded presidential influence. Ministers were more prone than usual to accept advice from a man of experience and prestige. The president's importance in these circumstances varied in direct ratio to the respect which the ministers held for Poincaré's opinions and in inverse ratio to the strength of the premier. Certainly the personality of the irresponsible Poincaré must have dominated that of the responsible Viviani in council sessions. In addition, frequent informal conferences with a few leading ministers at the Elysée enabled the president to take part in discussing plans for submission to the council. Poincaré has rarely complained about the "prison of the Elysée" in recalling the events of August 1914. When that familiar refrain does appear in *Au service de la France* it is directed against the pretensions of military headquarters.

It has already been pointed out that the war increased the president's freedom to choose new premiers in times of cabinet crisis. Poincaré did not stop there; more than once he interfered in the choice of ministers as well. A case in point occurred during the first month of the war.

From the outbreak of hostilities the president decided that the Viviani cabinet should be broadened. He held that all parties ought to be represented, in order to carry out the theme of the *union sacrée*. To his enemies his motives were less pure; they suspected a scheme to bring some of his friends back into

[2] *Chamber Debates,* July 5, 1922, p. 717. Cf., however, *Carnets de Georges Louis,* II, 149.

power.[3] Viviani resisted for three weeks but finally capitulated before the president's daily exhortations. It was agreed that portfolios would be given to two Unified Socialists, two Moderate leaders (Millerand and Delcassé), and the ubiquitous Briand. There remained, however, the task of fitting them into the cabinet and of deciding which members of Viviani's old combination ought to be sacrificed. This problem was worked out, not at the premier's office, but in a series of private conferences at the Elysée.[4] The chief stumbling block proved to be Millerand's refusal to accept any portfolio except that of war, held at the time by Adolphe Messimy. To satisfy Millerand, the Radical soldier-politician Messimy was finally sacrificed. Poincaré expressed displeasure at this transaction, even though he was somewhat doubtful of Messimy's ability as minister of war. He told the latter privately that an injustice had been done, and excused himself by saying: "I am without effective power . . . . You know how little personal power the constitution leaves me."[5] Poincaré was probably sincere, but certainly he made little effort to prevent Messimy's fall. In the president's eyes two prominent Moderates in the cabinet more than offset a minor injustice.

Different treatment was accorded to Doumergue, the min-

---

[3] Poincaré, V, 17, 165, 170; Colonel Converset, *Les trois ans de diplomatie secrète qui nous menèrent à la guerre de 1914* (Paris, 1924), p. 248; Joseph Caillaux, *Devant l'histoire; mes prisons* (Paris, 1925), p. 35.

[4] Poincaré, V, 171–75, 179–83; Adolphe Messimy, *Mes souvenirs* (Paris, 1937), p. 372.

[5] Messimy, *Souvenirs*, pp. 372–73. Poincaré failed to mention this conversation in his memoirs. The British ambassador heard "from a good source" that Joffre had demanded Messimy's replacement in a letter to Poincaré, who then forced the change (*The Diary of Lord Bertie of Thame, 1914–1918* [London, 1924], I, 68). The journalist William Martin heard a similar story from a Swiss diplomat ("Notes de Guerre," conversation with M. Henri Schreiber, August 18, 1915). This seems to have been a false rumor, for Messimy wrote to Joffre on August 27, "I have been dismissed by the president of the republic for having treated the public powers and the press too rudely" (*Mémoires du Maréchal Joffre, 1910–1917* [Paris, 1932], I, 321).

ister of foreign affairs, whose portfolio was similarly demanded by Delcassé. Doumergue was not sacrificed, but was shifted to another post which would keep him in the cabinet.[6] The fact that Doumergue was more "Poincarist" than Messimy probably was not the reason for his retention. It did prepare the ground, however, for a suspicion that the ministry was being packed with "king's friends."[7]

This cabinet reshuffle threw an interesting light on Poincaré's governmental influence at the time. The initiative was definitely his. Furthermore, most of the actual negotiations took place at the Elysée, even though custom would have left these entirely to the premier. The president was no dictator who could revise the ministry at will. He was able to bring three leading Moderates into the government; but Viviani balked at Poincaré's proposal to add his friends Albert de Mun and Denys Cochin of the extreme Right.[8] All the same, his role was not so insignificant as his complaint on August 18 would indicate: "I am deprived by the constitution of every means of personal action."[9]

Barely a month after the war broke out, Paris faced imminent capture by the Germans. Belgian resistance had proved futile; it did not even serve to delay the invaders appreciably. As in 1870, the question of evacuating the city became acute. During the night of September 2, shortly before the German troops reached the Marne, the government of France was trans-

---

[6] Poincaré, V, 182.

[7] As finally revamped, the cabinet contained still another Moderate— Alexandre Ribot. It was the president, not the premier, who called Ribot to the Elysée and offered him the finance portfolio (Ribot, *Journal,* p. 22). Ribot's earlier book, *Lettres à un ami,* had Viviani making the offer; and Poincaré left the same impression in his memoirs (V, 183).

[8] Poincaré, V, 182. Hanotaux has credited Poincaré with bringing two Socialists into the ministry during this reshuffle (Gabriel Hanotaux, *Raymond Poincaré* [Paris, 1934], p. 35). It was Viviani, however, who proposed their addition. Poincaré never pretended to have won their support for the cabinet (Poincaré, V, 174).

[9] Poincaré, V, 123.

ferred bodily to Bordeaux; and president and ministry remained in the Southwest until December 1914.

The three months at Bordeaux were rather colorless ones so far as the functioning of the government was concerned. Mornings spent in council meetings, afternoons in private conferences or in studying the papers sent to him by the ministers —thus Poincaré has pictured his existence there. Few glimpses have been permitted into his activity in the council of ministers. Ribot complained privately that council meetings were developing into presidential monologues: "he talks all the time, a great deal too much."[10] Apparently this criticism was based on fact, for it reappeared several times during the war. The president probably believed that he was merely presiding, but he placed rather wide limits on that function.

Poincaré, always thin-skinned, suffered acutely during this period from a sudden revulsion of public opinion against him. A large and vocal section of the population was unreasonably bitter at what it called the government's "flight" to Bordeaux. With even less reason, it loaded the blame for the evacuation of Paris on Poincaré, who had actually fought against it tooth and nail. As a result, the president devoted much of his energy in council sessions to urging an immediate return to Paris. Considerable friction resulted from this, as it did also from his repeated requests for permission to visit the front. In addition, there were two minor clashes between Poincaré and Millerand when the former demanded full information regarding military operations and munitions. Millerand replied politely that it was none of the president's affair, and objected when Poincaré consulted one of the war minister's subordinates directly.

Back in Paris in December, the government gradually settled into the routine of warfare. High officials, like ordinary citizens, began to find their places in the new system. The presi-

[10] *Carnets de Georges Louis,* II, 149. Ribot suggested the same thing in more reserved terms in his *Lettres,* p. 15.

dent's time was occupied to an ever increasing degree with journeys to the front, visits to hospitals, and other formalities. But he continued to preside over council meetings, which were now held three times a week, and he kept in close contact with the work of the various ministries. His habit of calling in subordinate officials for private conferences still drew intermittent objections, especially from Minister of War Millerand.[11] Most of the cabinet members, however, conferred with him readily, and sometimes even furnished him with information which they withheld from the council.[12] Private citizens more than once brought him details which were not given to any minister;[13] and frequently it was the president who acquainted the council with the situation at the front.[14] Apparently he continued to speak quite freely in council sessions, causing some ministers to complain that they could not get in a word.[15]

The French parliament ended its three-month vacation in December 1914. Its convocation brought a new factor into the complicated governmental situation and raised the problem of executive-legislative relations in time of war. Interpellation was impossible under the circumstances, so that the legislators had to find a new way to control the ministry. To fill this need, they sought to use as supervisory agencies the Chamber and Senate commissions. These groups were privileged to call in ministers for questioning at any time. Commission meetings, unlike regular legislative sessions, were secret; therefore the members felt justified in demanding complete information on the military situation and the state of munitions production.

Most implacable of all in asserting the legislative right of

[11] Poincaré, VI, 23.

[12] *Ibid.*, pp. 33–34.

[13] *Ibid.*, pp. 22–23, 26.

[14] *Ibid.*, p. 351.

[15] *Carnets de Georges Louis,* II, 197. In his memoirs, Poincaré has seldom mentioned his interventions in council; see, however, VI, 258, 346.

constant control was the Senate army commission, led by Clemenceau, Freycinet, and Boudenoot. Poincaré was soon dragged
into their realm of activity. When War Minister Millerand
evaded their questions, they addressed themselves directly to
the president. He alone, they contended, could break a wartime deadlock between the executive and legislative branches.
This senatorial appeal to the president against the cabinet was
something new under the sun of the Third Republic. The constitution limited his official contact with the Chambers to written messages, and even that power had rarely been used. Should
he receive the appeal, the way might be opened for far-reaching changes in the distribution of powers. Furthermore, the senators acted publicly, so that the implications of their *démarche*
were clear to everyone. This was exactly the sort of situation
to arouse Poincaré's hostility. He might be willing to expand
the presidential prerogative through privately exerted influence,
but his legalistic mind abhorred any infringement upon the
strict letter of the constitution. Therefore he agreed to receive the army commission's appeal only in the presence of two
ministers, and emphasized the fact that this act must not create
a precedent.[16]

Between preserving the letter and the spirit of the constitution, however, there was a broad difference. Poincaré sympathized with the members of the commission in their desire
to wring information out of Millerand. He remained silent
during the commission's visit in deference to Millerand's
presence. When the disappointed senators had gone, the president paid a private visit to chairman Freycinet and gave him

[16] According to Gabriel Terrail, the journalist, Poincaré avoided any
direct contact with the commission members during this audience. He insisted that their petition be handed to the war minister, who passed it to the
premier, who passed it to the president. This was supposed to illustrate Poincaré's strict adherence to constitutional forms ("Mermeix," *Au sein des commissions* [Paris, 1924], p. 260). The story is probably apocryphal; it is difficult
to believe that intelligent men would attach any importance to such hocus-
pocus.

the details which Millerand had refused to divulge.[17] Not long after, he convoked the commission at the Elysée to discuss their complaints with Joffre.[18] Poincaré's activity behind the back of a responsible minister was fully justifiable. It was necessary to reduce friction that impaired the work of the government. But at the same time it illustrated the president's incurable tendency to dig under constitutional fences even while insisting that they be maintained intact.

In spite of this backstage mediation, relations between Millerand and the senators only grew worse. Again Poincaré made a private visit to Freycinet; this time he found the commission's complaints so well justified that he urged Millerand to change his attitude.[19] The dispute flared up once more in July 1915. The commission made a second written appeal to Poincaré as "chief of the armies and supreme guardian of the great interests of the country." As before, the president replied that he was irresponsible and could not act except through a minister. "The president of the French republic presides and does not govern," he pointed out. "That is the A B C of the parliamentary regime."[20] The commission, forced at last to recognize that Poincaré would take no open step which might expose him to criticism, henceforth abandoned its effort to make the president a mediator. He continued to confer privately with acting chairman Boudenoot; and he tried to exert pressure on Millerand, but without apparent success.[21] Obviously he could go no further unless he should decide to adopt an extra-

---

[17] It was really Joffre rather than Millerand who opposed the commission's desires. Millerand sympathized with the commission's viewpoint but kept silent because he feared "leaks" in the commission (Poincaré, VI, 59–63). Some senators understood this but objected that Millerand was permitting headquarters to assume too much power.

[18] Poincaré, VI, 76.

[19] Ibid., p. 111.

[20] Ibid., pp. 308–10.

[21] Ibid., pp. 204, 277. Cf. Izvolsky to Sazonov, July 2, 1915, Russian Docs., VIII, 205.

constitutional role. It became clear that even in wartime the president would be little more than a shock absorber between the executive and the legislative.

No sooner had the Senate army commission abandoned its appeals to Poincaré than its counterpart in the Chamber made a similar attempt. Representatives of three Chamber commissions came to the Elysée on August 13, 1915, to urge that French reinforcements be sent to the Dardanelles. They received no encouragement from Poincaré.[22] Two months later the Chamber army commission under General Pédoya took a more daring step. It addressed a letter to the president through the new prime minister, Briand, calling on him to "end the alarming state of indecision" in the Balkans.[23] This was the sort of unconstitutionality to make the jurist Poincaré righteously indignant. It was a formal and literal illegality, written down in black and white; it was undeniable evidence for any law court. Poincaré condemned it as "the very negation of the parliamentary regime." Henceforth the Chamber commission, like that of the Senate, no longer looked to the Elysée for aid. The deputies had to develop a new device to replace the suspended practice of interpellation; they found it in the secret legislative session. This was merely the ordinary procedure of interpellation carried out *in camera;* the president was in no way involved.

The army commission incidents stood out as perhaps the clearest examples of Poincaré's formalism. His horror at the idea of direct contact with the legislature was no doubt genuine. But it did not prevent him from interviewing deputies and senators singly or in groups and presenting their opinions to the ministerial council. His conscience was clear so long as the visitors presented themselves as individuals and not as representatives of the legislative body. He may have been right

[22] Poincaré, VII, 30; General Pédoya, *La commission de l'armée pendant la grande guerre* (Paris, 1921), p. 351.

[23] Poincaré, VIII, 242; Pédoya, *op. cit.,* p. 364.

in religiously preserving the forms, but undoubtedly he exaggerated their importance.

The phase of the president's wartime activity which remains most obscure is that relating to foreign affairs. The reason is obvious—an almost complete dearth of source materials. Russia alone has extended its published documents beyond August 1914; and those papers show that Izvolsky saw Poincaré rather infrequently after that date.[24] Scraps of information available here and there, however, permit the tentative conclusion that the war did not change Poincaré's role in diplomacy a great deal. He remained what he had been in peace time—a secondary but not powerless factor in the making of foreign policy. The Quai d'Orsay was occupied during most of Viviani's term by the Moderate Delcassé. The latter sought Poincaré's advice on frequent occasions and kept him in day-to-day contact with events by sending copies of all important telegrams to the Elysée.

The government's chief concern during the first year of the war was to bring neutral nations into its camp. In the course of these negotiations Poincaré now and then took a personal part. The effort to win Italy was a case in point. Soon after the conflict broke out, the Italian commercial attaché in Paris approached Clemenceau with certain suggestions which he thought might eventually lead to an understanding between the two Latin nations. Clemenceau at once brought the attaché to the Elysée rather than to the Quai d'Orsay. Poincaré, however, was rather suspicious of the attaché's good faith, and refused to give him any encouragement then or in the weeks that followed.[25] He did hint at a Franco-Italian agreement

[24] The president also had two long conversations with the Russian finance minister, during which political, military, and economic questions were thoroughly discussed (Izvolsky to Sazonov, February 2, 1915, *Russian Docs.*, VII, 110; same to same, October 7, 1915, *ibid.*, VIII, 771. Cf. Poincaré, VI, 41, and VII, 56). Poincaré's account of the second interview is a remarkable example of his tendency to conceal important details.

[25] Poincaré, V, 30, 94.

during a conversation with Ambassador Tittoni.[26] But his suggestion had no effect, and it was not until six months later that Italy was brought into the war. Poincaré apparently had little to do with this successful negotiation in the spring of 1915. He confined himself to urging that too many promises ought not to be made to Rome.[27] At the last minute, though, it seemed that Russian resistance to Italy's demands might wreck the proposed alliance. Poincaré sent an urgent telegram to the Tsar on April 19, which helped to soften Russia's intransigeance and led to an immediate agreement.[28]

The president also played a secondary but not insignificant role in the effort to find new friends in the Balkans. In the case of Rumania Poincaré knew that success depended upon Russia's willingness to sacrifice some territory. He exerted pressure on both Delcassé and Izvolsky in an attempt to achieve this end.[29] Bulgaria was second on the list of possible allies, but the Serbs coveted part of the spoils which were to be used to win Bulgaria. Poincaré, along with the heads of the other Allied powers, sent the Serbian king a personal note and urged him to make concessions.[30]

The Allied offers were made in vain. By October 1915 Bulgaria was obviously on the point of joining the Central Powers. The French and British therefore decided to land troops at Salonika to protect the Serbs and to defend the railway by which munitions were being shipped to Russia. In an effort to win Russia's participation in this expedition Poincaré sent off another personal telegram to the Tsar.[31] He pointed out that the presence of Russian troops at Salonika

[26] Ibid., p. 80. [27] Ibid., VI, 149.

[28] Ibid., pp. 167–68; Poincaré to Nicholas II, April 20, 1915, Russian Docs., VII, 567–68. Cf. also Izvolsky to Sazonov, April 21, 1915, ibid., p. 577.

[29] Poincaré, VI, 205, 208, 220; Izvolsky to Sazonov, July 8, 1915, Russian Docs., VIII, 252.

[30] Nicholas II to George V, July 29, 1915, ibid., VIII, 375; Izvolsky to Sazonov, August 4, 1915, ibid., p. 400.

[31] Sazonov to the Tsar, October 1, 1915, ibid., VIII, 737–38.

might cause a last-minute change of heart among the Slavic brethren in Bulgaria. The Tsar refused this plea, whereupon Poincaré exerted severe pressure upon two Russian representatives in Paris. He warned Izvolsky that French opinion would be adversely affected; and he made a great impression upon the Russian finance minister, Bark, by returning to the subject several times in the course of a conversation.[32] The net result of all this was zero; Bulgaria joined Germany, and Russia sent no troops. But failure does not disqualify it as evidence of Poincaré's presidential activity.

Greece was still another state with which the Allies flirted. In April 1915 its government offered to enter the war in return for a pledge of its territorial integrity. The Greeks feared, and with reason, that one of their Macedonian ports would be used as a lure to win Bulgaria. Prince George of Greece saw Poincaré twice in April and May in an attempt to gain the president's support for this territorial guarantee. According to his own memoirs Poincaré confined himself to formulas of politeness and avoided any definite reply.[33] But the prince's report to Athens on April 20 contained the following assurance from Poincaré: "The territorial guarantee will certainly be accorded to us for the period of the war and during the peace negotiations."[34] Not a word was said of the port which Greece might lose in the treaty settlement itself. Obviously Poincaré was trying to keep the Greeks friendly by hints rather than solid commitments. His words served their purpose; they gave the Greeks hope, in spite of Foreign Minister Delcassé's refusal to make any promises. Prince George therefore returned to the Elysée two weeks later, only to have his illusions rudely shattered. This time he was told that a guarantee was impossible. Apparently Delcassé had convinced Poincaré that

[32] Izvolsky to Sazonov, October 6 and 7, 1915, *ibid.*, VIII, 766, 771.

[33] Poincaré, VI, 170-71, 201-2.

[34] "S. Cosmin," *L'entente et la Grèce pendant la grande guerre* (Paris, 1926), I, 85. "Cosmin" had access to the archives of the Greek foreign office.

Bulgaria was about to take the Allied bait. The president complained that the Greeks were too suspicious, but in vain; his reply ended the conversations.[35] The incident suggests three things: that Poincaré continued to speak quite freely to foreign agents in the absence of a minister; that foreign governments did not believe him powerless, since they thought it essential to secure his approval; and that in recalling such interviews Poincaré toned down his remarks and undervalued the part which he played.

The president was involved in one other incident during 1915. Early in the year the Russian government suddenly informed its allies that it would claim Constantinople at the end of the war. The French, though angry, were in no position to issue a flat refusal; they were forced to approve in the wake of England. But both Poincaré and Delcassé first tried to get the Constantinople question postponed indefinitely. The president went so far as to write a private letter to Ambassador Paléologue in St. Petersburg, outlining France's Near Eastern policy as he saw it, and showing how that policy conflicted with the Russian designs.[36] Such correspondence between president and ambassador was of course extraconstitutional. Poincaré has been careful to point out that it was his only aberration from strict legality. It would be more interesting, however, to know to what extent the president helped create French foreign policy through his influence on Delcassé. Unfortunately, no such analysis is possible.[37]

[35] *Ibid.*, pp. 86–89. William Martin received similar information in an interview with M. Streit, former foreign minister of Greece, on June 26, 1919 (Martin, "Notes de Guerre").

[36] Poincaré, VI, 92–94; Pingaud, *Histoire diplomatique*, I, 249.

[37] Izvolsky believed that Poincaré could still influence the cabinet's actions, despite his presidential chains. He wrote in one dispatch: "finally you are not ignorant of the fact that the personal opinion of Poincaré, remaining unchanged, always stamped with the old traditions of French foreign policy, will doubtless be an obstacle for us, even if the government has other views" (Izvolsky to Sazonov, March 28, 1915, *Documents diplomatiques secrets russes 1914–1917* [Paris, 1928], p. 258).

The Viviani cabinet was subjected to bitter legislative criticism throughout 1915. Most of these attacks fell upon the head of Alexandre Millerand, minister of war. Members of the Senate army commission bickered with him for months; they complained of his refusal to answer questions, found fault with the production of munitions, and concentrated special blame upon two of Millerand's aides whom he in turn defended vigorously. It was something of a paradox, therefore, that the fall of the cabinet was finally brought on not by Millerand but by Foreign Minister Delcassé. Nor did the legislature ever dare to vote nonconfidence in the cabinet.

During the long conflict over Millerand, Poincaré had staunchly opposed the sacrifice of the war minister. This was true even though the president sympathized with many of the legislature's complaints and repeatedly urged Millerand to change his ways. Besides, personal relations between the two men were not entirely happy. Friction had occurred several times when the president called in Millerand's subordinates for private conversations. Nevertheless Poincaré feared that the dismissal of the minister might destroy the *union sacrée* and perhaps even endanger the republic.

Viviani was more than once on the verge of throwing Millerand to the wolves in order to protect himself.[38] His failure to do so may be traced to the president. Time and again Poincaré urged the premier not to permit Millerand's resignation. At the ministerial council of July 27, for instance, he expatiated at length on the danger of opening the gates to a crisis which might lead to revolution.[39] Viviani heeded the warning; but three weeks later the dispute boiled up again. This time the

---

[38] Viviani had never been very friendly toward Millerand. Early in 1915 he proposed to resign in order to form a new cabinet without the war minister. He abandoned this scheme, however, for fear that Poincaré would seize the opportunity to get rid of him as well (Henri Leyret, "Delcassé parle," *Revue des Deux Mondes*, September 15, 1937, p. 349). Apparently Viviani did not trust the president too far.

[39] Poincaré, VI, 346; also pp. 292, 299, 300–301, 321, 342, 344.

distracted premier decided to give in, and reversed himself only when Poincaré repeatedly argued that one sign of weakness would only whet the legislators' appetites.[40] Viviani finally summoned up enough courage to make a vigorous defense of his cabinet before the Chamber (August 26), and was rewarded by a handsome vote of confidence. The crisis passed; hostility persisted toward the minister of war, but there was no more open talk of his resignation. The incident proved beyond doubt that Poincaré, a strong personality, standing behind Viviani, a weak premier, was sometimes able to guide the latter's policy.

It may be that the president's defense of Millerand was not entirely unselfish. He knew that certain legislators might seek bigger game if they succeeded in bagging the war minister. Henri Leyret, an intimate friend of Delcassé, hinted at this when he urged Viviani to stand firm: "Today Millerand, tomorrow Augagneur, Thomson, the day after tomorrow Delcassé, you soon, and—who knows?—the president himself, for Poincaré is mistaken if he thinks he will be spared." Whereupon Viviani replied, "Someone told him that at the last council, but he answered dryly that as for him he would never resign, no matter what happened!"[41] Whatever Poincaré's purpose may have been, however, the fact of his influence upon Viviani cannot be denied.

The cabinet's collapse was only postponed when the Millerand squall subsided. It loomed up again on October 8, when Delcassé resigned as minister of foreign affairs on grounds of illness. His health was indeed bad; but politicians were not slow to find other reasons for the resignation. It was said in the lobbies that Delcassé's self-confidence had been shattered by his failure to win Bulgaria to the Allied cause. In fact—so ran the rumor—Poincaré had been forced to take over active direction of French foreign policy for two months past.[42]

[40] Poincaré, VII, 25, 27, 28, 31, 34, 46, 192.
[41] Leyret, *loc. cit.*, p. 352.   [42] *Ibid.*, p. 354.

This talk was not entirely devoid of truth. Bulgaria's decision to join the enemy was a severe blow to the oversanguine foreign minister. The failure of his Balkan policy weighed heavily upon his mind. So preoccupied did he become that Poincaré began to exert daily pressure upon him through September—far heavier pressure than the president was accustomed to use.[43] Poincaré's activity redoubled in October. He telegraphed to the Tsar, urging that Russia join the Salonika expedition.[44] He and Viviani drew up all of Delcassé's diplomatic messages on October 2. Four days later Poincaré formulated a telegram of instructions for Ambassador Paléologue but stipulated that Delcassé sign it as usual.[45] Yet in spite of Delcassé's virtual abdication the president insisted that the foreign minister retain his post, declared that he would not accept his resignation, and wrote him a two-page letter of remonstrance when Delcassé finally did resign.[46] In order to uphold French prestige among the Allies Poincaré wished to keep a man at the Quai d'Orsay who had become nothing more than a figurehead. Protected by Delcassé's responsibility, the president was willing to direct foreign policy to a degree which none of his predecessors had approached.

The testimony of Henri Leyret has made it clear that Delcassé resigned because he differed with the cabinet over Balkan policy. The foreign minister opposed a landing at Salonika unless Greece should first enter the war. In spite of his attitude, the landing was carried out early in October. Why did Delcassé give formal consent to this and to other steps which he really disapproved? "After making all my reservations," Delcassé told Leyret, "I had to bow before the decisions of the council, provoked by the intervention and the insistence of the

---

[43] Poincaré, VII, 114, 116, 118, 121, 130, 137, 139, 141–42.

[44] Sazonov to the Tsar, October 1, 1915, *Russian Docs.*, VIII, 737–38.

[45] Poincaré, VIII, 145, 148, 156, 159, 162; Pingaud, *Histoire diplomatique*, II, 97–98.

[46] Poincaré, VII, 142, 166; Leyret, *loc. cit.*, p. 348.

president of the republic . . . ."[47] Delcassé's statement is a striking commentary upon Poincaré's conduct in council meetings, and upon his influence over the whole cabinet as well as over the ailing foreign minister.

This breach in the cabinet let loose all the complaints and ambitions which had been accumulating for a year. Viviani tried for three weeks to revive the ministry by an infusion of new blood, but eventually had to admit failure. Meanwhile Poincaré sought guidance in daily conversations with political leaders almost as though the cabinet had already fallen. One idea which entered his mind was to desert the Elysée for the premiership. He soon abandoned it, fearing opposition in the Chamber.[48] Someone also suggested that he combine the two presidencies, but he doubted the constitutionality of such a plan.[49]

Viviani's resignation left Poincaré with complete freedom to select a successor. His choice was Aristide Briand. Poincaré confronted the premier-designate with a single condition —that the ministry be one of "broad national union." This meant that few ministers would be replaced but that the center of gravity would shift slightly to the Right. Clemenceau refused a portfolio on the ground that "Poincaré wants to run everything . . . . and I am not the man to permit this interference."[50] Some thought that Clemenceau hoped to bring on

[47] Ill as he was, Delcassé was acutely aware of his differences of opinion with Poincaré. When Viviani returned from a trip abroad and learned of Delcassé's resignation, he asked the latter "if, during his absence, Poincaré had not offended me in one way or another, but he was speaking about the consideration due to the man and not the ideas of the minister: it is in this sense that I replied negatively" (Leyret, loc. cit., pp. 375-76). Cf. Martin, "Notes de guerre," conversation with M. Emile Haguenin, October 13, 1915; Marcellin, Politique, I, 136; Izvolsky to Sazonov, October 15, 1915, Russian Docs., VIII, 804.   [48] Poincaré, VII, 186.

[49] Ibid., p. 176; L'Action Française, October 25, 1915.

[50] Poincaré, VII, 204. Many people were already looking with favor toward a Clemenceau ministry but realized that it would inevitably lead to conflict with the Elysée (Martin, "Notes de guerre," conversation with M. Pierre Comert of the Quai d'Orsay, October 26, 1915).

a presidential crisis; but this sort of loose talk was not widely heard. In general, the cabinet crisis took place in an atmosphere of polite curiosity. The substitution of Briand for Viviani was not expected to produce profound changes in the conduct of government.

THE BRIAND MINISTRY (1915–1917)

When the Left-wing cabinet of Viviani had first come to power, not long before Sarajevo, it had seemed to mean a minimized role for the president. Three things had made it possible for Poincaré to avoid the King Log status during the seventeen months of Viviani's incumbency. One was the premier's weakness. The second was the outbreak of war, which had calmed the ruffled waters of party conflict. The third was the addition of three Moderate ministers in August 1914—a modification which had neutralized the government's Left-wing character. Viviani admired the president and had willingly co-operated with him, allowing him to offer advice and to intervene at length in council meetings. In fact, Poincaré had clashed more frequently with the Moderate Millerand than with any of the Left-wing ministers.

Briand's arrival in office in October 1915 seemed likely to improve still more the president's position. Viviani, after all, was a Socialist-Republican, while Briand was a leader of the Poincaré-approved Fédération des gauches. Briand's early days of militant socialism were past, and his post-war differences with Poincaré over foreign policy were still far in the future. During this intermediate period both men followed the same general trend of thought in politics. Furthermore, Briand had been the "great elector" in the presidential campaign of 1913 and had inherited the headship of the cabinet when his candidate Poincaré stepped up into the Elysée. Complete harmony between the two men seemed assured. Time proved these expectations false; Poincaré experienced far more friction in his relations with Briand than he had met in the case of Viviani.

When the list of ministers appeared in the *Journal officiel,* Clemenceau wrote in derision: "It is hard to tell whether we have had a ministerial crisis or a remodeling of the cabinet . . . . The premier has become vice-premier, and the vice-premier premier: there is the principal fact in this great revolution." "Nothing was changed or could be changed," he complained a few days later, "for there is only one Poincaré in the world, in his immutable successive incarnations."[51]

Clemenceau's first gibe did not miss the truth very far. There were a few significant replacements, however. Millerand disappeared from the war ministry, a change which removed the major point of friction both between cabinet and legislature and between cabinet and president. Some thought that Poincaré had intrigued against Millerand, in order to insure his exclusion from the new government.[52] Millerand apparently believed this was the case, for he was very cool toward the president immediately thereafter.[53] No positive proof could be found to justify the suspicion, but it was quite obvious that Poincaré did not regret the elimination of his old friend at this time. Replacing Millerand was a professional soldier, General Gallieni, whose presence was likely to create new relationships between military headquarters and the government. Another important change was at the Quai d'Orsay, where Briand himself took over the conduct of affairs. Briand was likely to resist presidential interference in foreign policy more than his predecessors had done.[54]

Briand's presence in the premiership itself was also signifi-

[51] *L'Homme Enchaîné,* October 31 and November 5, 1915.

[52] Germain Bapst, "Journal de la guerre de 1914," October 31 and November 1, 1915.

[53] Poincaré, VII, 212.

[54] Jean Malvy was retained at the ministry of the interior through Poincaré's insistence (Suarez, *Briand,* III, 168–70). Poincaré's friendship toward Malvy, a Caillautist, has never been satisfactorily explained. Suarez believes that Poincaré stood in terror of Caillaux, and hoped to mollify him by keeping Malvy in office.

cant. He was a stronger personality than Viviani; his arrival seemed to mean a more vital leadership at the head of affairs. For this reason the exponents of authoritarian government were somewhat mollified. Even the Socialists of *L'Humanité* approved the change, for they wished to see the war conducted to a rapid and successful conclusion.[55] But however decisive and however willing to assume responsibility Briand may have been, he was not a man of detail and close application. His specialty lay in brilliant oratory and in acute generalizations; besides, he was notably easygoing by nature. Ribot believed that Briand arrived at sessions of the council without having formed any opinion on the dispatches which had arrived at the Quai d'Orsay. He read them aloud in the meeting, observed the reaction of the ministers present, and adopted a spur-of-the-moment policy.[56]

The result was that Poincaré, the conscientious worker *par excellence,* soon became impatient at Briand's carelessness and continued to act as he had done during the Viviani period. He intervened continually in council; and his intervention carried weight, for it was generally realized that he was better informed than the premier himself.[57] While he was still legally unable to force the acceptance of his opinions, his influence under these conditions was almost as effective as real power would have been. Minister of War Gallieni was the only one who objected, and he did so only to his diary. "Always palavers, never decisions," he complained. "Poincaré, Briand, Bourgeois, Doumergue talk constantly, and about everything . . . . Always these useless discussions, where each

---

[55] *L'Humanité,* October 30, 1915.

[56] Ribot, *Lettres,* p. 128; cf. Poincaré, VIII, 177.

[57] Albert Thomas, the Socialist leader, told a Swiss news correspondent in 1917: "Poincaré has some great qualities. He is a worker, conscientious, he has dossiers, studies and understands questions. In the council of ministers, as neither Viviani nor Briand presided effectively, he intervened constantly and with authority, for he knew questions better than they" (Martin, "Notes de guerre," December 10, 1917).

one's character asserts itself: Poincaré, fault-finding, malevolent, suspicious of everyone, jealous, desirous of taking part in affairs, but without responsibility, of *presiding* always, with his name never forgotten in the press . . . ." Once Gallieni noted with satisfaction that the council had accomplished a great deal that day because the president had been absent— "this president without responsibility, who wants to meddle in everything."[58] Gallieni's irritation, however, had no effect on Poincaré.

Although the president had a chance to be heard three times a week, his words did not meet blind acceptance. Briand also possessed ideas, and he defended them with energy. Council meetings became interminably long; they turned into sharp debates between president and premier, in which Poincaré certainly forgot the meaning of the word "preside."[59] Conditions in Greece were responsible for the most serious clashes. Poincaré, backed by most of the ministers, nursed a deep distrust of King Constantine and of his professed neutrality or even benevolence toward the Allies. Poincaré favored the use of force to settle any differences with the Greek government. Such a case arose, for example, when the hard-pressed Serbian army was seeking permission to retreat across Greek territory. But Briand was convinced of Constantine's sincerity and believed that the king should be treated with respect. His personal friendship with certain members of the Greek royal family probably colored his viewpoint.

As Briand showed a tendency to give the council less and less information on foreign affairs, Poincaré took it upon himself to fill the gaps.[60] He purposely congratulated the minister of marine in Briand's presence when the minister pursued a Near Eastern policy at variance with that of the premier.[61] He

[58] *Les carnets de Gallieni* (Paris, 1932), pp. 217, 260, 230. Cf. Suarez, *Briand*, III, 256.

[59] Ribot, *Lettres*, pp. 23–24, 128.

[60] Poincaré, VIII, 303. [61] *Ibid.*, p. 330; cf. IX, 26.

openly assumed the role of pleader for the anti-Constantine
group, so that sessions of the council more than once degenerated into violent argument. Albert Thomas, the minister of
munitions, described one meeting as follows:

> In August 1916, at the moment of Rumania's entrance into the war,
> I recall a terrible scene dealing with Greece: "You lie, sir!" cried
> Poincaré to Briand, and the latter threw his portfolio on the table.
> Doumergue, between them, cried in a ridiculous voice: "There is
> France!" Finally they were brought together and embraced.[62]

But a passing embrace was not enough to hide their dissensions. Poincaré disguised his disapproval of the foreign minister so badly that even the British ambassador remarked it.[63]
It was just as plain to Prince Andrew of Greece, who visited
Paris in July 1916. The prince received a warm welcome from
Briand but a distinctly cool one from the president.[64] A condition such as this was not likely to make well-informed contemporaries believe that the French president's function was
confined to presiding only. Even though he could not enforce
his will, he could and did embarrass Briand by continual criticism and by acting as leader of an opposition group within the
ministry. Poincaré's sincerity and his patriotism were beyond
any question; they were so great, in fact, that he could not in-
cline gracefully when the responsible premier followed a course
that conflicted with the president's own ideas.

Greece was not the only scene of Poincaré's efforts to trace
the outlines of French foreign policy. Another example was
the protracted effort to bring Rumania into the war. The Ru-
manians played their cards like experienced gamblers; their
aim was profit, not glory. In 1914 Poincaré had already tried

[62] Martin, "Notes de guerre," December 10, 1917. Cf. Suarez, *Briand,*
III, 290–91.

[63] Bertie, *Diary,* II, 19.

[64] Izvolsky to Stürmer, July 21, 1916, *Die Europaischen Mächte und
Griechenland Während das Weltkrieges* (Dresden, 1932), p. 122. This interview received no mention in Poincaré's memoirs. Cf. Poincaré, VIII, 319;
and Suarez, *Briand,* III, 445.

to convince the Russians that certain Rumanian demands ought to be met.[65] His authority was utilized again in 1916. In March he once more urged the Tsar to make concessions; in August his appeal was repeated, this time with successful results.[66] Oddly enough, Poincaré has mentioned neither of these important messages in his well-stocked memoirs.

In several other instances Poincaré put pressure on the premier, with varying degrees of success. His ire was aroused when the Italian ambassador suggested a "rectification" of the Franco-Italian frontier. Briand's noncommittal attitude toward this piece of blackmail stirred Poincaré to write an indignant letter to the premier demanding a stronger stand.[67] The spoils of war in Asia Minor also drew the president's attention. He feared that a British proposal for the division of Turkey did not adequately insure French acquisition of Syria. His complaints in council forced Briand to seek added guaranties from the British.[68] Again, Poincaré condemned a scheme by which Briand hoped to resuscitate Albania; and the cabinet agreed with the president.[69]

It was Poincaré, too, who goaded Briand into defining the war aims of France. At every council session he complained, "You have no guarantee for Alsace-Lorraine on the part of our allies."[70] He urged that a letter of instructions be sent to Ambassador Cambon to guide him in conversations with the British government. Poincaré's "pressing insistence" finally overcame Briand's reluctance. While the premier was absent in Italy in January 1917, Poincaré had the proposition discussed and adopted in council. Faced by a *fait accompli* on

[65] *Supra,* p. 143.

[66] Pingaud, *Histoire diplomatique,* I, 178, 194; Paléologue, *La Russie des tsars,* II, 204–5, 330.

[67] Poincaré, VII, 350–51; Suarez, *Briand,* III, 228.

[68] Poincaré, VIII, 9.   [69] *Ibid.,* pp. 316–17.

[70] Martin, "Notes de guerre," conversation with Albert Thomas, January 23, 1919. Cf. Ribot, *Lettres,* p. 220.

his return, Briand consented to write the desired letter to Cambon.[71]

This same presidential insistence forced Briand into a war-aims agreement with Russia. Gaston Doumergue was sent to Petrograd in February 1917 and secured the signature of the so-called Paléologue-Pokrovsky letters, wherein the tsarist government promised to support French claims in Alsace-Lorraine and in the Rhineland.[72] When the Russian revolution brought these letters to light, French Socialists immediately attributed them to Poincaré. Technically the Socialists had no case. The president was protected by Briand's responsibility; he could even point to the fact that he had not so much as seen the Paléologue-Pokrovsky letters.[73] It is true, nevertheless, that these letters contained the exact assurance which Poincaré had been demanding for months. His influence started the diplomatic machinery, which proceeded to function under the control of the responsible officials.[74]

Briand's cabinet, like that of Viviani, stretched its span of power over seventeen months. Its foundations were never very solid, however. As early as December 1915 there were rumors of its overthrow and prospects of a Clemenceau ministry were discussed. The prediction was freely made that if "the Tiger" were called to office, Poincaré would resign.[75] Again at the end of 1916 the cabinet wavered, and hostile tongues accused

[71] Martin, "Notes de guerre," January 23, 1919; Ribot, Lettres, p. 222; "Mermeix," Le combat des trois, notes et documents sur la conférence de la paix (Paris, 1922), pp. 192–93. There is no mention of this Briand-to-Cambon letter in Poincaré's memoirs.

[72] Paléologue, La Russie des tsars, III, 183, 193; "Mermeix," Le combat des trois, pp. 191, 224.   [73] Ribot, Journal, p. 100; Poincaré, IX, 145.

[74] Georges Suarez (Briand, IV, 133–35, 220–21) argues that Poincaré controlled the machinery as well. In Briand's absence, someone at the Quai d'Orsay telegraphed Doumergue the authority to have the letters signed. Briand grudgingly approved ex post facto, but many Deputies heard and believed that Poincaré had given the order.

[75] Bertie, Diary, I, 277, 279; "Mermeix," Joffre, la première crise du commandement (Paris, 1919), p. 89.

Poincaré of trying to cause its fall.[76] It was finally subjected to a slight "replastering."

The fatal day at last came in March 1917. Minister of War Lyautey left office in a fit of irritation brought on by a slight skirmish with the Chamber of Deputies. His resignation resulted in the fall of the cabinet, just as Delcassé's resignation in 1915 had wrecked Viviani. Briand could find no one to replace Lyautey; and the legislature was so hostile that the premier decided to abandon his task.

Poincaré's part in this ministerial crisis was most obscure. Apparently he did not intrigue to cause Briand's fall, although some people hinted that such was the case.[77] In fact, he had helped to save the cabinet three months earlier by approving the replacement of Joffre as commander of the French armies.[78] He had even refused to accept Briand's proffered resignation in December 1916.[79] On the other hand, there was undeniable friction between the president and the premier over foreign policy, especially in regard to Greece. Poincaré wrote that "Briand is . . . . working against certain of his collaborators, notably against those who do not join in his complacency toward King Constantine."[80] Since the president led this anti-Constantine bloc in the council, perhaps Poincaré felt that Briand was intriguing against him too. In mid-March he even thought of forcing Briand to resign against his will, on the ground that the Chamber's opposition to the cabinet was continually increasing.[81] Before Lyautey's retirement broke up the ministry the president had started to confer with numerous politicians for suggestions in case of a crisis. In this way, he made it plain that he would not use his prestige to defend Briand. His attitude doubtless increased the hesitancy of men who might otherwise have agreed to replace Lyautey.

[76] Marcellin, *Politique,* I, 523; Bapst, "Journal," November 14 and 29, December 17 and 18, 1916; Suarez, *Briand,* IV, 14, 35, 59, 66–67.

[77] Corday, *L'Envers,* II, 63–66; Bapst, "Journal," March 18, 1917.

[78] *Infra,* p. 185.   [79] Poincaré, IX, 30–31.   [80] *Ibid.,* p. 72.   [81] *Ibid.,* p. 73.

As in 1915 Poincaré had complete freedom in selecting a new premier; there was no Chamber vote to guide him. His first choice, Paul Deschanel, declined; his second accepted. It was Alexandre Ribot—the aged, conservative financier whom Poincaré had already thrown in the teeth of the legislature in June 1914 with disastrous results. Although Ribot was said to bear some ill will toward Poincaré as a result of the presidential election of 1913, there was no real hostility between the two men. Ribot's advanced age made it unlikely that he would furnish aggressive leadership. The censored press was unable to state its opinion of the new ministry, but there was some privately expressed dissatisfaction. André Tardieu told a journalist: "Poincaré is playing a dangerous game; he does not understand the need of changing methods. Among the ministers who have foreseen nothing, old Ribot has foreseen less than all the others."[82] Men of authoritarian tendencies generally condemned the choice as weak. When it was announced that Paul Painlevé would become minister of war, one Right-wing critic was astounded at the "monstrosity" of Poincaré's and Ribot's conduct: "It can only be cowardice or jealousy, fear of seeing a superior man in office, which makes them act thus."[83] But if reactionaries groaned, the Radicals, who had destroyed Ribot's ministry in June 1914, applauded the change. For Ribot promised that he would govern in accord with the Chambers, whereas Briand had avoided legislative control as much as possible. "Let there be no mistake," wrote the Socialist-Republican Deputy Augagneur with more fervor than accuracy; "we have just seen the defeat of an attempt at personal power."[84] The Left, appeased for the moment, sat back to watch the experiment of war government under legislative guidance.

[82] Martin, "Notes de guerre," March 19, 1917.

[83] Bapst, "Journal," March 19, 1917.

[84] *La Grande Revue,* XCIII (April 1917), 367.

THE RIBOT AND PAINLEVÉ MINISTRIES (1917)

Poincaré did not exaggerate when he called the year 1917 *l'année trouble*. It did not bring actual revolution to France as it did to Russia; but this twelvemonth saw more unrest than any other period during the war. There were strikes behind the lines, grave military mutinies at the front. The government reflected this growing disorder. Four different cabinets held office during 1917, and one of them was overthrown by a hostile vote of the Chamber—the only case of its kind during the entire war.

The accession of Ribot to the premiership suggested no sharp change in the conduct of government except perhaps a reaffirmation of the legislature's right to exercise control. Ribot had been a member of the ministry since 1914, and he maintained many of his former colleagues in office. The exclusion of Briand, who had proved to be a rather ineffective wartime leader, left the way open for more firmness at the helm. The aged Ribot, however, was hardly the man to fill such a need. But at least there would be no more of the interminable Poincaré-Briand debates in council.

Ribot had sat through many of these clashes from 1915 to 1917 and was determined that they should come to an end. One of his first moves was to draw up a set of rules for future procedure in council sessions. One of them provided that "the president of the republic, who has been talking as much as the premier, will have his say only when the affair is worthy of his intervention; he will let the premier direct business." Poincaré answered this frank rebuke by admitting: "I departed from my role, and I realized the fact; but I was forced to do so because there was no premier."[85] Henceforth he could no longer use this excuse, for Ribot had openly shown the president his place.

[85] Ribot, *Journal*, pp. 50–51. Poincaré did not mention this conversation in his memoirs.

Another suggestive incident occurred twenty-four hours after Ribot had taken power. The premier called a meeting of the *conseil de cabinet* in which the president did not take part.[86] Sessions of this kind had been rare since the war had broken out; they had been replaced by frequent meetings of the *conseil des ministres* at which Poincaré presided. This apparent symptom of greater independence was not followed up, however. During the rest of the Ribot period the ministerial council and the war committee each continued to meet twice a week under Poincaré's chairmanship.[87]

If Ribot wanted the president to stay in his place, he was at least willing to accept advice from the Elysée. Poincaré objected to a phrase in Ribot's first official document, his ministerial declaration, and secured its change. In the original version, Ribot planned to tell the Chambers that France was fighting "with no spirit of conquest." Poincaré pointed out that the idea of annexing the left bank of the Rhine was spreading in France; he feared that Ribot's phrase might "destroy enthusiasm and discourage salutary hopes."[88] This incident, along with the Paléologue-Pokrovsky letters of February 1917, showed for the first time that Poincaré's war aims were not limited to Alsace and Lorraine. He did not yet publicly identify himself with the idea of wrenching the Rhineland from Germany; but in 1919 his sympathy turned into open support of this plan.

The war-weary year of 1917 brought with it several plans for a negotiated peace. By far the most important of these was the so-called Sixte affair, instigated by the new ruler of Austria. Emperor Charles had ascended the throne at Vienna in 1916. Only three months after his accession he began to explore the possibilities of a separate peace between Austria and the Allies. He chose as go-between his brother-in-law, Prince Sixte of Bourbon-Parma. Sixte's Bourbon blood made

---

[86] Poincaré, IX, 82.   [87] Ribot, *Journal*, p. 50.

[88] *Ibid.*, p. 48; Poincaré, IX, 79–80.

him ineligible for service in the French army; he had been fighting as a volunteer with the Belgian forces, where he had won the French *Croix de Guerre*. His family connections plus his war record made him an ideal intermediary.

Sixte arrived in Paris late in February 1917 with a memorandum from the emperor and asked for an audience with Poincaré. The latter refused at first on the ground that only the cabinet could undertake such negotiations.[89] But the president's scruples were soon overcome by Sixte's insistence as well as by his own curiosity. Sixte was admitted to the Elysée on March 5 and spent two hours outlining the Austrian proposal. Poincaré was careful to point out that he would have to inform the premier, Briand, of their conversation. "I can keep part of the details for myself," he added; "but I cannot act without the assent of the premier."[90]

Poincaré was favorably impressed by Sixte's sincerity and hastened to bring Briand into the negotiation. The premier proved much more skeptical, but he agreed that Charles's good faith might be tested by a four-point program of concessions to the Allies. Sixte set off at once for Vienna, much encouraged by the success of his entering wedge. He returned late in March with an autograph letter from Charles and secured a second interview with Poincaré on March 31. During his absence Ribot had displaced Briand in the premiership. Ribot was even less enthusiastic about the Austrian negotiation than Briand had been; but he sent Jules Cambon to represent him at the meeting of March 31. This time Sixte offered a definite promise of Austrian support for the French claim to Alsace-Lorraine; also Belgium and Serbia would be restored to full sovereignty. Poincaré objected that the return of the lost provinces would no longer compensate France for the injuries which she had suffered. He agreed, however, that the con-

[89] Poincaré, IX, 66.

[90] Prince Sixte de Bourbon, *L'offre de paix séparée de l'Autriche* (Paris, 1920), p. 65; there are some further details in Suarez, *Briand*, IV, 136–48.

versations had reached a point where the British ought to be brought in. The president took care to send a full written report of this discussion to the premier.[91]

Ribot, still hostile, went to London early in April to put Lloyd George *au courant*.[92] On his return, he joined Poincaré in a third conference with Sixte. In spite of the premier's presence Poincaré did a large share of the talking. He insisted, among other things, that Germany must give up all territory on the left bank of the Rhine. Ribot, however, declared bluntly that neither he nor Lloyd George would take another step until they had secured the approval of Italy. Sixte demurred, and Poincaré cautiously agreed with him. But Ribot was adamant. He insisted that the Italians must be informed of the peace offer at an Interallied conference to be held at St.-Jean-de-Maurienne on April 19. Reluctantly Sixte had to consent; but only on condition that the Italians be told nothing definite. Ribot promised that he would merely sound Italian opinion as to a hypothetical peace with Austria.[93]

The conference at St.-Jean-de-Maurienne virtually spiked Sixte's mission. When Ribot barely hinted at a separate peace, the Italian representative Sonnino flared up in protest. To quiet Sonnino's suspicions, the delegates had to pledge themselves against any separate negotiations. Prince Sixte, his optimism gone, journeyed to Vienna for further instructions. He found that the Emperor Charles refused to give up hope. Charles still believed that Poincaré's prestige and authority

[91] Ribot, *Journal*, p. 62; Poincaré, IX, 85–90; Sixte, *op. cit.*, pp. 102–5.

[92] David Lloyd George, *War Memoirs* (Boston, 1933–36), III, 234.

[93] Sixte, *op. cit.*, pp. 114–17. On April 16 Poincaré heard a report that Austria had joined Germany in proposing a separate peace to Russia. In his mind, this evidence of solidarity between Berlin and Vienna seemed to belie Austria's talk of a separate peace with the Allies. It proved, he wrote to Ribot, that the Central Powers really desired a white peace which would be equivalent to a French defeat (Ribot, *Journal*, pp. 65–66; there is no mention of this letter in Poincaré's memoirs). His suspicions doubtless increased the difficulty of Sixte's task.

might overcome the opposition of Ribot.[94] Sixte was doubtful, but was instructed to continue to work through the Elysée
rather than the Quai d'Orsay. Carrying a second autograph
letter from the emperor, he returned to Paris for one last
effort. On May 20 he was received at the Elysée by both
Poincaré and Ribot. He offered certain concessions to Italy,
but they were insufficient to satisfy Ribot. The president, however, was more willing to listen and had no qualms about sid-
ing openly with Sixte on some points.[95] The prince left the
Elysée with a very favorable opinion of Poincaré, but felt that
his position tied his hands.

Thus expired the peace negotiations begun by Emperor
Charles. Sixte returned to the front with Poincaré's promise
to call him back when the moment for further talks arrived.
But the moment never came. Italy had entered the war in
1915 only after securing a promise that all Italian territorial
ambitions would be fulfilled. Rome refused to reduce its demands; and, since Ribot would not act without Italian approval,
the peace plan ran into a stone wall.

The abortive nature of the Sixte affair does not invalidate
it as an illustration of Poincaré's subsurface activity. Every
move which the president made was strictly constitutional; he
took no personal action, never failed to keep the premier informed, and was always careful to be protected by a minister.
Yet the Sixte affair showed that he was something more than
a prisoner of protocol. The Paris end of the negotiations
centered in his office at the Elysée. Only four or five men in
France knew what was occurring, and Poincaré probably knew
more than any of the others. Even the cabinet remained in
ignorance of the peace offer; no official report was ever made.
Fortunately for Premier Ribot, the president cared little
whether Austria was in or out of the war. Had he seen great
value in a separate peace, Poincaré might have made things

[94] Sixte, *op. cit.*, pp. 167, 170.
[95] *Ibid.*, pp. 193–200.

very uncomfortable for Ribot and might possibly have forced the latter's hand.

The president's attitude toward a negotiated peace with Germany was more ambiguous. In June 1917 Baron von Lancken, the German governor of Brussels, approached ex-premier Briand through certain Belgian intermediaries. Briand became seriously interested in these conversations and kept Poincaré informed of their progress. The president, according to his own later account, gave Briand absolutely no encouragement.[96] He has recalled that he finally summoned several ministers to discuss the von Lancken affair, and secured a vote that the negotiation ought to be abandoned.[97] Briand's daily memoranda, however, tell another story. They suggest that Poincaré offered a guarded sort of approval, and that it was Ribot's opposition which killed the project.[98] Apparently the president spoke in such equivocal terms that Briand and Ribot could interpret his remarks in opposite ways.

Within four months after Ribot came to power, hostility to the government was in the air. The premier became so discouraged by July that he wished to resign, but Poincaré refused to permit it on the ground that the Chamber had given him no indication as to the choice of a successor.[99] This was a feeble excuse, for the fate of ministries had not been decided by Chamber votes since the war had broken out. The president looked with favor on a reconstruction of the cabinet, however, for he wished to reduce the number of Socialist ministers.[100] Poincaré's anger toward the Socialists stemmed from that party's growing agitation for an early peace. A second

[96] Poincaré, IX, 167, 286.

[97] According to Poincaré's memoirs, this conference took place on September 24 with Premier Painlevé present (IX, 299). Ribot, however, dates it September 25 and asserts that Painlevé did not attend (*Journal,* p. 216).

[98] Suarez, *Briand,* IV, 268–69, 271, 297–98.

[99] Poincaré, IX, 219.

[100] *Ibid.,* pp. 263, 269, 276.

source of his irritation, no doubt, was their bitter anti-Poincarist campaign in press and parliament.[101]

Early in September Ribot finally made up his mind to resign over Poincaré's protests. The president wasted little time in political consultations; he turned almost immediately to Paul Painlevé, minister of war in the outgoing cabinet. The premier-designate met a great deal of difficulty in forming a combination, for the Socialists refused to promise their support unless they received several portfolios. Only pressure from Poincaré kept Painlevé from granting their demands. He finally constituted his ministry without a single Socialist member.[102]

Of all the wartime premiers Paul Painlevé was least prepared for his high office. His reputation was great, but it had been made in mathematics rather than in politics. He had abandoned a distinguished career as a professor to enter the Chamber in 1910. Since then his record had been mediocre; he had filled only one important ministerial post. To justify his choice Poincaré declared that the presidents of the Senate and the Chamber had suggested it. All the same, it was strange that Poincaré unhesitatingly accepted their suggestion in a period of serious crisis like 1917. The time for a strong leader was becoming overdue, and Painlevé could not fill that need. As one of his critics said, "he shakes hands too much to have a fist."[103]

There were some who believed that the president had ulterior motives when he named the new premier. Caillaux and his entourage asserted that Poincaré's chief purpose was to get his friends into power. At a private dinner attended by Caillaux, Pierre Laval, Victor Margueritte, and others, someone remarked: "Are not all the men who took part in his 'national' ministry [1912–1913] called back into the present cabinet?

[101] *Infra*, p. 208.
[102] Poincaré, IX, 280–83.
[103] Corday, *L'Envers*, II, 153.

Poincaré never had so much power in his hands. Remember that he besought Painlevé to accept the premiership, for otherwise he would have been obliged to call Clemenceau."[104] Indeed, the Tiger had become almost the only acceptable alternative; and Poincaré still hoped that solution might be avoided. Clemenceau immediately dubbed Painlevé "M. Poincaré's premier," and continually referred to him thus during the weeks that followed.[105]

One thing was certain—and the president must have been aware of it—Painlevé was not likely to dominate the governmental scene. But the cabinet's eight-week span of power was too brief to furnish many indications of an enlarged role for Poincaré. As a matter of fact, several times Painlevé called *conseils de cabinet,* even though this practice of meeting without the president had been virtually abandoned since 1914.[106] There was one peculiar innovation in an opposite direction. Twice when the premier had to make trips abroad, *conseils des ministres* continued to be held in his absence.[107] If Poincaré had sometimes been the real director of council sessions when Viviani and Briand were in power, he probably did not hesitate to take over active leadership while Painlevé was not in Paris.

There might have been some interesting developments in

---

[104] Corday, *L'Envers,* II, 144.

[105] *L'Homme Enchaîné,* October 9, 1917, *et seq.*

[106] Poincaré, IX, 318, 320, 328.

[107] On October 30, and November 5, 6, and 9, 1917 (Poincaré, IX, 344, 352, 357, 359). Raoul Péret was minister of justice in the Painlevé government. In reply to the author's request for information, M. Péret wrote (letter to the author, March 28, 1938) as follows: "It is very difficult for me to divulge what went on in the council of ministers, the deliberations being secret and unrecorded. For that matter, M. Poincaré always confined himself to his constitutional role, always leaving the decision to the government. He limited himself to giving his advice but without insisting that it be followed." M. Péret's reply, written two decades after the event, suggests that details of cabinet sessions probably never will be known. It may be added that Péret was politically friendly toward Poincaré.

the president's position if Painlevé had stayed in office. But the cabinet never got under way; it floundered along under the weight of parliamentary criticism, internal dissension, and general discouragement throughout France. Foreign Minister Ribot, upon whose head fell many of the attacks, was jettisoned in October; but his replacement failed to buoy up the ministry. At last, on November 13, Painlevé was put in a minority by the Chamber. For the third time within a year, the president was faced by a ministerial crisis.

Informed politicians saw clearly that Clemenceau would have to be called to power. There had been talk of a ministry headed by the Tiger ever since 1914; but his bitter diatribes against the Elysée caused widespread belief that Poincaré would refuse to name him. By the end of 1917, however, the president decided to swallow his pride. He had been prepared to make Clemenceau premier in September if Painlevé had failed to form a cabinet.[108] He continued to express his intention to take the fateful step before the crisis arrived in November.[109] Yet when Painlevé finally fell Poincaré hesitated and consulted widely before he placed his chief adversary in the saddle.

The nomination of Clemenceau has often been used as a clinching argument to prove Poincaré's unselfish patriotism. There is much justice in the claim, for some presidents might conceivably have placed personal enmities above all other considerations. At the same time one may well ask just how much choice Poincaré really had in November 1917. He might have continued to avoid Clemenceau for a time, by renominating Viviani or some other secondary politician. But France had come to the point where these vacillating cabinets could no longer effectively control the process of government. Crisis

[108] Colonel Emile E. Herbillon, *Souvenirs d'un officier de liaison pendant la guerre mondiale* (Paris, 1930), II, 137. Painlevé believed at that time that Clemenceau's accession would force Poincaré to resign (Bertie, *Diary*, II, 175). [109] Poincaré, IX, 357; Ribot, *Journal*, pp. 236, 238.

would have followed crisis with increasing frequency, with a complete breakdown of the republican system as a possible result. The time had come when a strong hand was indispensable; and this meant either Caillaux or Clemenceau. Both were equally distasteful to Poincaré from a personal point of view. But Caillaux would probably have attempted to end the war by negotiation; Clemenceau alone was capable of demanding and achieving that imposed French peace which the president regarded as necessary.

Poincaré had no right to claim excessive credit for making a well-nigh inevitable decision. This does not imply, however, that he deserved criticism for his failure to call Clemenceau earlier. The Tiger's defects were enormous, and in the years before 1917 he was far from possessing that halo with which the postwar generation in France equipped him. If he had been chosen to form a cabinet in 1915 or 1916, his government might very well have broken up violently long before victory was in sight. He came to power at the psychological moment, and the president merited praise for realizing the fact. Nevertheless Poincaré was certainly forced into that realization by the pressure of circumstances. Dynamic leadership was necessary to restore French self-confidence. At the end of any other road lay not only danger for France but possible disaster for the man at the Elysée.[110]

[110] According to Georges Suarez, Poincaré strongly considered the possibility of combining the presidency and the premiership in his own hands just before he called Clemenceau to power. Marcel Sembat was said to have assured him of Socialist support for such a step (Georges Suarez, La vie orgueilleuse de Clemenceau [Paris, 1930], p. 481). Suarez does not indicate why Poincaré abandoned this plan. Several years after the war Poincaré told Gabriel Hanotaux that he had decided to resign the presidency and take over the premiership if Clemenceau had failed to form a cabinet (Hanotaux, Raymond Poincaré, p. 67). Poincaré's memoirs contain no suggestion of this, and Madame Poincaré informed the author that her husband had never considered resignation (letter, October 14, 1938). The liaison officer, Herbillon, who saw the president almost daily, favored such a step but did not believe that Poincaré would venture to take it (Souvenirs, II, 133).

THE CLEMENCEAU MINISTRY (1917–1918)

On November 16, 1917, the proofs of *L'Homme Enchaîné* carried an attack on President Poincaré. That paragraph had vanished when the journal appeared on the street: in the interval Clemenceau had been called to power.[111]

Thus the hostility of Poincaré's new collaborator persisted until the very eve of his nomination. The president could have no illusions; he realized clearly enough that a new and painful era had arrived for him. The two men exchanged polite assurances that they would co-operate whole-heartedly; but these phrases meant little. Poincaré had seen this moment looming before him for many months; he was aware that many people believed it would mean his own abdication.

Clemenceau's satisfaction at his arrival in power somewhat tempered his old antagonism toward Poincaré. He was resolved to be at least reasonably generous toward the president, even though he continued to be as suspicious as ever. He remarked to his military aide:

> In my relations with M. Poincaré, I intend to act . . . . with the greatest fairness, with the utmost candor. I will hide nothing from him, I will render an account of everything; but I will insist, on the other hand, that this confidence be reciprocal and that he shall not prevent me from fulfilling my difficult duties by giving himself over to lateral maneuvers.[112]

The new premier's misgivings arose from his conviction that Poincaré had intrigued against every ministry since 1914. His attitude hardly prepared the ground for sincere collaboration between the two men. The Tiger's suspicion flared into the open at intervals during the months that followed. As a matter of fact Clemenceau's extreme sensitiveness was unjustified. Poincaré did nothing to hinder the cabinet's activity—at

---

[111] Jean Martet, *Le Tigre* (Paris, 1930), p. 15.

[112] General Jean Jules Henri Mordacq, *Le ministère Clemenceau, journal d'un témoin* (Paris, 1930–1931), I, 5.

least until the eve of the armistice. No less a person than Georges Mandel, Clemenceau's *chef de cabinet,* later attested this fact; and he was no friend of Poincaré.[113]

But the president's loyal support, of which Mandel has spoken, was rather negative than positive. It was a new role which Poincaré now had to fill. Ministerial councils were reduced from two or three to one a week—a double or triple reduction of the president's opportunity to influence governmental decisions. Nor did the single weekly session give him much chance to intervene. He complained that it became more and more a mere formality where no real business was transacted.[114] Besides, Clemenceau, like Ribot, had warned the president not to speak so often in council.[115] Poincaré's private conferences with individual ministers continued, but declined in importance; for now each minister looked to the real leader, Clemenceau, for advice or approval.[116]

The president's patriotism was great, but not great enough to stifle all the bitterness he felt at his new position. He did not fit easily into his narrowed groove. Poincaré knew well enough that he must remain quiet, for Clemenceau's suspicions would have been aroused at the least indication of unauthorized personal activity at the Elysée. Years later he filled the final

[113] Interview with M. Mandel, October 29, 1938.

[114] Poincaré, X, 10, 28, 67–68, 105, 137, 196.

[115] *Ibid.,* IX, 371–72.

[116] A law adopted on February 10, 1918, considerably broadened the president's decree powers at the expense of the legislative branch. But these decrees still required the countersignature of a minister, so that under a Clemenceau ministry Poincaré's status was not enlarged.

In December 1916 Briand had asked the Chamber for a similar extension of the decree power. His request had been refused. Some deputies had attacked the Briand proposal on the ground that it dissimulated the truth in that it provided that the government rather than the president should issue the emergency decrees (*Chamber Debates,* December 29, 1916, p. 1875). Apparently they regarded it as a disguised effort to broaden the president's control. As a matter of fact the wording was a result of faulty drafting: it would not have affected Poincaré's powers. *Au service de la France* contains no inkling of the president's attitude toward the bills of 1916 or 1918.

volume of *Au service de la France* with plaintive remarks about his powerlessness during 1918. Such complaints had appeared in earlier volumes as well, but they reached an all-time high in his references to the Clemenceau period. By making so odious a comparison between the earlier and later periods of his presidency he has tacitly admitted that his activity before November 1917 was not completely insignificant.

There is no doubt that the burden of inaction weighed heavily on Poincaré. His memoirs indicate that he accepted silently and painfully this role of bedraggled queen bee and that he gave Clemenceau absolute freedom to save France. One may question, however, the alleged silence of his renunciation. Poincaré had a way of conveying to visitors his dissatisfaction with any policy which he disliked. Ministers or politicians who saw him in council or at the Elysée could easily enough divine from his words or his attitude when he was in conflict with Clemenceau.

Nor did he abdicate his privilege of giving advice by means of written notes to the ministers. Such had been his practice all through the war; now the activity of his pen redoubled, for he had fewer opportunities to intervene in council. Clemenceau, who usually refrained from asking the president's advice, became the principal recipient of his letters. This epistolary barrage thoroughly irritated the Tiger; he complained that he had no time to carry on a voluminous correspondence. Reminiscing about Poincaré in later years, he grumbled: "Oh, how he could write! Every time I saw his dainty little handwriting it threw me into a fury."[117] Received in this spirit, the well-meant but prolix missives of Poincaré were wasted, so far as influence on the government was concerned. Sometimes their effect was actually worse than nil because of Clemenceau's violent reaction.

[117] Martet, *Le Tigre*, p. 153. According to Gabriel Terrail, Clemenceau received a twenty-page memorandum from Poincaré on the day he reached office ("Mermeix," *Les négotiations secrètes et les quatre armistices* [Paris, 1919], p. 222).

One source of such friction lay in the projected evacuation of Paris in 1918. A crushing German offensive in March made Clemenceau consider the government's departure. Poincaré objected strongly, for the effects of the 1914 "flight to Bordeaux" were still fresh in his mind. He wrote several letters of protest to Clemenceau before the German drive was checked.[118] Again in June the enemy attacked with such fury that Hindenburg's troops reached the Marne. This time preparations were actually made to evacuate the capital. But Poincaré announced flatly that under no circumstances would he leave Paris. In several private conversations he made no effort to hide his disagreement with Clemenceau on this point.[119] Fortunately the German offensive was once more stopped and an open dispute was avoided. But this kind of thing intensified Clemenceau's belief that Poincaré was giving secret aid to the opposition in the Chamber. The Tiger gave voice to his suspicion now and again: for example, in May 1918 when he returned from a visit to the front and learned that the president had called a number of politicians to the Elysée during the interval.[120] Poincaré was justly indignant; he had probably done nothing worse than adopt a sour attitude toward certain acts of the government. All the same, this constant supervision forced him to be more careful than usual in his private conferences and therefore reduced his personal influence still further.

Clemenceau's exasperation at Poincaré's continual bombardment of advice reached a climax in October 1918. In the midst of the successful French offensive Clemenceau learned that the troops were tired and implied that an armistice might be arranged soon. Poincaré, who cherished visions of a march to Berlin, immediately took up his pen and wrote a sharp note to the premier complaining that an armistice would "ham-

---

[118] Martet, *Le Tigre*, p. 232; cf. Raymond Recouly, *Foch: My Conversations with the Marshal* (New York, 1929), p. 10.

[119] Poincaré, X, 206, 216, 222.

[120] *Ibid.*, pp. 202-3; Mordacq, *Le ministère Clemenceau*, II, 51-52.

string" the army.[121] Infuriated, Clemenceau submitted his resignation. It was only after the exchange of several long letters that he agreed to remain in office. Poincaré was forced to realize that free indulgence in his passion for offering advice did more harm than good. Nevertheless, he could not bring himself to give up the practice. His final contribution to this October dispute was an eight-page letter which Clemenceau decided to ignore in contempt.[122] Otherwise their post-office duel might have gone on indefinitely.

So long as the war continued Poincaré refrained from any act which might have impeded the cabinet in its accomplishment of victory. He even resigned himself to certain infringements on what he considered to be his inalienable right to advise and influence, simply because he wished to avoid trouble with Clemenceau.[123] But he always regretted the abandonment of any privilege which the constitution allowed him and which he had been accustomed to exercise. Whenever possible he tried to avoid the loss of his privileges.

Such presidential resistance was most noticeable in the conduct of foreign affairs. Poincaré resented the fact that Foreign Minister Pichon turned to Clemenceau for counsel, whereas his predecessors had all paid regular visits to the Elysée and had often followed the advice which they received there.[124] The president felt a special obligation in this regard, for when he had taken office in 1913 he had promised to assure the continuity of French foreign policy. Although deeply disturbed at being thus superseded, he dared not interfere openly for fear of Clemenceau's wrath. All he could do was to await Clemenceau's absences from Paris, when Pichon was loosed

[121] Poincaré, X, 379.

[122] Mordacq, *Le ministère Clemenceau*, II, 262–67. Poincaré's account fails to mention this last letter but makes it appear that he renounced any answer and withdrew into dignified silence.

[123] Poincaré, X, 158.

[124] *Ibid.*, pp. 18, 67–68.

from his leading strings. At such times the foreign minister would visit the Elysée and Poincaré would crowd his advice on all possible subjects into their conversation.[125] He observed with displeasure that Pichon did not always adopt the presidential point of view; he suspected that the minister awaited the return of Clemenceau to make decisions. Poincaré's regret over this situation apparently arose from injured pride rather than from any idea that Clemenceau's opinions were mistaken. He often expressed irritation when Clemenceau and Pichon took decisions first and consulted him afterward—even when the decisions were acceptable.

Among Poincaré's reasons for placing Clemenceau in office was his belief that agitators, defeatists, and traitors must be suppressed. Clemenceau had established himself as the most energetic champion of such a program when he publicly denounced Louis-Jean Malvy, the minister of the interior, in July 1917. The Tiger's philippic forced Malvy to resign before the former took power in November. A few other arrests had been made also; but it was after November 1917 that the campaign of repression really got under way. Not only shady characters like Miguel Almereyda of the *Bonnet Rouge,* Bolo Pasha, Duval, and Lenoir but bigger game as well fell under Clemenceau's bludgeon. Senator Charles Humbert, director of the prominent Paris daily *Le Journal,* and even Joseph Caillaux himself went behind bars.

Many of the accusations which led to war trials were mere products of war hysteria. Caillaux, for example, has long since been absolved of any treasonable dealings with the enemy. His only mistake, except for certain imprudences, was his willing-

[125] Poincaré, X, 47, 145, 336. General Mordacq also sketched Pichon as weak and susceptible to influence: "Unfortunately he sometimes lacked decision in difficult moments. In fact, during the whole duration of the ministry, it was M. Clemenceau who really directed foreign affairs. Every morning M. Pichon came to the ministry of war to confer with the premier, and he never took an important decision without the latter's approval." (Mordacq, *Le ministère Clemenceau,* III, 118.)

ness to accept a white peace.[126] Humbert and Malvy were also victims of circumstances. Men like Bolo and Almereyda, however, were mere adventurers and deserved their fate before firing squads or in prison cells.

Poincaré expended a great deal of energy in worrying about the danger to France from within. He had first heard talk of treason as early as July 1915. A deputy had received information concerning the questionable activities of Bolo Pasha, and had immediately brought the news to the Elysée. Poincaré hastened to turn the information over to the minister of justice, where it should have gone directly.[127] The president's suspicions were aroused, but he possessed no definite proof of treason. He therefore received Bolo twice at the Elysée during the following year.[128] By 1917 he had become convinced that Bolo ought to be arrested. For months he urged the government to examine Bolo's dossier, and when the arrest was finally made in September 1917 he proudly and justly claimed the credit.[129]

[126] Caillaux's case has been presented in his *Devant l'histoire; mes prisons* (Paris, 1920) and in two biographies: Gaston Martin's *Joseph Caillaux* (Paris, 1931), and Alfred Fabre-Luce's *Caillaux* (Paris, 1933). There is also an unpublished doctoral dissertation by W. Henry Cooke at Stanford University, entitled "Caillaux and International Relations, 1911–1920" (1928). Caillaux's memoirs have been written but are yet to be published.

[127] Poincaré, VI, 337; Charles Humbert, *Chacun son tour* (Paris, 1925), pp. 200–205; *L'Humanité*, April 16, 1919. During the Humbert trial in 1919, the woman who had turned informer in 1915 described this episode. The official *Gazette des Tribunaux* (April 7–8, 1919) concealed the fact that the information had gone through Poincaré.

[128] Some of Poincaré's enemies declared that the president had entrusted Bolo with a secret mission to Spain in 1916 (Humbert, *op. cit.*, pp. 254–55; Poincaré, X, 15). This effort to link the two men was absurd. Poincaré's willingness to receive Bolo was perfectly constitutional and aboveboard, for at the time he had no real proof of Bolo's guilt.

[129] Poincaré, IX, 38, 58, 304, 332; X, 42; Herbillon, *Micheler*, pp. 233–34. The Bolo case, like most similar treason cases during the war, has never been completely clarified. Bolo was a Frenchman who had received his title from the ex-khedive of Egypt. During the war he acted as agent of the German government in an attempt to bribe the French press. Apparently he

The Malvy case involved the president in a more indirect way. Malvy was a young Radical deputy with a reputation for ambition and political skill rather than strength of character. As minister of the interior he had been very lenient toward the unruly extremists of the Left wing. Malvy resigned in 1917 after Clemenceau had denounced him as a traitor. To clear himself he demanded that he be tried by the Senate sitting as a high court. This was done in 1918; the court absolved him of treason but convicted him on the charge of betraying the duties of his office, whatever that may have meant. Several years after the war the Senate rehabilitated Malvy. In the course of the proceedings Poincaré told the Senate that he had never seen any evidence of lack of patriotism on Malvy's part during the war.[130] An outcry resulted from anti-Poincarists, who asserted that the president ought to have defended Malvy in 1918 rather than in 1924.[131] In one sense Poincaré's silence when an injustice was being done did indicate weakness. On the other hand, his intervention on behalf of Malvy might have led to demands for his own resignation. So long as victory was the all-important goal, perhaps it was better to allow the sacrifice of a second-rate politician than to run the risk of a presidential crisis.[132]

It was the case of Charles Humbert which concerned Poincaré most directly. Humbert was publisher of Le Journal, one of the largest daily newspapers in France. A ponderous pro-

---

doublecrossed his employers and used most of the money in riotous living. He was executed seven months after his arrest for commerce with the enemy.

[130] Senate Debates, November 18, 1924, p. 64.

[131] General Mordacq, Clemenceau au soir de sa vie, 1920–1929 (Paris, 1933), II, 43; Maunoury, Police de guerre, p. 213.

[132] Poincaré was probably glad to see Malvy leave the important ministry of the interior, where he had refused to show severity toward Socialist agitators. It has been asserted that Poincaré was loud in his criticism of Malvy's policies in 1917 (Maunoury, op. cit., p. 149); this seems to be an exaggeration, for the president's personal relations with the minister were always friendly (see Malvy's book, Mon crime [Paris, 1921]).

vincial transplanted to Paris, his huge stature was matched only by his inflated ego. For several years he had sat in the Senate, where his colleagues regarded him as something of a parliamentary clown.

Humbert was a carping critic of the government throughout the war. He took upon himself the duty of saving France, and his daily demands for *"Des canons! des munitions!"* became well known wherever *Le Journal* was read. He was arrested in 1918 when it became known that Bolo had invested a large sum of money in his newspaper. The money was of German origin, but apparently Humbert was ignorant of the fact. In any event the policies of *Le Journal* had shown no appreciable change after Bolo had become its financial angel.

When Humbert was finally brought to trial in 1919 he introduced as evidence a voluminous correspondence exchanged between himself and Poincaré during the war.[133] Most of the president's letters were efforts to defend the government against Humbert's attacks. Several times the Senator was invited to come to the Elysée to receive personal explanations. Humbert's purpose in introducing this correspondence into the trial was not very clear, for it had no connection with the charges against him. Probably he meant to suggest that even the president had not questioned his patriotism. The result, in any event, was to drag Poincaré's name into the case.

Humbert's attorney went even further in the course of the proceedings. He charged that Poincaré had consciously schemed to bring about the Senator's arrest. According to the attorney's argument, Poincaré had intentionally withheld the evidence which he possessed against Bolo until Humbert was drawn into Bolo's trap.[134] Such use of the irresponsible president's name during a public trial was unprecedented. In order to reply, Poincaré had to break with precedent by sending a written

[133] These have been published in Humbert's apology, *Chacun son tour;* they occupy sixty-four printed pages.

[134] *Le Matin,* April 9, 1919; *Journal du Peuple,* April 9, 1919.

deposition before the court. He denied that he had wished to cause the fall of Humbert or that he had criticized the senator semipublicly during the war. He had not warned Humbert against Bolo, he said, because he feared that Bolo might get wind of the fact that he was under suspicion.[135] This reasonable explanation satisfied the court, whereupon the president's part in the case was closed. The whole episode was a sorry business, without vital importance for an analysis of Poincaré's presidential activities. He did not conspire against Humbert, even though he disliked and suspected *le gros Charles.* His correspondence with the senator was merely a useless piece of imprudence. The affair proved nothing except Poincaré's unwillingness to let any accusation pass without a reply.

The climax of the government's campaign against defeatism was the arrest of Joseph Caillaux in 1918. After several months of imprisonment he was tried in 1920 by the Senate and was banished from France. Caillaux's friends placed the blame for his arrest upon the shoulders of Poincaré. They believed that the president had made Clemenceau premier in return for a promise that Caillaux would be prosecuted.[136] No proof has been adduced for this charge, though Poincaré has admitted that he hoped Clemenceau would be "resolute" in judicial affairs.[137] His reasons for naming the Tiger were more profound than mere hatred of Caillaux. The president certainly took a keen interest in the investigation of Caillaux's affairs and was not sorry when the latter disappeared behind prison doors. Existing evidence, however, does not support the theory that Poincaré sponsored the prosecution.

So far as political affairs were concerned, the end of the war found Poincaré less influential than he had been at its outbreak. It was not the war, however, which was responsible for this decline. The immediate effect of the conflict had been

[135] *Le Matin,* April 12, 1919; *L'Humanité,* April 12, 1919.
[136] Maunoury, *Police de guerre,* p. 149.
[137] Poincaré, IX, 368.

rather to broaden his powers. The *union sacrée* extricated him from the toils of party conflict in which he had become involved during the first half of 1914. For the first time he was regarded as president of all the French rather than as a Moderate president. His prestige and experience, too, carried more weight than before in council sessions. For three years, so long as authority was lacking in the premiership, Poincaré was more influential than he had been since the honeymoon period of his presidency.

On the contrary, the twelve months from November 1917 to November 1918 made the president an almost useless cog in the political machine. He was called upon only to second the work of Clemenceau in certain military crises. Authority again became centralized in the hands of the premier, as past constitutional practice in France had decreed. A French journalist wrote soon after: "Clemenceau . . . . tolerated him [Poincaré] only after having annexed him, by confiscating the Executive. He authorized him only to warm his place at the Elysée, to decorate cities, to give speeches; commercial traveler of the government, zero in the state."[138] With due allowance for literary exaggeration this statement contained more truth than error. The strong-presidency hopes of 1913, it seemed, had proved to be empty illusions.

[138] Ernest Judet, *Le véritable Clemenceau* (Berne, 1920), pp. 26–27.

CHAPTER VII

MILITARY AFFAIRS

The French republic faced many thorny problems between 1914 and 1918, but none were more difficult than the relations between military headquarters and the civil regime. The army's prestige had been severely shaken by the Dreyfus affair, which it had never been able to live down completely. But the outbreak of war restored its leaders to public favor. Even the most ardent Dreyfusard could not deny that the high command needed more freedom of action in wartime. The extent of that freedom, however, was sharply disputed.

It soon became evident that a solution would be hard to find. Joffre and his staff were reluctant to send news from the front to Paris. Accustomed to treat civilians with a certain disdain, the generals went ahead with their task and ignored the government's angry demands for information. Poincaré and the ministers have been called weak for permitting headquarters to set up a quasi dictatorship during the first months of the war. The charge is unjust. After all, they could not have cashiered Joffre at such a moment of crisis. They could only complain; and this they did ardently, with the president leading the way.[1] As usual, Poincaré blamed his Elysian prison for his inability to secure news from the front. It was not the presidential earmuffs, however, which shut out military information; for the minister of war could learn no more than Poincaré. On the contrary, Joffre was more willing to consider himself nominally subordinate to the president than

[1] Poincaré, V, 66, 104, 123, 142, *et seq.*

to the cabinet.[2] On August 9, desiring to speed up the arrival of British troops, he wrote directly to Poincaré rather than to the minister of war.[3] If the president had cherished illusions of future dictatorship, this might have served as a first step: an alliance with headquarters against the cabinet. But to him the letter of the constitution was sacred; he was willing to exercise influence, but only within the boundaries traced by his jurist's mind. Therefore he joined forces with the cabinet in objecting to the military viewpoint and insisted that Joffre consider himself subordinate to his hierarchical chief at the ministry of war.[4] The incident proved once more that Poincaré set rigid limits to the exercise of his power. He wished to exercise every privilege which the constitution granted him, but not one privilege more than that.

After the German drive had been turned back at the Marne, the strain between civil and military leaders eased somewhat. Headquarters sent information to Paris with less reluctance. Poincaré's demands for permission to visit the front began to be granted more frequently. Yet civil-military relations were still far from being completely harmonious. Among other things, Poincaré did not hesitate to interrogate subordinate generals during his journeys to the front and to collect their usual crop of complaints about the conduct of the war. Joffre sharply resented the president's activity, on the ground that civil authorities should have contact with no one but the commanding general. On one occasion Joffre ordered General Sarrail to answer none of Poincaré's questions about military operations and to report their conversations in full.[5]

---

[2] J. M. Bourget, *Gouvernement et commandement: les leçons de la guerre mondiale* (Paris, 1930), pp. 131–35; Jacques Echeman, *Les ministères en France de 1914 à 1932* (Paris, 1932), p. 16.

[3] Poincaré, V, 45–46.

[4] *Ibid.,* p. 169.

[5] General Sarrail, "Souvenirs de 1914–1915," *Revue Politique et Parlementaire,* CVIII (August 1921), 235; Poincaré, VI, 137.

It was essential that Paris and Chantilly (where headquarters were located until 1916) remain in steady contact with each other, in order to insure smooth co-operation. To meet this need Joffre was frequently called to the Elysée for ministerial conferences. These soon evolved into regular weekly affairs, attended by Joffre, Poincaré, and three or four ministers.[6] They were often held informally, although the membership was the same as that of the official council of national defense, later called the *comité de guerre*. The president's attitude there, as in the council of ministers, caused some irritation. Early in 1917 Deputy André Tardieu told a journalist: "Poincaré presides over the war committee, which the King of England does not do. He and Briand have made it into a debating society, which lasts two and a half hours in place of three-quarters of an hour and in which they never arrive at a result. Lyautey, Loucheur, all the competent people complain of it."[7]

The president had other ways of keeping informed on military affairs. Two liaison officers, Colonels Pénelon and Herbillon, brought him all the important news in their regular trips between Chantilly and Paris. He had private conversations with various officers. He read the letters which General Micheler wrote regularly to Antonin Dubost, president of the senate.[8] In addition, he participated in a number of special conferences at headquarters, both French and Interallied.[9]

[6] Poincaré, VII, 49.

[7] Martin, "Notes de guerre," March 19, 1917. Cf. Duff Cooper, *Haig* (London, 1935–36), II, 42.

[8] Emile E. Herbillon, *Le général Alfred Micheler* (Paris, 1934), p. 248.

[9] For example, on May 18, 1916, in Poincaré's railway car near Châlons, the Somme offensive was agreed upon in order to relieve Verdun (Herbillon, *Souvenirs*, I, 279; Poincaré, VIII, 223–24). Poincaré opposed this strategy, favoring a fight to the finish at Verdun (Herbillon, *Souvenirs*, I, 284; cf. *ibid.*, pp. 302–8 for Poincaré's undisguised criticism of headquarters and his double reversal of opinion on the Somme offensive). On May 31 and again on August 27, 1916, he took part in Franco-British conferences of generals and ministers (Poincaré, VIII, 250–51, 326).

Poincaré had no scruples about speaking his mind during sessions of the council of national defense. A notable instance occurred in a meeting of March 21, 1915, when the president challenged Joffre's pretension to ignore control from Paris. There was a sharp exchange of words between the two men, during which Joffre melodramatically threatened to get himself killed on the battlefield.[10] The president objected to the general staff's ambition to become what he called "a government above the government."[11] During a visit to Chantilly in June 1915 he demanded such precise explanations from Joffre that their interview became quite stormy. He irritated the general still more in the course of dinner by questioning the truth of military communiqués.[12] He complained repeatedly to the liaison officers that Joffre ignored the advice of subordinate generals. He freely expressed his hostility to Joffre's proposed offensive in the autumn of 1915, and warned that it would have to be stopped after twenty-four hours if no break-through should occur by then.[13] That Joffre became highly offended at all this interference was not unnatural. The president's activity, however, contained no hint of personal spite.[14] Although he often differed with Joffre, he defended the general against those who wished to remove him. Poincaré believed that a change in the leadership of the army would undermine public confidence; therefore he resisted it as long as possible.

More than once Poincaré made himself chief barrister for

[10] Poincaré, VI, 124–25; C. E. Callwell, *Field Marshal Sir Henry Wilson, His Life and Diaries* (London, 1927), I, 216.

[11] Herbillon, *Souvenirs*, I, 135–36.

[12] *Ibid.*, pp. 160–62.

[13] *Ibid.*, pp. 164, 181, 187. Joffre was profoundly vexed at Poincaré's freely expressed opposition to an offensive in 1915. Poincaré demanded that the government examine and pass on the military project. Joffre considered this a dangerous interference in the conduct of operations (Joffre, *Mémoires*, II, 86–87).

[14] Michel Corday (*L'Envers*, I, 114) has made the preposterous statement that Poincaré regarded Joffre as a rival for power and popularity.

a plan of strategy. The outstanding example occurred in the long dispute over a Balkan expedition. The president had heard this suggested by General Franchet d'Espérey as early as 1914.[15] He soon became convinced that an Allied diversion in the Balkans had great military and diplomatic possibilities. He presented it to the council on January 7, 1915, and brought it up at every possible opportunity thereafter. Joffre was absolutely opposed to such a diversion of troops; but Poincaré continued to argue for it in and out of council sessions.[16]

A new factor entered the situation in September 1915: Bulgaria mobilized in preparation for joining the Central Powers, so that Serbia was seriously threatened with attack from the rear. At about the same time Winston Churchill's attempt to force the Dardanelles was coming to a disastrous end. With some of the troops from Gallipoli available for use, the project of a Balkan base was hurriedly revived. On October 5 a small French and British army began to land at Salonika.

Poincaré naturally felt some paternal pride when the Balkan expedition came into being. There was another man, however, who claimed and generally received the credit for establishing the new Balkan front. That man was Briand. Like the president, he had been preaching such a plan since 1914. He did not become premier until a few days after the Salonika base was established; but his long-time sponsorship was well known, and Frenchmen could easily regard him as the real father. Poincaré's pride was hurt by this failure to recognize his role. A number of politicians believed that the president's jealousy contributed to the friction between him and Briand during the war.[17]

---

[15] Poincaré, V, 360.

[16] *Ibid.*, VI, 41, 45; Herbillon, *Souvenirs,* I, 88, 90, 104, 129, 144, 187, 203. In London, Poincaré was credited with the proposal for a Balkan expedition (Benckendorff to Sazonov, February 10, 1915, *Russian Docs.,* VII, 151).

[17] Marcellin, *Politique,* I, 372; cf. Suarez, *Briand,* III, 90–91, 149.

The French and British were unwelcome guests at Salonika from the start. They had been invited to land there by Prime Minister Venizelos, a thorough Francophile. Venizelos had immediately been dismissed by the pro-German King Constantine. This seemed to annul the invitation, but the Allies went serenely ahead as though nothing had changed. Constantine dared not protest, but he intrigued against the occupiers and refused to give them the aid which they expected. This extraordinary situation, together with the weakness of his little army, prevented General Sarrail from bringing any effective aid to the Serbs. Bulgarian forces soon overran Serbia, and the original excuse for the expedition ceased to exist.

For diplomatic reasons, however, the Allied troops remained. Great Britain desired to withdraw its contingent, and was on the verge of doing so in December 1915. French and British leaders conferred at Calais on the 4th; Briand argued valiantly for continuing the expedition but failed to shake the Britons' resolution.[18] When he returned to Paris and reported failure, he ran into more trouble. A majority of the cabinet, supported by Poincaré, refused to hear of evacuation. They voted that new pressure should be exerted on London. In the face of this intransigeance the British reluctantly changed their

---

[18] Briand's attitude at Calais is not entirely clear. Both Joffre and Gallieni, who were present, have asserted that Briand held out to the last against withdrawal from Salonika (Joffre, *Mémoires*, II, 139, 181–82; Marius-Ary Leblond, *Gallieni parle* [Paris, 1920], p. 273). Other evidence, however, indicates that Briand finally backed down before the British. Both Lloyd George and Poincaré were so informed by the returning delegates (Lloyd George, *Memoirs*, I, 452; Poincaré, VII, 312). Furthermore, Briand himself told Izvolsky two days later that if the British left Salonika the French would have to follow (Izvolsky to Sazonov, December 6, 1915, *Die Europaischen Mächte und Griechenland*, pp. 54–55). Briand's latest biographer believes that Briand gave in at Calais but argued his case so ably that the British spontaneously reversed themselves four days later (Suarez, *Briand*, III, 213–15). According to another recent account Briand capitulated at Calais but reverted to his original position that same night under the influence of Philippe Berthelot (Bréal, *Berthelot*, pp. 144–45).

minds.[19] Whether for good or ill, the expedition was maintained until the end of the war, partly as a result of Poincaré's insistence.

The decision to stay at Salonika was only half a solution. It was now necessary to determine what use should be made of Sarrail's army. This question lay at the heart of a Poincaré-Joffre duel which went on throughout 1916.

General Joffre had never been friendly toward the eastern diversion. He believed that the war would be won or lost on the western front, and that every soldier should be kept there to increase the Allies' striking power. In the autumn of 1915 he had grudgingly agreed to send a few thousand men to Salonika. This did not mean that Joffre had become converted to the "easterners'" plan. The general's prestige had suffered considerably from the failure of his offensives of 1915, and he felt it advisable to mend his fences. He considered this sacrifice of troops necessary to keep the support of Poincaré, Briand, and Minister of War Gallieni.[20]

This gesture made, Joffre thought that he had gone far enough. He was willing to let the army remain at Salonika, but his attitude toward the expedition was never more than lukewarm. He obstinately refused to send additional men and supplies which Sarrail needed in order to attack.[21] Probably he wished to embarrass Sarrail, whom he had already removed from command of an army on the western front in 1915. Poincaré had no axe to grind in favor of Sarrail; but he

---

[19] The minister of war, Gallieni, told his secretaries that the president was back of this French resistance (Leblond, *Gallieni parle*, p. 273). Poincaré has given himself less of the credit in his memoirs (VII, 312). Cf. also Lloyd George, *Memoirs,* I, 452–54.

[20] Lloyd George, *Memoirs,* II, 5–6.

[21] Joffre went to London in June 1916 to argue for a stronger Salonika army. The British refused, "much to the secret satisfaction of General Joffre" (*ibid.,* II, 9). Poincaré (VIII, 224) has confirmed the fact that Joffre undertook this mission unwillingly. The insistence of the president, Briand, and War Minister Roques forced him to carry it out.

wanted the Salonika project to succeed, no matter who was in command there. All through 1916 the hopeless deadlock continued: Sarrail refused to move until he received reinforcements; Joffre refused to send the reinforcements. Poincaré used all his influence to change the mind of the commanding general, but in vain.[22] He began to grow quite bitter toward Joffre late in 1916, accusing him of petty animosity toward the eastern army.[23]

The Salonika dispute was one of two major military problems which occupied the president during 1916. Moving along parallel to it was the question of Joffre's replacement as head of the French armies.

Parliamentary opposition to Joffre had been rising for over a year. He was accused of trying to set up a dictatorship at Chantilly with the assistance of his entourage, popularly called the "Young Turks." Millerand, as long as he remained minister of war, defended Joffre vigorously against the legislative critics. By October 1915 the rumblings had become so loud that Viviani decided Joffre would have to be sacrificed. Apparently that was Viviani's purpose when he attempted to remodel his cabinet in October 1915.[24] In order to get rid of Joffre it was necessary first to eliminate his chief defender, Millerand. Viviani's effort failed, however, and the premier himself had to leave office. Joffre survived until December 1916, when he was finally removed from his post and was given a marshal's baton as compensation.

Poincaré's part in this first crisis of the high command is not entirely clear. For many months the president defended Joffre, in spite of considerable friction between the two men. They had clashed a number of times in council meetings, where Poincaré's cold, insistent, aggressive manner of cross-examination sometimes irritated the general, much to the surprise of

[22] Herbillon, *Souvenirs,* I, 144, 147, 338–39, 341–42.

[23] *Ibid.,* pp. 349–50; Poincaré, VIII, 208, 337.

[24] Herbillon, *Micheler,* p. 47.

the president.[25] Poincaré's temper had flared up once when Joffre advised him to adjourn a projected visit to Verdun.[26] There had been the incident when Joffre ordered General Sarrail not to discuss military affairs with the president. They had debated continually and acridly over the Salonika expedition.

In spite of all these open differences Poincaré did not favor the replacement of the commanding general in 1915 or early 1916. Nor did the president intrigue against Joffre. He reserved much of his hostility for the "Young Turks" rather than for Joffre himself.[27] He actually opposed Gallieni's attempt to "clean the stables of Chantilly," when Gallieni became minister of war late in 1915. The latter had once been Joffre's superior officer; there was probably an element of professional jealousy in his desire for a shake-up at headquarters. Poincaré resisted on the ground that any change might injure public confidence in the army.[28] Thus he helped the general survive Gallieni's threat, as Joffre had already survived that of Viviani.

By the end of 1916, however, the president apparently had changed his mind. His memoirs furnish little indication of how the anti-Joffre agitation finally crystallized. They leave the impression that the idea of kicking Joffre upstairs arose suddenly, out of a clear sky.[29] The truth is that Poincaré was not quite so innocent of all connection with the change. He had finally become convinced that either Joffre or the Briand cabinet must fall, for the legislature was becoming violent about what it considered the misdeeds of Chantilly. Deputies had long been crying out against the ineffectiveness of Joffre's "nibbling" policy. His failure to prepare for the German attack on Verdun began to be noised about. The deadlock at Salonika

---

[25] Herbillon, *Souvenirs,* I, 160–62; cf. Joffre, *Mémoires,* II, 86–87.

[26] Herbillon, *Souvenirs,* I, 310.

[27] *Ibid.,* I, 135–36, 160, 227.

[28] Poincaré, VIII, 104–5; Joffre, *Mémoires,* II, 87; Leblond, *Gallieni parle,* p. 94.

[29] Poincaré, IX, 28, 33.

added another cause for complaint; and this was one with which Poincaré could sympathize. The president therefore abandoned his support of the general and agreed that the latter should be transferred to a purely honorary post.[30] Joffre was replaced by Nivelle, a comparatively young general, who had distinguished himself in the fighting at Verdun.

The fall of "Papa" Joffre brought a change in the spirit of headquarters. Joffre had resented every effort by civilians to interfere in the direction of military policy. He had not been a dictator, as some professed to believe. But in disputes between military and civil leaders the prestige given him by the victory of the Marne was usually enough to carry the day. After all, it was easier to sacrifice a minister than a general in time of war. The Joffre legend gradually lost its potency, however, and had evaporated by the end of 1916. With it disappeared the idea of military predominance. At Poincaré's urgent request Nivelle even moved his headquarters from Chantilly, the very name of which had come to be anathema to many deputies.[31] Joffre's fall was a victory above all for the Chamber; it seemed to suggest a revival of legislative control. Henceforth Poincaré and the cabinet had to keep a more careful eye focused upon the Palais-Bourbon.[32]

Paris was determined that no new Chantilly should arise to infringe upon its prerogatives. The character of the new commander seemed to be a guaranty of this. Nivelle was not a well-known general. Catapulted into prominence by his suc-

[30] Herbillon, *Souvenirs,* I, 365–68; Joffre, *Mémoires,* II, 420. Joffre refused to accept this sinecure and was then offered a marshalship.

The removal of Foch from his command during 1916 has also been laid at Poincaré's door by Clemenceau, who claimed to have information from Foch himself (Georges Clemenceau, *Grandeur and Misery of Victory* [New York, 1930], p. 21). More impartial evidence shows that it was Joffre who caused the fall of Foch (Herbillon, *Souvenirs,* I, 371, conversation with Poincaré; II, 128, conversation with Foch. Cf. Paul Allard, *L'oreille fendue* [Paris, 1933], p. 174, conversation with Admiral Lacaze).

[31] Joffre, *Mémoires,* II, 440.

[32] Herbillon, *Souvenirs,* II, 13.

cessful recovery of the Fort of Douaumont in 1916, he had been promoted over the heads of many officers who outranked him. He was therefore faced by some hostility among his new subordinates. Nor did he have time to build up solid support in civilian circles. The choice of Nivelle had been approved by Poincaré, although the president apparently took no active part in his nomination.[33]

Nivelle knew that his future career depended upon immediate action. The French demanded an end to Joffre's sluggish strategy—"I nibble at them." Nivelle came into office with a plan all prepared. It called for a daring offensive over an eighty-kilometer front, designed to make a clean break through the German line. Confident that it would be successful, he prepared its execution for the spring of 1917. But the revolution in Russia, the imminent entry of the United States into the war, and the Germans' unexpected retirement to the new "Hindenburg line" altered many perspectives. Men who had already questioned Nivelle's sanguine hopes now declared openly that the offensive could not succeed, that it ought to be delayed until American troops could arrive. Chief among the doubters was Paul Painlevé, who became minister of war in the new Ribot cabinet in March. Many high-ranking generals took a similar position.

Premier Ribot wavered in the face of this opposition. Poincaré knew of Ribot's hesitancy and was aware that a movement was on foot to postpone or limit the offensive. He believed that a last-minute change of policy would be dangerous. One of the liaison officers recalled later: "How often during this period Poincaré repeated: 'If only the Germans do not attack us first; that would be disastrous. When will we be ready to take the offensive? The more we delay, the more our chances diminish.' "[34]

At last the president proposed a special session of the war

[33] Herbillon, *Souvenirs,* I, 370; Ribot, *Journal,* p. 36.

[34] Herbillon, *Micheler,* p. 144; cf. Herbillon, *Souvenirs,* II, 31, 46–47, 49.

committee in which all the objectors could air their opinions. He did not mean to secure a free discussion and an impartial vote for or against the offensive. His aim was to give Nivelle unquestioned authority to proceed. His private remarks on April 5, the day before the war committee met, made this purpose evident:

> I was the promoter of this meeting, for I consider it necessary to put a stop to underhanded intrigues, to the campaigns of various people, to the distrust of some. General Nivelle will explain his reasons and his plan of action to us; if his generals have objections to make, they will make them before us and before him, thus engaging their responsibility. Once the decision is taken, there will be no question of changing it; this conference has only one aim: to permit General Nivelle to explain himself and to assure him of the government's confidence.[35]

On April 6 ministers and generals gathered in Poincaré's railway car at Compiègne.[36] Nivelle first outlined his plans to the committee. Poincaré at once asked permission to question all the subordinate generals in the presence of the commander. This remarkable request was granted, even though it was entirely alien to the spirit of military discipline. The president himself did much of the questioning. Several participants did not hide their opposition to the offensive; Nivelle therefore announced that he would resign. Poincaré, Ribot, and Painlevé at once surrounded the general in one corner of the car and succeeded in calming him. The president then proceeded to summarize the discussion as indicating that the offensive must go on, even though unanimous support could not be

---

[35] Herbillon, *Souvenirs,* II, 53; cf. Ribot, *Journal,* p. 77.

[36] Several participants have left accounts of the Compiègne conference. General Micheler's contemporary notes furnish the fullest and most objective description available (Herbillon, *Micheler,* pp. 169–71). Poincaré and Painlevé have confided almost no details to their memoirs; the president has implied that he was a mere observer (Poincaré, IX, 107–8). The official account, based on documents submitted to a legislative inquiry in 1917, adds virtually nothing (France, Ministère de la Guerre, *Les armées françaises dans la grande guerre* [Paris, 1922], V [Ier vol.], 563–66).

secured.[37] The meeting showed openly how great was the lack of confidence, but it ended all talk of abandoning the offensive. At the same time Nivelle made it clear that if victory did not come in the first few days he would call a halt.

If the Nivelle offensive had succeeded in crushing the enemy, Poincaré might justly have claimed much credit for the victory. Unfortunately for him and for France the German line was pushed back but not broken. Nivelle had proclaimed the coming attack so loudly that the Germans had plenty of time to prepare for it. Their sudden retirement to the new "Hindenburg line" forced the French to cross a broad expanse of no-man's land in the face of machine-gun fire. Nivelle's troops managed to win a narrow strip of territory, but at terrible cost.

Back in Paris irate legislators set out to establish responsibilities. Seizing upon the war committee session of April 6, they presented it as evidence of presidential interference in military affairs. The title "Nivelle offensive" disappeared; it was replaced by "Poincaré-Nivelle offensive." Hostile deputies declared that the plan of attack originated with the president, that he had assembled the war committee on April 6 in order to break the opposition to his protégé, Nivelle.[38] Poincaré was subjected to severe criticism in secret sessions of the Chamber during June and July; the uproar finally led to the creation of a commission of inquiry to investigate the charges.[39]

[37] Herbillon, *Micheler,* pp. 169–71; cf. Ribot, *Lettres,* pp. 189–90.

[38] Poincaré, IX, 154; Marcellin, *Politique,* II, 124; Aristide Jobert, *Souvenirs d'un ex-parlementaire (1914–1919)* (Paris, 1933), p. 138.

[39] In the Chamber on July 4, 1917, Léon Accambray declared, with some reason: "For my part, I consider that the mere presence of the president of the republic at Compiègne must have weighed considerably on opinions." And Deputy Raffin-Dugens interjected: "It was his offensive" (*Journal officiel,* July 4, 1917, p. 390). The official proceedings at secret sessions of the Chamber were published at intervals from 1919 to 1923 as supplements to the *Journal officiel.* They can be most conveniently consulted at the Bibliothèque de Documentation Internationale Contemporaine at Vincennes, where they are bound in a single volume, *Journal officiel, les comités secrets.*

The inquiry was useless. There was not the least hint of illegality about the conduct of the president. He had acted according to the constitution, covered by the responsible ministers. It was difficult to accuse him of trying to control military policy when he was supporting the plan of the general in command. Yet these technical loopholes, added to Poincaré's efforts to minimize his role, cannot hide the fact that the Compiègne meeting was his most remarkable intervention in military affairs. True, the offensive was conceived and planned by Nivelle; but Poincaré also had been an open partisan of an Allied attack for several weeks. If he had not called the war committee into session on April 6, Ribot and Painlevé would probably have forced Nivelle to abandon his plans. In this sense the phrase "Poincaré-Nivelle offensive" was not entirely unjustified. It is strange that Poincaré has written in his memoirs, under the date of April 4, 1917, this phrase: "I know nothing except by chance and after decisions are made."[40]

Poincaré has explained that he supported Nivelle because the government—notably Painlevé—was trying to interfere in the conduct of operations. He regarded this meddling as very dangerous, for headquarters alone had the right to determine strategy.[41] The president's duty, he argued, was to see that each organ of the government functioned in its own orbit and did not infringe upon others. But Poincaré's reasoning has been weakened by the fact that he himself was guilty of interference two weeks later. The offensive, after several delays, had begun on April 16. Nivelle failed to break through in forty-eight hours as he had expected; it was generally supposed, therefore, that the commander would call a halt. On April 22, Deputy Ybarnégaray, who had been fighting at the front, appeared at the Elysée. He informed Poincaré, on behalf of two subordinate generals, that the attack was to be continued in at least one sector. The generals in question insisted that it be stopped. Poincaré caused an "extremely urgent" mes-

[40] Poincaré, IX, 101.   [41] *Ibid.*, pp. 99, 101, 106.

sage to be telephoned to headquarters; "deeply anxious," he recommended that Nivelle confer at once with the doubtful generals.[42] Nivelle was furious at his subordinates for this breach of military discipline and at Poincaré for giving them support.[43] The president's act, well-intentioned beyond any doubt, was certainly an interference in military operations. His original support of the Nivelle offensive, then, must have had some other reason than a desire to protect headquarters from civilian interference. It must have been based partly upon his own current belief in the necessity for an Allied attack.

Nivelle staked his whole future on the April offensive. When it failed, his replacement became almost inevitable. Poincaré continued to defend Nivelle for a time; he felt that too many changes were dangerous.[44] Painlevé and then Ribot, however, came to the conclusion that the high command should be turned over to General Pétain, with Foch as his chief of staff. They proposed this change on May 8, barely three weeks after the offensive bogged down.[45] It is not entirely clear whether or not the president still tried to save Nivelle from the ministerial wrath. Ribot wrote later that Poincaré not only refrained from any objection but offered and gave his full support to the change.[46] In his own account Poincaré has asserted that he continued to oppose the replacement of Nivelle.[47] Moreover, he told a liaison officer on the evening of May 10 that Nivelle would not be removed.[48] Perhaps Ribot made his statement in an effort to protect the irresponsible president.

[42] *Les armées françaises dans la grande guerre*, V (Ier vol.), 710; Herbillon, *Souvenirs*, II, 68–69; Ribot, *Journal*, p. 83.

[43] Especially since Nivelle had already countermanded the offensive. His order did not reach the subordinate generals until after they had made their complaint (*Les armées françaises*, V [Ier vol.], 712).

[44] Poincaré, IX, 120–22; Herbillon, *Souvenirs*, II, 71, 75.

[45] Paul Painlevé, *Comment j'ai nommé Foch et Pétain* (Paris, 1923), pp. 83–85, 113.

[46] Ribot, *Lettres*, p. 189.

[47] Poincaré, IX, 135.   [48] Herbillon, *Souvenirs*, II, 84.

Whatever the truth may have been on this point, the war committee did vote on May 10 to request Nivelle's resignation.[49] Nivelle proceeded to shock everyone by refusing to resign. There was consternation in government circles, for Ribot and Painlevé dared not take the responsibility of openly cashiering the commanding general. At last, on May 15, the president was called upon to use his influence. Nivelle was brought before Poincaré and Ribot; Poincaré declared that he was personally opposed to a change in command but that it was necessary to prevent the fall of the ministry. Faced by this appeal, Nivelle finally gave in.[50] The president had been one of his few defenders in Paris, and now this support was gone.

In a secret session of the Chamber a month later, Left-wing deputies bitterly attacked Poincaré for having protected Nivelle for so long. They accused him of consciously blocking action by the responsible government.[51] If this was the truth, it was served up in such exaggerated form that it became false. Poincaré had no power to controvert the will of his ministers if the latter were fully determined to act. His role on May 15, when he won Nivelle's resignation in spite of his own beliefs, furnished sufficient proof of his correctness.

The accession of Clemenceau to the premiership caused Poincaré's influence in both political and military affairs to shrink sharply. He could no longer propose strategic plans in the war committee nor make himself the outspoken sponsor of any given policy. Yet he remained something more than a lifeless figurehead, able only to offer unwanted advice and express ineffectual complaints. Several times his prestige was invoked by the premier to help solve knotty problems. It was in the

[49] Painlevé, *op. cit.*, p. 114.

[50] Herbillon, *Souvenirs*, II, 88; Callwell, *Wilson*, I, 352 (General Wilson talked with Nivelle on May 16). Both Poincaré and Painlevé have failed to mention this incident in their memoirs. Painlevé was always careful to avoid references to the president in his book.

[51] *Journal officiel, les comités secrets*, June 30, 1917, pp. 343–44.

military sphere that he was called upon most frequently, when disputes arose among the Allied governments. Under Clemenceau, however, he could never take the initiative in such cases. His intervention was usually requested only as a last resort, or when his action would furnish mere secondary support.

One such case occurred late in 1917 when large numbers of American troops were beginning to pour into France. Both Clemenceau and Pétain wished to incorporate American regiments in French divisions at once. General Pershing, however, doggedly refused to place any of his men under a foreign flag, even though the organization of an independent American army meant considerable delay. The Tiger, baffled by this stubborn resistance, at last decided to appeal to President Wilson over Pershing's head. He asked Poincaré to plead the French case in a telegram to the White House. Poincaré acquiesced, in spite of his own doubts as to the advisability of amalgamating the American regiments.[52] His message drew a polite but noncommittal reply from Wilson, and the attempt to force Pershing's hand had to be abandoned.

The most notable incident of all was the Interallied council at Doullens in March 1918. The Germans had just launched a desperate offensive which seemed to be carrying all before it. Faced by imminent disaster, civil and military representatives of France and Britain gathered hastily at Compiègne and Doullens on March 25–26 to meet the crisis. Poincaré, invited by Clemenceau to attend and preside, was the only irresponsible statesman present. After considerable debate, the delegates made a far-reaching decision: they placed the Allied armies under the single command of Foch.[53]

[52] Poincaré, IX, 435–38; Herbillon, *Souvenirs,* II, 185, 190–91.

[53] The single command was not fully adopted until April. But the Doullens conference on March 26 established the principle of unified control, giving Foch the right to co-ordinate the French and British armies on the western front.

This concentration of authority in the hands of one general helped turn the tide of battle against the Germans. Legends immediately began to spring up about the Doullens conference; and prominent among these legends was one which described Poincaré as the savior of Paris and of France. Thus Colonel Herbillon (who was not present) wrote on the morrow of Doullens that the president's action there had been decisive.[54] Likewise a cabinet minister later described Poincaré as the "supreme counsellor and final arbiter" at Doullens.[55] Such statements were far from the truth. Several participants in the conference of March 26 have left accounts of what happened, and not one has implied that Poincaré's role was anything but secondary. Most of them have barely mentioned the fact that the president attended.[56] Oddly enough, Clemenceau was the only one to suggest that Poincaré deserved some credit. The Tiger told his military aide just after the first session at Compiègne that "in this conference M. Poincaré intervened very skillfully, and that, as a result, he was very well satisfied at having caused him [the president] to take part."[57]

Although his very presence at Doullens must have carried some weight, Poincaré was sufficiently honest to deny the legend which exaggerated his role.[58] Yet at the same time he resented the fact that most Frenchmen regarded Clemenceau rather than himself as the hero of Doullens.[59] This spiteful

---

[54] Herbillon, *Souvenirs*, II, 235.   [55] *Le Matin*, January 1, 1919.

[56] E.g., Lord Milner, "Memorandum to the cabinet by Lord Milner on his visit to France, including the conference at Doullens," *New Statesman*, April 23, 1921, p. ii; Ferdinand Foch, *Mémoires pour servir à l'histoire de la guerre* (Paris, 1931), II, 19-23. The official account is no more revealing (*Les armées françaises*, VI [Ier vol.], 321-24).

[57] Mordacq, *Le ministère Clemenceau*, I, 239.

[58] Poincaré, X, 134.

[59] *Ibid.*, p. 137. Clemenceau always maintained that he was the author of the single command. For his case, see his *Grandeur and Misery of Victory*, pp. 37-38, 126; General Mordacq's volumes, *Le ministère Clemenceau*, I, 236-37, and *La vérité sur le commandement unique* (Paris, 1930), p. 90; and

attitude reveals a curious weakness in Poincaré's character. His conscience refused to let him accept undeserved praise. He knew that Clemenceau's invitation had allowed him to take part, and then only as more or less brilliant second. But as strong as his conscience was his pride, revolted by the idea that praise should go to his collaborator and personal enemy.

A corollary to Doullens occurred two weeks later. The Belgians had not taken part in the agreement for a unified command. Clemenceau, unable to win King Albert's accession to the plan, suggested that Poincaré visit the king and try to obtain his consent. The president's mission proved successful, for Albert promised that his army would carry out all orders from Foch.[60]

Until the autumn of 1918 Poincaré played the role which Clemenceau assigned him in military affairs. The approach of victory encouraged him to begin rattling his chains. Late in August, when Clemenceau wanted to stop the bloody Saint-Mihiel offensive, Poincaré privately suggested to Marshal Foch that he ignore the premier.[61] Again in October, when Clemenceau spoke of an armistice to spare the tired allied troops, the president balked. His acrid letter of protest came near causing an open break between the two men.[62] Faced by the Tiger's threat of resignation, Poincaré shifted from a frontal to a flank attack. He turned to Foch, urging the marshal to resist any

---

Colonel Herbillon's *Souvenirs*, II, 175, 201, 206. Most evidence, however, suggests that Clemenceau wished to limit Foch's authority to a force in the Amiens region and that it was British pressure which gave Foch wider powers. (See Lloyd George, *Memoirs*, V, 356–58; Lord Milner, *loc. cit.*, p. ii; Duff Cooper, *Haig*, II, 258–59; Foch, *Mémoires*, II, 23; General***, *La crise du commandement unique* [Paris, 1931], p. 178; Jules Sauerwein interview with Foch, *Le Matin*, November 8, 1920.) Poincaré himself said privately in 1920 that the British rather than Clemenceau deserved the credit for the unified command (Ribot, *Journal*, p. 285).

[60] Poincaré, X, 124, 129; Herbillon, *Souvenirs*, II, 247.

[61] Poincaré, X, 316.

[62] *Supra*, p. 195.

pressure for an early armistice. It was the president's only serious attempt to cross Clemenceau in the military sphere.[63]

Poincaré's appeal to Foch proved vain. The marshal asserted that his armistice terms were the equivalent of unconditional surrender and that nothing more could be gained by a march to Berlin. Members of the French government agreed when they saw Foch's terms on October 26. Even Poincaré considered them severe; he said hopefully to Foch, "My dear general, they will never sign that."[64] But the president was mistaken. The Germans signed, however rigorous the terms, and their armies were permitted to withdraw in good order. Poincaré never fully forgave Foch and Clemenceau for this "error," which his position made him powerless to correct.[65]

In summary, the war years gave the president numerous opportunities to make his presence felt in military affairs. His words carried particular weight in Interallied negotiations and in disputes between headquarters and the cabinet. So true was

[63] Clemenceau suspected another case of presidential interference in October. At that time, the French believed that confusion in the American supply service in the Argonne was slowing up the Allied advance. Foch therefore proposed that a number of American divisions be placed under French command. Pershing refused; and Foch did not insist further, for he knew that insistence would only cause friction. The marshal's attitude infuriated Clemenceau, who demanded that Foch exercise his authority and order Pershing to hand over the divisions. The Tiger attributed Foch's refusal to Poincaré's secret encouragement (*Grandeur and Misery of Victory*, pp. 77–87). No evidence exists, however, to confirm this suspicion. In fact, Clemenceau told his military aide soon after the incident that the president had helped him seek a solution (Mordacq, *Le ministère Clemenceau*, II, 248–49, 266–67; cf. Herbillon, *Souvenirs*, II, 319 n.).

[64] General Weygand, "Le maréchal Foch et l'armistice," *Revue des Deux Mondes*, November 1, 1938, p. 29.

[65] Poincaré, X, 461; Ribot, *Journal*, p. 262; Herbillon, *Souvenirs*, II, 343; John J. Pershing, *My Experiences in the World War* (New York, 1931), II, 364. Poincaré told Pershing ten years later: "Clemenceau threatened to resign if an armistice was not granted, and it was out of the question for me to envisage a cabinet crisis at that moment" (T. Bentley Mott, *Twenty Years as Military Attaché* [New York, 1937], p. 277).

this that even Clemenceau called upon Poincaré for aid in military crises. But, just as in the field of politics, the president dared make himself no more than a secondary cog in the governmental machine. He was willing to utilize the prestige of his office, to offer advice, and to exert personal pressure on his friends; but beyond that he would not go. According to Poincaré's code of political ethics, no crisis could justify genuine responsibility in the hands of an irresponsible president.

CHAPTER VIII

WARTIME PUBLIC OPINION

Poincaré's place in the hearts of his countrymen from 1914 to 1918 did not lack variety. There were some Frenchmen who, in the course of the war, never faltered in their support of the president. There were others, perhaps more numerous and certainly more vocal, who criticized without remission. Between these two extremes fluctuated the bulk of French opinion, shifting as public confidence in victory rose and fell.

Poincaré's prestige had suffered during the first six months of 1914 as a result of partisan strife. His friends of the Right and Center were disappointed by his failure to fulfill their expectations. His enemies of the Left regarded their electoral victory in May as a victory over the president. The last critical days of peace, however, restored him to the good graces of the populace. Factional quarrels slipped into the background. Opinion demanded that the government act with firmness and dispatch; therefore the French looked to Poincaré rather than to Viviani.

This spontaneous outburst of confidence was not destroyed by the outbreak of war. References to "presidential dictatorship" disappeared during August, even though dozens of mysterious interviews took place at the Elysée. One reason for this was the shift of popular interest from the government to the army. Another, no doubt, was the fact that Frenchmen no longer feared to see a prominent man in the presidential palace. The crisis seemed to justify strong men in every high office.

Poincaré was not to enjoy this second honeymoon very long. It came to an abrupt end when, at the beginning of September, the government abandoned Paris for Bordeaux. This departure, which would seem so advisable under the circumstances, was extraordinarily unpopular in Paris. Perhaps the Parisians, lulled by the censorship, did not realize the full gravity of the moment; at any rate they regarded the transfer of their government as a cowardly and almost treasonable flight to safety.[1] And now that the first surge of patriotic fervor had passed it was Poincaré who began to serve as the target for dissatisfaction—not Viviani, but the irresponsible Poincaré. The unpopularity with which this episode clothed the president clung to him through the first half of the war. Always abnormally sensitive to criticism, he was made keenly aware of this bitterness by the flood of anonymous letters which began to pour in.[2]

The reader of *Au service de la France* cannot fail to observe the effect which this outcry had upon Poincaré's mind. His memoirs point out repeatedly and with peculiar emphasis that he fought the departure of the government from start to finish. His self-justification proves little except his susceptibility to hostile opinion. All the evidence goes to show that it was Joffre who exacted the departure; nor has any sensible argument ever been presented to show that the commander was wrong in doing so.[3] Reason required that the government be

[1] Parisians spoke of "the retreat of the fifteen thousand," and called the departing statesmen *"les tournedos à la Bordelaise"* (Germain Bapst, "Journal de la guerre de 1914," September 17, 1914). Rumor had it that Poincaré, terrified, wished to sue for peace. The president had *"une mauvaise presse,"* Bapst wrote, and feared that he would be taken as a hostage (*ibid.,* September 8, 1914). Even the sympathetic American ambassador saw something ridiculous in the departure: "I shall never forget the picture presented by that train-load of ambassadors, ministers, secretaries, women, babies, servants, dogs, cats, birds, and a collection of baggage that reminded me of a gypsy camp. There were no sleeping cars. It seemed to me it would have taken most of the sleeping cars in Paris to give each one a berth." (Thomas Bentley Mott, *Myron T. Herrick, Friend of France* [New York, 1929], p. 160.)

[2] Poincaré, V, 284–85, 383, 398, 402, 404.

[3] Bertie, *Diary,* I, 138; Ribot, *Lettres,* p. 11; Herbillon, *Souvenirs,* I, 17, 25. According to one canard, the terrified president begged Joffre to order the government's departure (Marcellin, *Politique,* II, 51; Corday, *L'Envers,* I, 175).

removed from the danger of German capture. The average Parisian, however, let his emotions sway his reason; and it was Poincaré who suffered the consequences. The existence of unjust criticism led to much friction between president and ministers at Bordeaux, for the former daily exhorted the cabinet to return to Paris at once. It also increased Poincaré's desire to make flying trips to the front or to Paris in order to prove his lack of cowardice.[4]

The blind hostility of public opinion did not slacken during the remaining months of 1914. Absurd rumors circulated in Right-wing circles in Paris, charging Poincaré with a desire to treat for immediate peace. In their search for an explanation, these critics seized upon what they called the president's terrible fear of Caillaux, who led Poincaré "by the end of the nose." They believed that Poincaré was planning to introduce Caillaux into the ministry.[5]

The president's first visit to the front and to Paris in October made him the butt of sarcasm from both Socialists and reactionaries. Germain Bapst, elderly scion of a prominent and wealthy family of the extreme Right, made odious comparisons between Poincaré and Gambetta. "This poor Poincaré has declined a great deal in public opinion," he wrote. "I do not know how he will be received at Paris." After the journey, Bapst added: "Yesterday evening M. Poincaré came to sleep at the Elysée. . . . . He came secretively. This morning he departed by auto with Gl. Gallieni. No newspaper has mentioned his presence within our walls or his ride this morning. They were afraid that people would cry as he passed: 'Vive Gallieni.'"[6] The president was attacked for having announced a

[4] Bapst, "Journal," October 4, 1914; Corday, *L'Envers*, I, 23.

[5] Bapst, "Journal," almost daily references from September 6 to September 30, 1914.

[6] *Ibid.*, October 6 and 7, 1914. Gallieni, military governor of Paris, had won to his person much of the popularity which the government lost by its "flight" to Bordeaux. Several ministers expressed fears that Gallieni might have dictatorial dreams.

trip to the front to visit the soldiers when as a matter of fact he saw no one but generals.[7] The Left-wing *Guerre Sociale* avoided the rigid censorship with a bit of doggerel which described him as a coward:

> Avant de revenir à Paris
> Monsieur Poincaré sûr'ment s'est dit:
> L'populo dirait que j'ai eu peur;
> Il aurait raison, y a pas d'erreur,
> Si je n'allais pas dans la bataille
> Saluer ceux qui nargu'nt la mitraille.
> Quand je reviendrais, ça c'est reglé,
> Par tout's les mèr' je m'f'rais siffler ...[8]

When he returned to Paris a second time in November there were unconfirmed rumors that his presence had drawn catcalls as well as applause.[9]

Poincaré later complained that Paris critics had branded him as a dictator during the Bordeaux period—"responsible for everything that happens, and especially for everything that happens in spite of me."[10] Yet no such charge found its way into print except for Clemenceau's veiled hints in his newspaper.[11] It is true that Viviani and Briand were rumored to be angry at Poincaré for the latter's "monopoly, encroachment, jealousy."[12] But there still existed an opposite tendency, among men of authoritarian sympathies, to scoff at Poincaré as a "wet dishrag" and to evoke the memory of Gambetta.[13]

1915

The year 1915 brought Poincaré little relief from the barbs of his enemies. The unexpected dragging out of the war brought a new type of dissatisfaction, which joined itself to the heritage left by the "flight" to Bordeaux.

---

[7] Bapst, "Journal," October 8, 1914.   [8] *La Guerre Sociale,* October 8, 1914.
[9] Corday, *L'Envers,* I, 37–38.   [10] Poincaré, V, 438.
[11] *L'Homme Enchaîné,* November 22 and December 22, 1914. (This was the new title of *L'Homme Libre,* adopted by Clemenceau after a clash with the censorship.)
[12] Corday, *L'Envers,* I, 41.   [13] Bapst, "Journal," December 10, 1914.

Among the president's wartime duties was one which he took with particular gravity. He represented France; therefore he felt obliged to carry France's greetings to the front on all possible occasions. At first hostile tongues branded these as "triumphal tours."[14] But it was not long before they changed their tune. Poincaré adopted for his excursions a ridiculous semimilitary costume which made him resemble a liveried servant. The French penchant for irony could not resist such a temptation, so that stories of "King Albert's chauffeur" at the front began to circulate in a dozen forms. Other reports, less innocuous, declared that the soldiers received him coldly, or that they even cried "Vive la paix!" when he passed.[15]

In reactionary circles, where a dictatorial regime was considered a necessity, Poincaré was "regarded more and more as a man without character and even without honesty."[16] Yet at the same time Clemenceau's tirades were growing increasingly bitter, despite the censorship. There was a flood of allusions to Poincaré's "omnipotence," *"la monarchie fleurdelysée,"* the "Poincaresque censorship," a "Louis-quatorzien reign in a Versailles of gilded cardboard," the "sun king." The Tiger wrote one day in a burst of fury: "Of all the sovereigns under whom I have lived (I began with Louis Philippe), M. Poincaré is to me the most insupportable."[17]

An especially severe outbreak occurred in July and August, 1915, coincident with an attempt to drive Millerand out of the cabinet. Anti-Poincarist deputies launched their shafts at the war minister but hoped to bring down bigger game in the process. Anonymous letters began to flood the Elysée again,

[14] Marcellin, *Politique,* I, 57. On the other hand, a secret service man who accompanied Poincaré on his first visits to the front was asked how the president was received; he replied that Poincaré "was not received at all. He passed unnoticed" (Corday, *L'Envers,* I, 204).

[15] Marcellin, *Politique,* I, 81; Poincaré, VI, 337; VII, 29.

[16] Bapst, "Journal," March 30, 1915.

[17] *L'Homme Enchaîné,* notably January 14 and 18, February 5 and 28, March 8, May 1, June 12, August 12, 21, and 26, September 22, 1915.

criticizing the conduct of affairs or demanding peace.[18] Stories
spread of the president's imminent fall and of his replacement
by Caillaux at the head of a committee of public safety.[19] There
were absurd whispers that Poincaré considered the situation
desperate and wanted the Socialists to start a pacifist campaign
which would end the war.[20] Meanwhile those same Socialists
were busy condemning the president for his aggressive "fight
to a finish" speech of July 14, 1915.[21]

On the other extreme, reactionaries complained of his "extraordinary weakness." "The president of the republic and
M. Viviani are completely devoid of will-power," wrote Germain Bapst. "They do not understand that the responsibility
of the country rests in their hands . . . . The most serious
fact in France is the absence of all government. The weakness
of M. Poincaré and M. Viviani is incredible; they are incapable
of having an idea and of saying yes or no."[22] When the cabinet finally rode out the Millerand storm in August, the editor
of the *Journal des Débats* said privately: "During the recent
crisis, M. Poincaré was perfect. That will do him good in
public opinion. He needs it. He is accused of fearing that
Caillaux will publish some things about Mme Poincaré which
everybody knows."[23]

The attacks on the president had abated somewhat by October, when the cabinet fell at last. Delcassé's resignation early

[18] Poincaré, VI, 307, 317.

[19] General Palat, "Souvenirs de guerre 1914–1916," *Archives de la
Grande Guerre,* Vol. XV, No. 44, p. 1785.

[20] Aristide Jobert, *Souvenirs d'un ex-parlementaire (1914–1919)* (Paris,
1933), pp. 149–50.

[21] Corday, *L'Envers,* I, 131.

[22] Bapst, "Journal," August 21, 22, 25, 1915. One provincial newspaper
called on the president to make himself dictator (cited in *L'Homme Enchaîné,*
August 26, 1915).

[23] Martin, "Notes de guerre," conversation with M. Etienne de Nalèche,
August 25, 1915. Others said that Viviani, buoyed up by his victory in the
Chamber, immediately told Poincaré to talk less in council sessions (Corday,
L'Envers, I, 149).

in that month and his replacement by Viviani as temporary minister of foreign affairs caused some unwarranted inferences to be drawn. In the Right-wing salons, for example, it was said that Poincaré had intrigued against Delcassé and that "in naming M. Viviani, who is absolutely incapable of directing foreign affairs, he counts on directing the department . . . ."[24] This was far from the truth. On the contrary, the president made valiant efforts to keep Delcassé in office; his own control of foreign policy actually decreased when Delcassé resigned. Rumor also blamed him for the absence of Millerand from the new Briand cabinet. In general, however, the October ministerial crisis passed quietly. This seemed to indicate that Poincaré was gradually returning to the customary obscurity of presidents, so far as public opinion was concerned. But the public really knew little about the government's activity during the war. Behind the walls of the Elysée, doubly protected by the censorship, Poincaré's activity had by no means gone into decline.

1916

Gustave Hervé, a Paris editor with wide contacts among the working class, assured Poincaré early in 1916 that his popularity among the French masses had regained its prewar level.[25] This was hardly the case. It is true that active criticism became less severe during the Briand era, which roughly coincided with the year 1916. Memories of the "flight" to Bordeaux began to dim, while the president's indefatigable travels to the war zone ended all talk of cowardice. But most Frenchmen apparently regarded him with indifference rather than enthusiasm. Clemenceau continued his caustic comments, denouncing the president's "personal government," charging that he had blocked legislative efforts to control the executive, railing at "appear-

[24] Bapst, "Journal," October 13, 1915; also October 14, 28, 30, November 1, 1915.

[25] Poincaré, VIII, 56.

ances of authority, and not a shadow of responsibility," jeering at "the setting hen of the Elysée."[26] Early in 1916 Clemenceau and others undertook a campaign of abuse against René Besnard, undersecretary for aviation. Their real target was Poincaré, for Besnard was generally regarded as the president's protégé.[27] But as time went on even the attacks of *L'Homme Enchaîné* gradually degenerated into mere passing insinuations; and during the last six months of 1916 Poincaré's name virtually disappeared from its columns.

On the extreme Right wing hostility to the president showed little sign of abating. Habitués of the Étoile-quarter salons declared that the Salonika expedition was Poincaré's personal project, and that if it failed the president would fall with it. These critics believed that Clemenceau had made himself the loudest opponent of Salonika in an effort to bring on a presidential crisis.[28] Unfriendly as they were toward Poincaré, the reactionaries were not yet prepared to go as far as Clemenceau. Bapst recorded in his diary late in 1915: "Certainly M. Poincaré is very weak, but it would be a crime to cause his fall at this moment."[29]

As the months of 1916 passed, the Right began to pay less attention to the obscure man of the Elysée. The daily notes of Germain Bapst reflected this tendency. Bapst's references to "this president of the republic who cannot take a decision or accept a responsibility" grew more infrequent. His circle still believed that Poincaré's "cowardice" was traceable to fear of

[26] *L'Homme Enchaîné*, December 4, 14, 17, 30, 1915; January 18, 19; February 22, April 3, May 14, June 19, 1916; cf. Suarez, *Briand*, IV, 264.

[27] Corday, *L'Envers*, I, 192; Marcellin, *Politique*, I, 189; *L'Homme Enchaîné*, January 3, 1916. Germain Bapst recorded in his diary (February 2, 1916): "Now all of M. Poincaré's enemies are attacking M. Besnard, not because he is incompetent, the honorable deputies don't care much about that; but because they hope by demolishing M. Besnard to strike M. Poincaré, his wife being the real author of the said Besnard's nomination."

[28] Bapst, "Journal," November 28, December 8, 11, 1915.

[29] *Ibid.*, December 14, 1915.

Caillaux and Malvy, whom they regarded as Caillaux's official mouthpiece. "If he [Poincaré] would speak to the country," wrote Bapst, "if he would say that he wants M. Caillaux's intrigues to stop, and if he would dismiss Malvy and prorogue the Chamber, he would win back all his popularity." The Right, however, no longer had much hope that Poincaré might take a strong stand. A flicker of optimism appeared when the president made an aggressive speech at Nancy in May 1916, but it soon died. At mid-year Bapst again spoke of "a malaise and general anxiety at Paris." "One feels," he continued, "that there is no government and that M. Poincaré and M. Briand do not know how to will."[30] The disgruntled authoritarians gradually began to seek another savior in Briand. They lost all confidence in the president, sneering that "M. Poincaré doesn't exist."[31] When the Briand ministry tottered in November-December, 1916, they charged that the premier was victim of an intrigue led by the president, who was "actuated by injured pride and by a spirit of rancor." *"M. Poincaré lui tire dans les jambes,"* went the phrase of Briand's defenders.[32] Only a year earlier, the reactionaries had treated Poincaré with contempt but had condemned any effort to force him out of office. At the end of 1916 they spoke without emotion of a possible presidential crisis.[33]

Poincaré's frequent visits to the front during 1916 failed to increase his popularity. He was not the man to buoy up confidence and encourage the will-to-victory among the poilus; his glacial personality often did him more harm than good. As one critic wrote: "M. Poincaré has a gift of lowering the temperature below zero when he appears."[34] When he pinned the *Croix*

[30] *Ibid.,* February 21, May 13, June 5, 1916. From June to November, Bapst did not mention Poincaré's name.

[31] *Ibid.,* November 12, 1916.

[32] *Ibid.,* November 14, 19, December 17, 1916; cf. Marcellin, *Politique,* I, 199; II, 64.

[33] Bapst, "Journal," December 18, 1916.   [34] *Ibid.,* February 21, 1916.

de Guerre on heroic soldiers, he sometimes mumbled his congratulations so low that the individual decorated did not understand him.[35] Such an incident occurred at Lyon in a munitions factory, where Poincaré was asked to present several medals: "They stopped all the machines, and in the greatest silence he pinned on all the crosses without saying a single word."[36] The president was remarkably devoid of tact when he addressed groups of soldiers at the front. In one case he began his remarks by saying, "The best of you are dead."[37] In spite of all these weaknesses, the reports which reached Paris about his growing unpopularity at the front were probably exaggerated. The poilus hated him, it was said, for his harsh coldness, his haughty blundering, his incapacity to address to them a *mot du cœur*. Once some soldiers were supposed to have shouted at him, "Go on back to Bordeaux!"[38] Poincaré was aware of these rumors and denied them indignantly; but, whether he realized it or not, much coolness did exist. His dignity suffered also from the ridicule which continued to greet his "chauffeur's costume." Even in the cinema his appearance on the screen sometimes brought laughter.[39]

The Briand period brought one new and significant development in the field of public opinion. This was the appearance of the war-guilt question. As early as 1913, at the moment when Poincaré had attained the presidency, a few Leftists had spoken of *"Poincaré-la-guerre."* In 1914–15, however, all France had turned in blind patriotism to the task of saving the country. As the war dragged on, Frenchmen were given time to think, to puzzle out explanations for this endless digging of trenches and throwing of grenades. Here and there individuals recalled

[35] Sixte, *L'offre de paix séparée de l'Autriche,* p. 15.

[36] Martin, "Notes de guerre," November 5, 1915, conversation with M. Ernest Sautter, Genevese financier; cf. also Suarez, *Briand,* IV, 119.

[37] Reminiscence of Captain Georges Varenne, 1938.

[38] Corday, *L'Envers,* I, 263, 270; II, 41.

[39] *Ibid.,* II, 14.

and analyzed the events of 1914. They began to wonder if this slaughter had been inevitable; they even took a second look at the official French publications on the origins of the war, in an effort to determine just how far they were trustworthy. A little group of Socialists founded the Société d'études documentaires et critiques sur la guerre. Poincaré denounced it as a German propaganda effort, but took it seriously enough to write a long letter of self-defense to the Société.[40] The anonymous letters which flowed steadily to the Elysée began to denounce the president as responsible for the war. The same idea appeared among war-weary soldiers at the front.[41] One day in September 1916 Germain Bapst heard a Socialist assert that Poincaré, the Tsar, the Kaiser, and Francis Joseph had agreed to make war in order to kill off the workers. On the same day Bapst was told by a scion of the highest nobility that Poincaré and the Tsar had planned the war in July 1914.[42] Here were the two extremes with a vengeance! Fed by war-weariness, the campaign was helped along by Poincaré's belligerent speeches, which demanded a fight to the finish and the recovery of Alsace-Lorraine. His addresses of May 14 and July 14, 1916, were severely attacked by the Socialists as evidence of the *revanchard* spirit.[43]

Few people dared assert in public that a French official might have been partly responsible for the war. Men of the Left wing sometimes expressed their suspicions in the form of implications that Poincaré had usurped power—for if he had caused the war he must have been more than a republican King Log. Third-rate newspapers like Almereyda's *Bonnet Rouge* escaped the censorship by means of dark hints:

[40] Poincaré, VIII, 79, 214, 217, 220.

[41] *Ibid.*, p. 52; Corday, *L'Envers*, II, 29.

[42] Bapst, "Journal," September 20, 1916.

[43] The first speech was delivered at Nancy, the second at Paris. Corday, *L'Envers*, I, 274; Hubert Bourgin, *Mémoires pour servir à l'histoire d'une sécession politique (1915–1917)* (Paris, 1924), p. 92; *Le Bonnet Rouge*, August 14, 1916.

There is a monarchy without the name, whose return is still to be feared . . . . Certain men . . . . are thinking seriously of again imposing the regime of personal power on France, of strengthening, to the detriment of popular and legislative sovereignty, the authority and the attributes of . . . . the president of the republic. These unhealthy dreams appear not only in the minds of men who frequent the salons and the clubs of the Etoile quarter; these projects found sympathy at the very head of the republic, at the Elysée, during the presidency of Félix Faure . . . . Félix Faure thought of setting up, with the aid of war . . . . , a sort of dictatorial presidency . . . . These times are not so distant . . . . [remainder of article cut by censors].[44]

The *Bonnet Rouge* was a journal of infinitesimal circulation, with little influence. It was more serious when the Socialist deputy Pierre Brizon dared to criticize Poincaré. Brizon wrote a long article for the *Bonnet Rouge* entitled "Le mauvais président." Although he declared that he was referring to the president of China, the allusion was grotesquely transparent. The censors cut out the whole article, whereupon Brizon rose and read it in the Chamber.[45] Printed in the *Journal officiel,* it drew far more public attention than it would have received in the *Bonnet Rouge.* Even this, however, made few Frenchmen aware of the war-guilt charge against Poincaré. The majority, if they had known of such an insinuation, would certainly have rejected it at this time.

1917

The troubled course of events during the year 1917 was inevitably reflected in public opinion. By this time, France had become restless under the incessant strain of war. Dissatisfaction and lassitude not only produced strikes and military mutinies but also increased criticism of every branch of the government. Confidence suffered as cabinets and military commanders were frequently replaced. Only Poincaré stayed on at the Elysée, a continuous target for those who wished to complain.

[44] *Le Bonnet Rouge,* September 5, 1916.
[45] *Chamber Debates,* June 14, 1916, pp. 1252–53.

Only a shadow of the *union sacrée* continued to exist. Socialists in the Chamber began to make undisguised attacks on
the president. Deputy Aristide Jobert, an obscure and ill-bal-
anced man, spoke of him as "the malevolent genius which di-
rects the country's destinies."[46] The phrase was typical of the
extreme Left-wing attitude, for those circles affected to believe
that Poincaré was the guiding spirit behind every act of government. Although the censorship kept such things out of the
newspapers, the "malevolent genius" speech was reprinted in
pamphlet form and was circulated even among soldiers at the
front.[47] Deputy Brizon's article on "Le mauvais président,"
written in 1916, was also distributed as a brochure. Still another deputy, the Socialist-Republican Augagneur, rebuked authoritarians who spoke of augmenting the president's powers.
Augagneur asserted that the prerogatives of the office were
already very great. He added meaningfully that there ought
to be a rule which would prohibit a premier from stepping directly into the Elysée.[48] The allusion was obvious, for only one
premier had ever been so elected. In such devious ways was
the censorship circumvented.

These incidents in the Chamber were products of the war-
guilt controversy. Little attention had been paid to the early
investigators of war origins; but 1917 with its crop of troubles
brought the question out of the shadows. In May it was noised
about that the new Russian government had found in the Petrograd archives certain letters written by Poincaré in 1914 urging
the Tsar to declare war. The president was alleged to have said
in one letter: "The French army has never been stronger; you
can march."[49] When this rumor reached Poincaré's ears he
became so agitated that he wished to open an investigation.
The cabinet managed to dissuade him. Still nervous, he wrote
a long letter of self-defense to Ribot on May 26, denying that

[46] *Chamber Debates*, July 7, 1917, p. 1715; cf. October 19, 1917, p. 2842.
[47] Corday, *L'Envers*, II, 147.
[48] *Le Bonnet Rouge*, July 8, 1917.   [49] Ribot, *Journal*, p. 132.

he had ever acted without approval from the responsible ministers. On the same evening he wrote to Ribot a second time.
The rumor was growing worse, he said; people were quoting
from his alleged letters to the Tsar; there was talk of his resignation.[50] He feared that the Socialists would exploit these criticisms when they assembled for their annual party congress a
few days later. Nor was he mistaken. One delegate at this
congress furiously denounced the president as the principal obstacle to peace. Others spoke with passion of interpellations,
of resignation, even of the guillotine.[51] These Socialist outbursts led directly to a secret session of the Chamber in June,
when the president's name was repeatedly dragged into the
debate.

Poincaré was well aware of what was going on. Abnormally sensitive to criticism, he followed the campaign in its
most minor details. He even read obscure journals of insignificant circulation to discover attacks against him. He asked
Ribot to publish a "Yellow Book" on the Balkan wars of
1912–13 in order to prove his pacific attitude. Ribot's irritation grew as Poincaré kept bombarding him with letters full
of complaints about the war-guilt campaign. Ribot knew that
such nervousness only augmented Socialist suspicion.[52]

The president's efforts at self-justification were largely
wasted. His enemies continued to find new excuses for attack.
When the Russians published the Paléologue-Pokrovsky letters, which promised support for French claims along the Rhine,
the Socialists wrongfully accused Poincaré of full responsibility for them.[53] The campaign of criticism reached a climax in
the Chamber secret session of June 29–30. The question up
for debate was the ill-fated Nivelle offensive, and the obvious

---

[50] *Ibid.,* p. 130.

[51] Bourgin, *Mémoires,* pp. 221–23.

[52] Ribot, *Journal,* pp. 153, 161–63.

[53] Bourgin, *Mémoires,* p. 221 ; Ribot, *Journal,* pp. 100, 129. On the Paléologue-Pokrovsky letters, see *supra,* p. 155.

aim of Socialist deputies was to load the blame on Poincaré. Repeated insinuations and open attacks were censured by the presiding officer, but not until after they had been placed in the record. Poincaré's presence at the war council of April 6, 1917, was branded as an unconstitutional attempt to direct military policy. A Radical deputy named Albert-Favre arose and described a visit he had made to the Elysée on the second day of the Nivelle offensive. Albert-Favre had demanded that Poincaré intervene to stop the attack; Poincaré's answer had been that he lacked constitutional authority for such a step. Albert-Favre told the Chamber: "I replied to him that a man who chose the premier, who intervened in the making of cabinets, who presided over ministerial councils, war committees, and *conseils de guerre* could not argue—," whereupon his words were drowned out by "lively applause" from the Socialist benches. Poincaré was accused of having defended Nivelle after the offensive, when the commander should have been removed at once. Some deputies even cried, "We must go to Versailles!"[54] All these accusations, however, were based on nothing better than suspicion, and it required more than suspicion to force a presidential crisis.

While politicians in Paris criticized and intrigued against Poincaré, his meager popularity at the front suffered also. To the common soldier the idea that Germany might not have been responsible for the war came as a shock. In addition, military morale had been weakened by three years in the trenches. Poincaré's journeys to the war zone began to bring more unpleasant incidents. Just before one trip an official warned him that his train might be showered with stones.[55] The soldiers' distaste for these presidential visits was bruited about in Paris, doubtless with considerable exaggeration; it was mentioned in one

[54] *Journal officiel,* June 29–30, 1917, pp. 322–49; cf. *ibid.,* July 4, 1917, p. 390, and Bertie, *Diary,* II, 147. "Secret" was a euphemism when applied to these sessions.

[55] Poincaré, IX, 164.

public session of the Chamber, and was perhaps responsible for the censorship's redoubled vigilance in suppressing newspaper references to Poincaré.[56] The Parisian populace was also affected by the wave of pessimism. The police actually wished to cancel the military review of Bastille Day, 1917, because they feared that the president would be in danger. The review was held in spite of this anxiety, and officials were relieved when Poincaré was hissed only once.[57]

In view of this extensive hostility, it was remarkable that Clemenceau was less outspoken in 1917 than in the past. The Tiger was supposed to be hoping still for a presidential crisis;[58] but his editorials included only sporadic insinuations against the Elysée.[59] Perhaps Clemenceau had decided that his continual clashes with the censorship harmed no one but himself. The same explanation cannot be applied to another long-time critic, the ultraconservative Germain Bapst. References to Poincaré virtually disappeared from his private journal during 1917. Whatever the reason, opposition to the president by now had found its chief center among the Socialists. There it remained throughout the rest of his septennate.

1918

Just as Clemenceau's accession to power pushed Poincaré into the political background, so the Tiger's presence eclipsed him in the eyes of the public. *L'Homme Enchaîné* had been the only journal which dared to criticize Poincaré regularly; now its attacks ceased. In the press there remained only the insinua-

---

[56] *Chamber Debates,* September 25, 1917 (Edouard Barthe). The censors suppressed reports of Barthe's speech (Marcel Berger and Paul Allard, *Les secrets de la censure pendant la guerre* [Paris, 1932], pp. 199, 218).

[57] Bertie, *Diary,* II, 152. Painlevé declared in his postwar memoirs that the police did not ask for cancellation of the review, even though they had received pessimistic warnings (Painlevé, *Comment j'ai nommé Foch,* pp. 162–63).

[58] Bertie, *Diary,* II, 139–40.

[59] *L'Homme Enchaîné,* April 25, July 24, August 5, 6, September 12, 14, 1917.

tions of obscure Left-wing sheets which had adopted the thesis that Poincaré desired war in 1914, and that his intransigeance since then had blocked a possible peace. All eyes were turned on Clemenceau, whose insolent willingness to bear full responsibility acted as a lightning rod for the Elysée. No one could possibly accuse Poincaré of dictatorship when Clemenceau was at the head of affairs.

Conservative editors showered the president with praise when he called Clemenceau to power.[60] In Right-wing circles he thus regained some of the ground which he had lost since 1913. But it was Clemenceau who now became the hope of the authoritarians, just as Poincaré had been in 1913. "In France, M. Clemenceau is awaited at work," wrote Germain Bapst. "He arouses as much hope as M. Poincaré caused the day after his election . . . . I trust that he will not bring the same disillusionment."[61] The conservatives still resented Poincaré's failure to fulfill their ideal of strong leadership. His nomination of Clemenceau served only to end the campaign of injurious remarks which had circulated in the salons at his expense. Henceforth he was quite generally ignored.

There were many Frenchmen, in the Chamber and out, who had feared and opposed the accession of Clemenceau. They had tried to exert pressure on the Elysée to avert the choice.[62] These were men of the Left, who knew that the old Jacobin stood for a fight to the finish, with the ruthless sacrifice of everyone who might stand in the way of that purpose. Clemenceau's position had been doubly clear since July 1917, when he had turned his guns on Malvy and on those whom he called pacifists. This was one issue on which president and premier saw eye to eye; for Poincaré too had demanded a fight to the finish in all his wartime speeches.

It was natural, therefore, that such attacks as were made on

[60] E.g., *L'Opinion,* X (November 24, 1917), p. 369.

[61] Bapst, "Journal," November 19, 1917.

[62] Herbillon, *Souvenirs,* II, 165.

Poincaré in 1918 should come only from the Left. Socialists believed that he had made an alliance with Clemenceau in order to suppress their evidence of presidential belligerence and war-responsibility. It was his head or theirs, they declared.[63] But they had little opportunity to spread their beliefs, for the censorship continued to be as severe as ever, and the government undertook a series of arrests and trials which frightened the opposition into silence. In the Chamber the uncomplimentary remarks about Poincaré which had been made so frequently in 1917 almost died out. Once, early in the Clemenceau period, a large number of deputies were said to have interrupted proceedings by chanting "Poincaré!" to the tune of a popular ballad.[64] There was a second anti-Poincarist incident in March 1918, when the Socialists criticized his prewar visit to Russia.[65] From that time on, the opposition went underground. Thus passed 1918: the Left repressed into quiet, the Right satisfied by Clemenceau's authoritarianism. Poincaré's name and figure faded into obscurity. It was the first time since his election that opinion treated him as presidents of the republic had customarily been regarded in the past.

[63] Fabre-Luce, *Caillaux*, pp. 144–46.

[64] Corday, *L'Envers*, II, 179. Naturally, there was no reference to such an incident in the official *Chamber Debates*.

[65] *Chamber Debates*, March 1, 1918, pp. 662–63.

CHAPTER IX

TREATY-MAKING AND AFTER

Fifteen months remained of Poincaré's septennate when the bells of Paris signaled the Armistice. He looked forward to those months without great pleasure, for there was little hope that he could escape the domination of Clemenceau. The premier, entrenched in the hearts of Frenchmen as Père la Victoire, could safely ignore any signs of revolt at the Elysée. The arrival of peace, therefore, had little effect on Poincaré's governmental status. He remained what he had been ever since the Tiger had come into power—an official who could not act without the premier's permission.

But if his status was little changed, Poincaré's attitude was altered greatly. During the war he had effaced himself before Clemenceau, in relative silence if not with good grace. Victory then had been all-important. Once the danger was past, injured pride plus blind confidence in the correctness of his own opinions led him to react against the Clemencist dictatorship. Knowing that Clemenceau always held the whip hand in an open dispute, he never dared push their differences to a public breach. His efforts had to be confined largely to using his influence on men of his own trend of thought who might be able to convert the Tiger.

It seemed to Clemenceau's entourage that the Elysée had become the nucleus of an antigovernmental party, working to overthrow the ministry. Their suspicions may or may not have been justified; a backstairs intrigue is seldom open to proof or disproof. Part of Poincaré's activity during the treaty-making period has come to light, however. His relations with Marshal Foch were of particular interest in this regard. It may be added

229

that Poincaré himself made no effort to hide his jealousy of Clemenceau, who was receiving most of the praise for France's victory.[1] The president sincerely felt that he deserved a larger share of the credit for this victory. Clemencists have therefore declared that Poincaré began to conspire even before the Armistice, as soon as the prospect of peace became a certainty. It is true that there were signs of a growing restlessness at the Elysée in October. Until then Poincaré had put no obstacle in the path of the premier. More than once he had used his influence to second Clemenceau. It was all the more noticeable, therefore, when Poincaré twice encouraged Marshal Foch to resist Clemenceau during the month of October.[2]

This Poincaré-Foch rapprochement was little more than a tendency in 1918. It did not ripen into a full understanding until the Peace Conference met several months later. The president had never hidden his desire for rigorous punishment of the German aggressor. In his wartime speeches he had outlined the essentials of an adequate treaty: full reparations, adequate guaranties for the innocent victors, no compromise with justice. Poincaré realized, however, that he could take no active part in the Peace Conference. It was necessary that he find a man of great prestige to argue his case before the delegates. He could have found no abler advocate than Ferdinand Foch, who saw eye to eye with the president.

Poincaré did not wait until the conference convened to begin his campaign. December found him actively disseminating his ideas in speeches and interviews. At Strasbourg late in 1918 he showed his distrust of League of Nations idealists by declaring: "The only guarantee of peace is that symbolized by the representatives of friendly and allied nations when they accompanied the French government to Strasbourg."[3] When President Wilson arrived in Paris a few days later, Poincaré's address of welcome contained hints of the Franco-

---

[1] Poincaré, X, 406, 415.

[2] See *supra,* p. 195.   [3] *Le Temps,* December 11, 1918.

American differences which were soon to arise. Poincaré again made it plain that he had no faith in a League of Nations unless it could be set up as a new Holy Alliance against Germany. He insisted that Wilson visit the war-torn departments of northeastern France before the conference sessions began. Obviously he feared that the idealistic American might try to restrain France in her demands for reparation.[4]

At last came the great occasion, the opening of the Peace Conference. Poincaré delivered the address of welcome; but his greetings were buried beneath a long plea for innocent France, chief sufferer from the war. The president asserted that the delegates possessed full authority to draw up any peace terms which they saw fit. He disguised his misgivings about the premature armistice by a bit of bravado:

> This victory is total, since the enemy asked for an armistice only to avoid an irremediable military disaster: and from this total victory it is your right to draw the total consequences today, in the interest of justice and of peace.

Continuing, he warned the peacemakers against any weak sentiment of generosity:

> You will seek only justice . . . . But justice is not inert; she does not resign herself to injustice; her first demands when she has been violated are restitutions and reparations for the peoples and the individuals who have been despoiled or mistreated . . . .
>
> Justice further demands . . . . sanctions against the guilty, and effective guaranties . . . . And she is logical when she asks that these guaranties be given, first of all, to the nations which have been and

---

[4] Raymond Poincaré, *Messages, discours, allocutions, lettres et télégrammes de M. Raymond Poincaré* (Paris, 1919–1921), II, 98–102. *L'Humanité* (December 15, 1918) pointed out the contrast between the toasts of the two presidents. Poincaré made only a brief indirect allusion to the League of Nations and asserted that it should exclude the Central Powers. From start to finish, there was no love lost between Poincaré and Wilson. The latter once branded Poincaré as "a cheat and a liar"; at another time he called him "a ——" (David Lloyd George, *The Truth about the Peace Treaties* [London, 1938], I, 241; Allan Nevins, *The Letters and Journals of Brand Whitlock* [New York, 1936], II, 566).

which may still be exposed to aggressors or to threats; to those which have many times run the risk of being submerged by the periodic flood of the same invasions.[5]

The conference was open; decision passed into other hands than those of Poincaré. He had used the preparatory weeks to fix in the minds of his countrymen an idea of what France ought to receive and to impress upon the conference his belief that there was but one straight and narrow pathway to justice. France, it appeared, expected every Allied delegate to do his duty.

Poincaré soon became aware that his extreme demands might be compromised by another Frenchman—Clemenceau himself. One article in the Poincaré program called for the creation of an autonomous buffer state on the left bank of the Rhine. This means of crippling Germany had become quite widely advocated in France during the war. Although Poincaré had never made a public statement in support of the plan, he had long looked upon it with favor. His appeal to the Peace Conference for "effective guaranties" was an obvious allusion to Rhineland autonomy. He was careful, however, to keep his sponsorship veiled, leaving Foch to become the public exponent of Rhenish separatism. On January 10, 1919, before the Peace Conference assembled, Foch had summarized his program in a note submitted to Clemenceau. The Tiger approved, and argued fervently for the plan in meetings of the Big Four.[6] But while Foch and Poincaré regarded Rhineland autonomy as a sine qua non of the peace, Clemenceau considered it an item which might be bartered for other concessions if that should prove necessary. It did so prove; Wilson and Lloyd George refused to set up this new Alsace-Lorraine on the other side of the frontier. After negotiations which lasted through March and April, Clemenceau finally secured a compromise. It provided for a fifteen-year Allied occupation of

[5] Poincaré, *Discours*, II, 140–41.

[6] André Tardieu, *La paix* (Paris, 1921), p. 164.

the Rhineland, plus a promise of Anglo-American treaties guaranteeing aid to France against future aggression.

Clemenceau won this partial victory over the bitter opposition of Foch and Poincaré. On the surface it was Foch alone who protested; but all Paris knew that the president sympathized thoroughly and remained in regular contact with the marshal. Foch learned late in March that Clemenceau had decided to abandon the idea of a Rhineland buffer state. The marshal demanded a hearing before the Big Four, and was received by them on March 31; but his arguments glanced off Wilson and Lloyd George.[7] Frustrated, he returned to the attack at once. Twice in April he wrote to the Tiger, asking to present his case to the cabinet and the French Peace Conference delegation. Clemenceau took no notice of this request until Poincaré intervened in support of the marshal on April 17.[8] Faced by this dual pressure, Clemenceau agreed to let Foch appear before the council of ministers on April 25. The Tiger prepared for a showdown battle against his two chief critics. To his surprise, however, the president maintained an attitude of utmost reserve during the session. Clemenceau told his military aide the next day that "Poincaré . . . . showed himself most correct, remaining constantly in the role which the con-

---

[7] Recouly, *Foch,* pp. 186–87; Mordacq, *Le ministère Clemenceau,* III, 202.

[8] Recouly, *Foch,* pp. 192–94; Ribot, *Journal,* p. 268. Also on April 17 Clemenceau ordered Foch to summon the delegates of Germany to Paris, where the treaty draft would be presented to them. Foch replied that he would not deliver the message until he had had a final opportunity to plead with the cabinet for Rhineland autonomy. Clemenceau was enraged by this "insubordination," and blamed Poincaré for it. The Tiger and others viewed it as an effort to precipitate a crisis in the midst of which both Foch and Poincaré would resign. Whether or not this suspicion was justified, any immediate danger of such a crisis was averted when Clemenceau promised Foch a hearing at the council session of April 25. Foch's act was excused as a misunderstanding, based on the obscure wording of the message to the Germans. On this incident, see: Clemenceau, *Grandeur and Misery of Victory,* pp. 131–36; Mordacq, *Le ministère Clemenceau,* III, 226–30; and Recouly, *Foch,* pp. 215–16.

stitution assigned to him, and intervened only to put very exactly to the point all the questions which were raised . . . ."[9]

The president's conduct on April 25 did not mean that he had abandoned Foch and Rhineland autonomy. No doubt he knew that his intervention in council would only annoy Clemenceau, and so he left Foch to carry the burden of the debate. Only three days later, in fact, Poincaré submitted a long memorandum on the Rhineland situation to the premier, and asked that the document be placed before the Peace Conference. In this memorandum the president objected that an occupation limited to fifteen years would be too short. Allied troops, he declared, would have to remain in the Rhineland until every mark of reparations should be paid. By reading between the lines it was easy to see that Poincaré expected the Rhenish provinces to break away from Germany before long if French soldiers were there to encourage separatist tendencies.[10]

Although this remarkable memorandum was not published at the time, it circulated rather widely by the grapevine route. It became the Bible of Germanophobes in France, who cited it in order to emphasize the weakness of Clemenceau's compromise plan.[11] The premier cherished no illusions about Poincaré's apparent neutrality in the council of April 25. When Foch threatened on May 4 that he would resign unless the treaty was altered, Clemenceau blamed the president for the threat. He told one of his aides that Foch had been continually at the Elysée for two weeks.[12] Perhaps Clemenceau exagger-

[9] Mordacq, *Le ministère Clemenceau*, III, 246. A year later, Foch recalled that "M. Poincaré supported me, he alone" before the council (Sauerwein interview in *Le Matin*, November 8, 1920). Foch's memory seems to have been at fault here; he even dated the session April 7. Later Foch said that Poincaré had agreed with him privately but had been forced by his constitutional bonds to remain silent (Recouly, *Foch*, pp. 206–7).

[10] This letter has been published in Lloyd George's *The Truth about the Peace Treaties*, I, 427–32.

[11] Stéphane Lauzanne in *Le Matin*, February 4, 1920.

[12] Mordacq, *Le ministère Clemenceau*, III, 258–59.

ated somewhat; but Poincaré later admitted that he too had considered resigning in protest and had discussed such a step with Foch and others.[13] He gave private support to Clemenceau's critics, even though he did not speak out in sessions of the council.[14] For example, the president complained to certain politicians that the Chamber was shirking its duty when it failed to overthrow the ministry. He feared to make such a demand publicly, however.[15] The temper of the Elysée was so well known that a guest at dinner there, a "high military personage," felt free to declare his hope for a cabinet crisis which might bring revision of the yet unsigned peace treaty. He was not rebuked by the president, although several deputies were present.[16] Well-informed journalists believed that Poincaré inspired all the press campaigns which were being carried on against the government.[17]

Clemenceau branded this activity as unconstitutional. Technically the charge was false; the president certainly was free to consult whomsoever he wished. According to the spirit of the constitution, however, he was not justified in giving aid and comfort to a group which was hostile to the premier. Strict honesty would have forced him to choose one of two courses: either a flat refusal to co-operate with the cabinet, thus provoking a crisis; or complete neutrality on the question at issue. His halfway position was inexcusable.

The Rhineland again took the spotlight briefly at the end of May 1919. By this time, Foch's buffer-state plan had been defi-

---

[13] *Chamber Debates*, November 23, 1923, p. 151; Ribot, *Journal*, p. 274.

[14] Mordacq, *Clemenceau au soir de sa vie*, I, 291–93; Lloyd George, *Treaties*, I, 581.

[15] Ribot, *Journal*, p. 273.

[16] Mordacq, *Le ministère Clemenceau*, III, 308.

[17] Martin, "Notes de guerre," May 6, 1919, interview with M. Pierre Comert, journalist attached to the Quai d'Orsay. Cf. Martin's interview with Wickham Steed on May 3, when the latter said: "Marshal Foch is playing a very dangerous game at this moment. He is in the midst of a political intrigue, and the threads appear traceable to the Elysée."

nitely rejected by the peace conference. A tiny group of separatist agitators in the Rhineland therefore took things into their own hands. With the undisguised aid of General Mangin, commander of the French army of occupation, they seized power in several cities and proclaimed an autonomous Rhenish republic within the framework of Germany. Mangin's first act after the coup was to telegraph the news to Poincaré. Why he informed the president rather than the minister of war, Mangin has never explained. Perhaps this procedure meant that Poincaré had been privy to the preparation of the coup. More probably the general simply wished to utilize Poincaré's well-known sympathy for the buffer-state program.[18]

Whatever the reason for Mangin's act, the president knew that such direct correspondence might arouse criticism. Therefore he forwarded the message to Clemenceau at once. But he appended a note stating his belief that the autonomy movement ought to be encouraged. "In my opinion," Poincaré declared, "it would be very unfortunate to take part against these as yet very shy dispositions toward independence."[19] It was clear that the president favored moral support to the separatists, at the very least. Clemenceau, however, ignored this suggestion, for he knew that it would mean a new conflict with Wilson and Lloyd George. Two days later Senator Ribot found Poincaré "grieved by his inability to make Clemenceau understand that he is serving the interests of France badly . . . ."[20]

In the important dispute over the Rhineland, Poincaré adopted a strategy of indirect action; he encouraged Foch to become the spearhead of the buffer-state plan. At the same time, he did not abandon the direct method in his relations

[18] When questioned as to her late husband's foreknowledge of the separatist coup, Madame Poincaré gave only the following reply: "President Poincaré was a partisan of an autonomous Rhineland, he was entirely in accord with General Mangin who worked for this end" (letter to the author, October 14, 1938).

[19] Clemenceau, *Grandeur and Misery of Victory*, pp. 223–24.

[20] Ribot, *Journal*, p. 272.

with Clemenceau. All through the treaty-making period he continued to write long and frequent letters to the premier presenting his views on various aspects of the settlement. When reparations were being discussed, for example, he "harried Clemenceau daily with exhortations not to give in."[21] His letters had little or no effect; often they did not reach their destination or, if they did, the premier ostentatiously ignored them.[22] Poincaré became particularly agitated when the Italian delegates withdrew from the conference on April 24. He demanded full information about the cause of the rupture, showed his disapproval that Orlando had been allowed to go, and even hinted that he would sign no treaty in which Italy did not take part.[23] Clemenceau's exasperation increased; but he did ask Poincaré to write a soothing letter to the king of Italy on April 30. News of the president's attitude got abroad; and when the Italians returned to Paris in May they were said to be basing their hopes on support from certain French statesmen, one of whom was Poincaré.[24] When the final draft of the treaty appeared, however, it contained no clause which could be attributed to Poincaré's influence.[25] With Clemenceau as chief negotiator that influence was virtually zero.

[21] Lloyd George, *Treaties*, I, 498–99.

[22] Interview with Professor Harold Temperley, British expert at the conference. Cf. Lloyd George, *Treaties*, I, 250–51. Albert Thomas was another who was annoyed by Poincaré's incurable letter-writing. He complained privately in 1919: "M. Poincaré writes too much and espouses too many things. He sends me useless bits of notes all the time." (Martin, "Notes de guerre," May 7, 1919.)

[23] Mordacq, *Le ministère Clemenceau*, III, 255–56.

[24] Steed, *Through Thirty Years*, II, 331; cf. *Le Matin*, May 2 and 3, 1919.

[25] Frenchmen who disliked both Clemenceau and the treaty singled out Article 428 (providing for Interallied occupation of the Rhineland) as one of the rare good clauses, and said that it had been included through the influence of Poincaré and Foch (*Le Matin*, February 5, 1920). The truth is that Clemenceau himself argued steadily for occupation, and finally secured Article 428 as it stood. (Mordacq, *Le ministère Clemenceau*, III, 202; Tardieu, *La paix*, pp. 202–205.)

Poincaré has often been criticized for his failure to resign rather than sign a treaty which, in his opinion, sacrificed the interests of France.[26] That the president did consider resignation has already been pointed out. The fact that he decided to stay in office does not reflect upon his integrity. After all, it was his right to weigh the utility of such a step. At best, his resignation would have been only an empty gesture; at worst, it might have led to an open breach with Britain and the United States.

By mid-1919 the treaty was signed and ratified and the separatist movement suppressed. Poincaré's seven years of "servitude" were nearing their end. The last few months were spent in marking time; for the president's relations with Clemenceau made it certain that he would exercise no influence in the government. Brief pilgrimages to the devastated regions filled much of his time. He drifted along in the obscurity of ordinary presidents; the press no longer reported the delirious acclamations of 1913. His public appearances were restrained in nature. It was Clemenceau's figure which drew the greatest applause. Yet during these obscure months, Poincaré achieved a quiet sort of popularity which he had never before known. Victory quickly dissolved the ill-will of most Frenchmen. Poincaré, like every wartime public servant, became a living symbol of Germany's defeat.

There were some who wished to see him accept a second term at the Elysée. In July 1919 L'Echo de Paris reported this desire, attributing it to the splendid fashion in which he had represented France during the war.[27] The president immediately let it be known that he had had his fill of the Elysée. Nevertheless, when the election approached in January 1920 there was new talk of drafting Poincaré. Many people pointed

[26] *Chamber Debates*, November 23, 1923, pp. 150–51; Ernest Renauld, *1914–1919, Histoire populaire de la guerre* (Paris, 1921–1923), II, 186; Louis Sonolet, *La vie de Paul Deschanel 1855–1922* (Paris, 1926), p. 250.

[27] *L'Echo de Paris*, July 27, 1919.

out that, although the retiring chief magistrate would not ask for a second term, he might accept it if it were offered.[28] The fact that Clemenceau was the leading candidate only strengthened their belief that Poincaré might agree to run. One rabidly anti-Clemencist periodical accused the Tiger of planning to set himself up in the Elysée as a virtual dictator, and added that Poincaré would probably accept re-election in order to prevent such a contingency.[29] Here was a strange spectacle: Poincaré called upon to block an attempt at strengthening the presidency, even though he had been elected in 1913 as the representative of presidential revival! Only a minority at the Left expressed horror at the very thought of a second term for "the president of war and reaction."[30]

All these hopes were in vain. Clemenceau was unexpectedly beaten in a preliminary caucus and withdrew from the race.[31] It seemed likely that an orthodox Radical would gain the Elysée; and in the face of this threat, many of Clemenceau's nationalist backers turned to Poincaré as a last hope.[32] But their dream of a spontaneous demonstration which would force Poincaré to accept failed to materialize. Delegates who rushed to the Elysée were sent away with a flat refusal. Paul Deschanel was elected, and in February Poincaré left his "prison" to its new occupant.

Clemenceau was convinced that his defeat had been caused by intrigues set on foot by the outgoing president. The Tiger's military aide, General Mordacq, has pointed out that Poincaré

---

[28] *L'Echo de Paris*, January 15, 1920.

[29] *Le Progrès Civique*, II (January 10, 1920), 29.

[30] *Journal du Peuple*, October 29, 1919.

[31] Clemenceau received 389 votes to Deschanel's 408 in the caucus. Since 120 legislators did not vote, Clemenceau might still have won at Versailles had he not withdrawn. His friends recalled Poincaré's persistence in similar circumstances in 1913, and used this to prove that Clemenceau was a truer republican. (Mordacq, *Le ministère Clemenceau*, IV, 264.)

[32] *L'Echo de Paris*, January 16, 1920; *Le Gaulois*, January 17, 1920; *Le Matin*, January 17, 1920; *La Victoire*, January 17, 1920; *L'Opinion*, XIII (January 17, 1920), 82.

must have feared a Clemenceau presidency more than anything else. It would probably have meant a seven-year famine for Poincaré, so far as cabinet posts were concerned.[33] But even Clemenceau was forced to admit the president's right to indicate his preferences to his friends. For that matter, no sane politician needed to be told what those preferences were. Poincaré was scarcely to be condemned on this score.

Poincaré departed from the Elysée in a sort of apotheosis. Men recalled that he alone had sat in the councils of government through all the years of the war, carrying on during the darkest days when hope burned low. They looked at him in sudden awe: he personified victorious France. In a generous mood inspired by success they forgot his faults and remembered only his virtues. Had he sometimes failed to fulfill their desires? The constitution had "imprisoned" him.[34] Had he avoided responsibilities even in times of severe crisis? He had simply wished to preserve the republican system inviolate.[35] Then had he been nothing but a figurehead? No; history would one day reveal that his benevolent activity had guided the government every step of the way.[36] The Chamber ex-

[33] Mordacq, Le ministère Clemenceau, IV, 287.

[34] Arthur Meyer in Le Gaulois, December 3, 1919.

[35] Ibid., September 23, 1919; Gustave Hervé in La Victoire, January 7, 1920.

[36] Some interesting expressions of this viewpoint follow:

"M. Poincaré has been a great, a very great president . . . . Posterity . . . . will ratify this judgment, and its admiration will increase with the revelation of documents in which the clear-sighted patriotism, the tenacity, the patience, the courageous confidence of the outgoing president are affirmed. It is known what he said . . . . and he was an incomparable orator. It is hardly suspected how much good he did and how much evil he prevented, without ever departing from constitutional correctness." (Louis Barthou in L'Excelsior, February 18, 1920.)

"It is the walls of his office in the Elysée, and those of the ministerial council and war committee chamber, which must be questioned as to his activity" (Louis Madelin in L'Echo de Paris, February 18, 1920).

"The president of the republic is too careful not to infringe upon the constitutional rights of his ministers to make known the part which he took

pressed the national feeling when it voted that he "deserved well of *la patrie*"; only the Socialists protested that, since he was irresponsible, his acts could not be approved thus until they were thoroughly examined.[37]

Praise for the president came from some unexpected quarters. *Le Radical* joined the chorus when it said:

> What remains of the emotion, of the underhanded but incontestable hostility with which certain republican circles greeted his election to the supreme magistracy on January 17, 1913? Nothing, except perhaps the conviction, shared by all republican patriots from the most moderate to the most extreme, that the decision of the congress was the happiest and most judicious choice.[38]

Even Germain Bapst, the unwavering and caustic critic of the president through seven years, suddenly reflected upon Poincaré's work and found it good. On February 18, 1920, the day when Deschanel entered the Elysée, Bapst wrote in his diary:

> I recall the nomination of M. Poincaré seven years ago. It was almost a revolution . . . . A man of great talent, sprung from a family of high morality and worthy in every respect, he succeeded M. Fallières . . . ., without talent . . . ., without energy . . . .
>
> The coming of M. Poincaré was greeted as announcing the dawn

---

in their decisions. Those who are or who believe themselves informed as to the secret of things affirm, however, that this part has been much greater than was supposed; that his intervention always showed itself vigilant, active, efficacious, down to the smallest details . . . ." (Count d'Haussonville in *Le Gaulois,* July 26, 1919.)

The most notorious article of this type appeared in *L'Opinion* (XI [December 14, 1918], 427). It asserted: "Metz and Strasbourg regained is the conclusion of a policy" which Poincaré had carried out by sacrificing "the means to the end, the men to the task." Summing up, the article declared that history would put each man in his true place: ". . . . and . . . . M. Poincaré in the first—not only for the admirable series of his speeches, but also . . . . for the admirable continuity of his acts." Anti-Poincarists seized upon these statements as semi-official, for editor Maurice Colrat was a close friend of the president. Poincaré discomfited them by showing that Colrat was not serving as editor at the time the article appeared.

[37] *L'Humanité,* February 11, 1920.

[38] *Le Radical,* February 11, 1920.

of a new era. A patriotic policy was about to succeed a regime of diminution and debasement. It was expected that this Lorrainer, an orator, an upright man, a patriot . . . ., would revive the country . . . .

Has he given what was expected of him? Well, I should say "Yes."

Certainly I have not spared him in this journal. I have showed his weakness . . . ., his defects of character . . . . All that is exact; but one must consider the circumstances, think of the difficulties with which he had to contend, and especially judge his role in its entirety.

Well, I do not hesitate to say that the total of good in his activity is greater than the total of bad.

He kept up appearances; he never weakened; even though he lacked warmth and courage, he was correct, straightforward, and honest.

He followed foreign policy carefully, and I think that many times his influence and his action were judicious, useful, and even very effective.

If Clemenceau led us to victory, it must be said that M. Poincaré called him to power at the propitious moment . . . .

Finally, if the country has maintained an honorable and worthy appearance, it is because he who represented it knew how to be worthy and honest himself.[39]

This eulogy from a customarily vitriolic pen gave striking evidence of Poincaré's place in the hearts of Frenchmen at the end of his septennate. In 1913 he had been regarded as the outstanding active statesman of his country. In 1920 Clemenceau had replaced him in that role, but Poincaré had won a deeper and more vital sort of confidence among his countrymen. When he left the Elysée for his old senatorial desk he possessed a prestige which no other politician could hope to attain. Never before had a retiring president returned to active political life. For Poincaré the road back to power was all prepared—even inevitable. His presidency became a basic ingredient in the legend which made him the statesman-type of twentieth-century France.

[39] Bapst, "Journal," February 18, 1920.

CHAPTER X

CONCLUSION

The Poincaré presidency presents the strange phenomenon of a relatively strong statesman in a weak governmental post. A study of his septennate raises a doubled-edged question: What effect did the office have upon the man, and what effect the man upon the office?

Beyond any doubt the presidency placed sharp limitations upon Poincaré's activity. Some of his enemies have asserted that nothing changed in 1913: that he remained the real as well as the nominal chief executive of France for seven more years. Only blindness or animosity can have motivated such a statement. On the other hand, the disgust with which Poincaré subsequently recalled his term at the Elysée was equally unjustified. He told a friend in 1920 that his wartime memoirs would be entitled "My Prisons."[1] Not long after, he wrote that a president could be nothing more than an experienced counselor. "Some optimists," he declared, "imagine that . . . . it is the manner of interpreting and applying the constitution, rather than the constitution itself . . . . which has taken all effective power away from the president and has reduced him to a double role of representative and [adviser] . . . . I do not share this illusion . . . ."[2] And yet, in his inaugural message seven years before, he had promised to maintain the continuity of foreign policy throughout his term. Those were not the words of a man who expected to be nothing more than an adviser. Either his opinions had changed in the interim or for some reason he wished to minimize his presidential activity.

[1] Stéphane Lauzanne in *Le Matin,* January 15, 1920.
[2] *Le Temps,* August 9, 1920.

Poincaré's postwar attitude, which was partly sincere and partly affected, had a triple root. In the first place, his election in 1913 had sent him directly from the strongest office in France into the Elysée. The sudden contrast between real and nominal power inevitably aroused in him a spirit of discontent. As premier he had been able to act directly; as president he could act only through someone else. And it was not always easy to find officials who would follow suggestions from the Elysée.

The second and most important root was disillusionment. Poincaré had expected that his prestige would inject new life into the presidency. He would never have aspired to the office had he believed that it would plunge him into the obscurity of his predecessors. His election in 1913 was the climax of a minority campaign in favor of a stronger presidency. Power exists in the constitution, ran the argument; it has been allowed to lapse; a man of character will revive it. Many of his electors hoped for such a result, and most of his opponents feared it. The election was marked by unprecedented popular interest, which arose largely from the novel idea of leadership at the Elysée. Although Poincaré made no campaign promise that he would try to revive the presidency, his earlier speeches and his political record clearly augured such an attempt. His inaugural message gave further evidence; so did his continual public appearances during 1913 and his direct contact with diplomacy.

Previous presidents had indulged in similar activity, but on a much more limited scale. Nothing in the constitution forbade it; several years of practice might have made it a precedent. But Poincaré's extreme nationalism soon led him into trouble. He identified himself with a definite political program, notably with the law for three-year military service. By doing so he injured his status as a moderator above parties; he came perilously near setting up a "policy of the Elysée." Enemies of that policy automatically became his enemies; some of them even suspected him of an intention to break his constitutional bonds. This was not the case. He simply regarded the three-year law as a national issue, an issue above parties, by a process of mental gymnastics. Proof that he had no desire to be a MacMahon was given in the crisis of June 1914 when he backed down before the Chamber. Yet his ill-fated effort to set up a Ribot ministry showed his willingness to fight up to the very limits of his constitutional prerogative.

Forced into a partial capitulation when he called Viviani to power, Poincaré might have abandoned his office before 1920 if the war had not come. Wartime conditions allowed the president to expand his influence somewhat, for experience and ability were at a premium. But active leadership could not occupy the Elysée so long as responsibility belonged to the ministers. Friction, delay, inefficiency were the inevitable results, and they endangered victory. Poincaré was finally forced to combine leadership and responsibility in the same hands—those of Clemenceau. For the president this meant abdication of virtually all his rights. The peacetime crisis of June 1914 had already blocked his effort to build a more influential presidency. The Tiger's arrival in November 1917 represented a similar wartime defeat. It is not surprising that Poincaré left office a disillusioned man.

There was still a third reason for Poincaré's derogatory attitude toward the presidency. It constituted a reply to the charges of war-guilt critics. For purposes of self-justification he exaggerated his weakness and confessed only to such activity as could not be concealed. One cannot expect to find a fair, objective account of the Poincaré presidency in *Au service de la France*.

It may be concluded, therefore, that the effect of the office on the man was great but not so great as he would have us believe. It removed him from active control for seven years, and he often chafed at his restrictions. But the presidency did not make him a useless King Log. Except during the Clemenceau period, he exercised effective influence over the members of the government. As one commentator has remarked: "In the dubious borderland between deliberation and decision he probably exerted an authority closely resembling in kind and surpassing in quality that of a responsible minister."[3] His contacts with politicians and ambassadors were frequent, and several times his intervention in governmental affairs had genuine significance. Stéphane Lauzanne, editor of *Le Matin* and friend of Poincaré, wrote in 1920: "Of 2,556 days as president of the republic, M. Poincaré . . . . had exactly 10 days of omnipotence."[4] Lauzanne's statement was misleading. If Poincaré was not omnipotent during the 2,546 ordinary days of his septennate, neither was he impotent. The presidency limited Raymond Poincaré, but did not stifle him.

There remains the opposite face of the question: the long-run effect of the man upon the office. Some earlier presidents, like MacMahon and Grévy, had left their stamp on the presidency, for practice tended to develop into constitutional rules. It is safe to say that Poincaré left the office almost exactly as he had found it. His rigid legalism was responsible for this fact. He had the jurist's respect for rules, whose spirit might be infringed but whose form had to be respected.

Poincaré expected to be a more important factor in the government than his predecessors had been. As a matter of fact, he went beyond the Loubet-Fallières tradition, although to a more limited degree than he had hoped. He achieved that result without altering a single constitutional rule; his method was simply to exert personal influence and pressure at every possible opportunity. So long as he remained at the Elysée the presidency was a stronger office than in the past. But that strength could not last beyond 1920 unless Poincaré's successors possessed his personal qualities.

This temporary change in the presidency passed unnoticed by most Frenchmen, especially during the war years. While a

[3] W. L. Middleton, *The French Political System* (New York, 1933), p. 199.

[4] *Le Matin,* January 15, 1920.

few on the Left wing cried "Dictator!", the Center and Right grumbled at what they called his refusal to assume responsibilities. Externally he seemed to be an ordinary chief magistrate who performed decorative functions and made innocuous speeches. Few people could see behind the scenes, where Poincaré tried to supervise everything and advise everyone.

In the immediate postwar months a swarm of brochures gave evidence of widespread dissatisfaction with the functioning of the French government. The authors invariably declared that the crisis had revealed the excessive weakness of the executive branch. Although each critic had his own reform program, almost all of them agreed that the presidency had not met the wartime test. In most cases, they demanded that the chief magistrate be strengthened by providing for his popular election, or by making the cabinet responsible to him. A few simply ignored the president in their plans for the cure of governmental ills.[5] As for the prewar idea of presidential revival by a strong man in the Elysée, it was abandoned by even its most sanguine sponsors.[6]

Disillusioned though they were by the apparent failure of the "Poincaré experiment," the advocates of a strong presidency felt a sudden resurgence of hope only a few months later. Paul Deschanel suffered a mental breakdown late in 1920, and the

[5] Representative articles and brochures include the following: *L'Opinion,* XI (December 7 and 28, 1918), 416 and 461; XII (February 22, 1919), 137; Comte de Fels, *Essai de politique expérimentale* (Paris, 1921); Olivier Bascou, *L'anarchie et la guerre* (Paris, 1921); Paul Féron-Vrau, *Après la guerre, une réforme urgente et nécessaire* (Paris, 1919); Charles Briand, *Donnons une constitution à la France* (Paris, 1919); Paul Gruet, *Vers la constituante* (Paris, 1919); B. Kemmel, *Etudes sur quelques réformes politiques et administratives* (Paris, 1918); Georges Lachapelle, *L'œuvre de demain* (Paris, 1917); Jules Roche, *Quand serons-nous en république?* (Paris, 1918); Charles Sancerme, *La confession d'un républicain* (Paris, 1917); "Un docteur ès-sciences politiques," *Un chef d'état qui gouverne* (Paris, 1918); H. Pineau, *La France en ordre* (Paris, 1919); Georges Renard, "L'organisation urgente de la démocratie," *Le Progrès Civique,* I (November 16, 1919), 11–13.

[6] Notably Henri Leyret in *Le gouvernement et le parlement* (Paris, 1919), pp. 52–58. Cf. Simonsson, *Millerands Presidentur,* p. 53.

Bloc National chose Alexandre Millerand to succeed him. The new president, a man of authoritarian temperament and sublime self-confidence, was known to favor a constitutional amendment to strengthen the executive. He proposed it in his inaugural message, but made it clear that even if no amendment were forthcoming, he would use all the powers which the constitution gave him. There was an explosion of approval from the Moderate and the Right-wing press.[7] Poincaré had "failed" them, to be sure; but perhaps a man of Millerand's determination could really revive the atrophied presidency. For almost four years they applauded while Millerand frankly identified himself with the policies of the *Bloc National*. He intervened openly in the elections of 1924, but the *Bloc* suffered a major defeat. The triumphant Left-wing parties did not even give him the choice that faced MacMahon in 1877—"give in or get out." They went on strike against any ministry which he might appoint, thereby forcing his resignation. Millerand's fall was the consequence of his own mistakes. A wiser man than he would have profited from Poincaré's recent experience. Poincaré had discovered just how far a president might safely go, and what methods might be used. He chose quieter, more limited, more personal ways to extend his authority; and he was far more successful than Millerand.

In summary, Poincaré proved to be no irresistible force, and the presidency no immovable object. His septennate showed that there were definite limits to the expansion of presidential power. When the chief magistrate used his influence behind the scenes he met no serious objection from those who jealously guarded the republican system. But whenever he tried to espouse a controversial issue a presidential crisis at once appeared on the horizon. Poincaré was never tempted to venture beyond the juridical boundaries of his office. Always in the back of his mind was the thought, "No Second of December!

---

[7] *Le Parlement et l'Opinion* (October 1920), pp. 1745–66; Simonsson, *op. cit.*, p. 94.

No new Louis-Napoleon!" His parliamentary background, his cautious temperament, his deep repugnance toward anything resembling a coup d'état—all these things made it certain that he would never embark on an adventurous policy. One may even doubt whether he was actually the strong man that Frenchmen have often thought him to be. Yet he was strong enough to test the presidency as it stood, strictly within its legal limits. The result of the "Poincaré experiment" was conclusive: It showed that a president could be influential, but never powerful; important, but never dominant. So long as the constitution of 1875 remained unchanged, the Elysée would never house the real chief executive of France.

BIBLIOGRAPHY OF MATERIALS CITED

NOTE ON SOURCES

Like any study in recent French political history, this monograph must depend to a rather dangerous degree upon memoirs. The basic source is, of course, Poincaré's *Au service de la France*. This ten-volume work describes his septennate from 1913 through 1915 in great detail, and from 1916 through 1918 in more sketchy fashion. Two projected volumes on the treaty-making period were not completed before Poincaré's death. It is obvious that these memoirs are not contemporary notes from a diary but that they form an elaborate reply to the author's critics. The ex-president culled his materials carefully so that his activity might appear in a favorable light. Poincaré's personal papers for the period are not available.

A great number of officials who collaborated with the wartime president have left memoirs as well. Four of the seven premiers have published reminiscences of some sort; but only Alexandre Ribot's *Journal* is of great value. In it appears Ribot's diary, apparently without revision for purposes of special pleading. A comparison between this volume and Ribot's earlier *Lettres à un ami* shows how many important facts disappear when contemporary notes are watered down. The books of Viviani, Painlevé, and Clemenceau fall into the class of polemics. Briand's daily memoranda are being used by Georges Suarez for his biographical study, but their cryptic brevity is disappointing. The *Carnets* of General Gallieni, Briand's war minister, furnish a candid and unrevised account of political affairs as seen through military eyes. The diary of Colonel Herbillon, a liaison officer, contains a wealth of details about Poincaré. General Mordacq's four volumes on the Clemenceau ministry are somewhat less useful because of their pro-Clemenceau bias. Mordacq was the Tiger's military aide. Almost every French general has left a volume or two defending himself before the bar of history. Herbillon's biography of Micheler stands out among these, for he has used Micheler's papers and has quoted liberally from them.

It is easier to discover what people thought about Poincaré than what the president actually did in office. Newspapers and periodicals furnish an overabundance of material for the prewar years, but the wartime censorship dried up this source. The gap may be partially filled through published diaries like that of Michel Corday, *chef de cabinet* of a wartime minister but excessively hostile to Poincaré. More useful is the manuscript "Journal de la guerre de 1914" of Germain Bapst, elderly member of a prominent Paris family of Right-wing sympathies. This enormous pile of daily notes has been bound into eight volumes at the Bibliothèque Nationale. The unpublished "Notes de guerre" of William Martin furnish many details, often interesting and sometimes significant. Martin, correspondent of the *Journal de Genève,* was one of the ablest journalists in Paris. His wide acquaintanceship enabled him to sound opinion in various circles.

Several men who held official posts between 1913 and 1920 have been kind enough to furnish the author with certain information orally or by letter. These include: M. Joseph Caillaux, former premier and minister; M. Georges Mandel, *chef de cabinet* of Clemenceau from 1917 to 1920; M. Gabriel Hanotaux, a close personal friend of the president; M. Charles Dumont, minister of finance in the Barthou cabinet of 1913; M. Raoul Péret, minister of justice under Painlevé in 1917; and M. Paul Allard, journalist attached to the wartime censorship. Madame Raymond Poincaré also consented to answer several questions concerning the presidency of her late husband.

The materials used in this study are drawn from the Hoover Library on War, Revolution, and Peace at Stanford University; the Library of Congress; the Bibliothèque Nationale; and the Bibliothèque de Documentation Internationale Contemporaine at Vincennes.

MANUSCRIPTS

BAPST, GERMAIN. "Journal de la guerre de 1914." 1914–21. Bibliothèque Nationale, Paris.
MARTIN, WILLIAM. "Notes de guerre." 1915–20. Hoover Library on War, Revolution, and Peace, Stanford University.

PUBLISHED DOCUMENTS

AUSTRO-HUNGARIAN MONARCHY, MINISTERIUM DES K. UND K. HAUSES UND DES ÄUSSERN. *Österreichs-Ungarns Aussenpolitik von der Bosnischen Krise 1908 bis zum Kriegsausbruch 1914, diplomatische Aktenstücke des österreichisch-ungarischen Ministeriums des Äussern (ausgewählt von Ludwig Bittner, Alfred Francis Pribram, Heinrich Srbik und Hans Uebersberger).* 8 vols. Vienna, 1930.

BELGIUM, MINISTÈRE DES AFFAIRES ETRANGÈRES. *Amtliche Aktenstücke zur Geschichte der Europaischen Politik 1885–1914 (Die Belgischen Dokumente zur Vorgeschichte des Weltkrieges.) Vollständige ausgabe der vom Deutschen Auswärtigen Amt herausgegebenen diplomatischen urkunden aus den Belgischen Staatsarchiven. Hrsg. von Bernhard Schwertfeger.* 1 Ergänzungsband. Berlin, 1925.

FRANCE, ASSEMBLÉE NATIONALE. *Annales de l'Assemblée Nationale, comte-rendu in extenso des séances.* Tomes 36 and 39. Paris, 1875.

———. *Annales du Sénat et de la Chambre des Députés.* Session ordinaire de 1877, tome 3; session ordinaire de 1879, tome 2. Paris, 1877–79.

———. *Annales de la Chambre des Députés, débats parlementaires.* Session extraordinaire de 1898, tome unique; sessions ordinaires et extraordinaires, 1912–24. Paris, 1898, 1912–24.

———. *Annales du Sénat, débats parlementaires.* Sessions ordinaires et extraordinaires, 1913–14. Paris, 1913–14.

———. *Chambre des Députés, Journal officiel (les comités secrets).* [The stenographic reports of the secret sessions held in 1916 and 1917 were published at intervals from 1919 to 1933. They have been collected in a single volume at the Bibliothèque de Documentation Internationale at Vincennes.]

FRANCE, MINISTÈRE DE LA GUERRE, ETAT-MAJOR DE L'ARMÉE, SERVICE HISTORIQUE. *Les armées françaises dans la grande guerre.* Vols. V–VI. Paris, 1931.

FRANCE, MINISTÈRE DES AFFAIRES ETRANGÈRES, COMMISSION DE PUBLICATION DES DOCUMENTS RELATIFS AUX ORIGINES DE LA GUERRE DE 1914. *Documents diplomatiques français 1871–1914.* 28 vols. Paris, 1929–39.

GERMANY, AUSWÄRTIGES AMT. *Die Grosse Politik der europaischen Kabinette, 1871–1914, Sammlung der diplomatischen Akten des Auswärtigen Amtes (im Auftrage des Auswärtigen Amtes, herausgegeben von Johannes Lepsius, Albrecht Mendelssohn-Bartholdy, Friedrich Thimme).* 40 vols. Berlin, 1922–27.

GREAT BRITAIN, FOREIGN OFFICE. *British Documents on the Origins of the War, 1898–1914* (edited by G. P. Gooch and Harold Temperley). 11 vols. London, 1927–36.

RUSSIA, MINISTERSTVO INOSTRANNYKH DIEL. *Der diplomatische schriftwechsel Iswolskis, 1911–1914, aus den geheimakten der russischen Staatsarchive, im auftrage des deutschen Auswärtigen amtes in deutscher übertragung, herausgegeben von Friedrich Stieve.* 4 vols. Berlin, 1925.

RUSSIA, MINISTERSTVO INOSTRANNYKH DIEL. *Documents diplomatiques secrets russes 1914–1917, d'après les archives du ministère des affaires étrangères à Petrograd* (translated by J. Polonsky). Paris, 1926.

————. *Iswolski im Weltkriege; der diplomatische schriftwechsel Iswolskis aus den jahren 1914–1917; neue dokumente aus den geheimakten der russischen Staatsarchive, im auftrage des deutschen Auswärtigen Amtes, nebst einem Kommentar von Friedrich Stieve*. 2 vols. Berlin, 1925.

————. *Komissiia po izdaniiu dokumentov epokhi imperializma. Die Internationalen Beziehungen im Zeitalter des Imperialismus; Dokumente aus den Archiven der Zarischen und der Provisorischen Regierung*. 8 vols. Berlin, 1931–36.

PRIVATELY PRINTED DOCUMENTS

CAILLAUX, JOSEPH. "Les responsables," *Les Documents Politiques, Diplomatiques, et Financiers*, March, 1926, pp. 81–96.

MARCHAND, RENÉ (ed.). *Un livre noir, diplomatie d'avant-guerre d'après les documents des archives russes, novembre 1910–juillet 1914*. 6 vols. Paris, 1922–31.

MILNER, LORD. "Memorandum to the Cabinet by Lord Milner on His Visit to France, Including the Conference at Doullens, March 26th, 1918," *New Statesman*, April 23, 1921, pp. i–iv.

PARTI RÉPUBLICAIN RADICAL ET RADICAL-SOCIALISTE. *Treizième congrès du parti républicain radical et radical-socialiste tenu à Pau le 16, 17, 18 et 19 octobre 1913*. Paris, 1913.

POINCARÉ, RAYMOND. *Messages, discours, allocutions, lettres et télégrammes de M. Raymond Poincaré*. 3 vols. Paris, 1919–21.

[RAFALOVICH, A.] *"L'abominable vénalité de la presse ..." d'après les documents des archives russes (1897–1917)*. Paris, 1931.

DIARIES AND MEMOIRS

ADAM, H. PEARL. *Paris Sees It Through; a Diary, 1914–1919*. London, 1919.

BENOIST, CHARLES. *Souvenirs de M. Charles Benoist*. 3 vols. Paris, 1933–34.

BERTIE, SIR FRANCIS. *The Diary of Lord Bertie of Thame, 1914–1918*. 2 vols. London, 1924.

BIENVENU-MARTIN, JEAN-BAPTISTE. "Mon interim de chef de gouvernement (15–27 juillet 1914)," *Revue de France*, XIII (August 15, 1933), 639–52.

BOURGIN, HUBERT. *Mémoires pour servir à l'histoire d'une sécession politique (1915–1917); le parti contre la patrie.* Paris, 1924.

BUCHANAN, SIR GEORGE. *My Mission to Russia and Other Diplomatic Memories.* 2 vols. Boston, 1923.

CAILLAUX, JOSEPH. *Devant l'histoire; mes prisons.* Paris, 1920.

CLEMENCEAU, GEORGES. *Grandeur and Misery of Victory* (translated by F. M. Atkinson). New York, 1930.

COMBARIEU, ABEL. *Sept ans à l'Elysée avec le président Emile Loubet; de l'affaire Dreyfus à la conférence d'Algéçiras, 1899–1906.* Paris, 1932.

CORDAY, MICHEL. *L'envers de la guerre, journal inédit.* 2 vols. Paris, 1932.

DAUDET, LÉON. *La pluie de sang; nouveaux souvenirs 1914–1918.* Paris, 1932.

DELL, ROBERT. *My Second Country (France).* New York, 1920.

FOCH, MARSHAL FERDINAND. *Mémoires pour servir à l'histoire de la guerre de 1914–1918.* Paris, 1931.

GALLIENI, GAETAN (ed.). *Les carnets de Gallieni.* Paris, 1932.

GÉRARD, AUGUSTE. *Mémoires; la vie d'un diplomate sous la troisième république.* Paris, 1928.

GOBLET, RENÉ. "Souvenirs de ma vie politique," *Revue Politique et Parlementaire,* CXXXVII (November 10, 1928), 177–97; CXLI (October 10, 1929), 5–29.

HANOTAUX, GABRIEL. "Jules Méline," *Revue des Deux Mondes,* January 15, 1926, pp. 440–53.

HERBILLON, COLONEL EMILE E. *Souvenirs d'un officier de liaison pendant la guerre mondiale; du général en chef au gouvernement.* 2 vols. Paris, 1930.

HUMBERT, CHARLES. *Chacun son tour.* Paris, 1925.

JOBERT, ARISTIDE. *Souvenirs d'un ex-parlementaire (1914–1919).* Paris, 1933.

JOFFRE, MARSHAL JOSEPH JACQUES CÉSAIRE. *Mémoires du Maréchal Joffre (1910–1917).* 2 vols. Paris, 1932.

KAROLYI, COUNT MICHAEL. *Fighting the World, the Struggle for Peace* (translated by E. W. Dickes). London, 1924.

KOKOVTSOV, COUNT. *Out of My Past: the Memoirs of Count Kokovtsov* (edited by H. H. Fisher). Stanford University, 1935.

LAUZANNE, STÉPHANE. *Great Men and Great Days* (translated by L. B. Williams). New York, 1921.

LEBLOND, MARIUS-ARY. *Gallieni parle. Entretiens du "sauveur de Paris" ministre de la guerre avec ses secrétaires.* Paris, 1920.

LEYRET, HENRI. "Delcassé parle," *Revue des Deux Mondes,* September 15, 1937, pp. 346–81.

LLOYD GEORGE, DAVID. *The Truth About the Peace Treaties.* 2 vols. London, 1938.

———. *War Memoirs of David Lloyd George.* 6 vols. Boston, 1933–36.

LOUIS, GEORGES. *Les carnets de Georges Louis.* 2 vols. Paris, 1926.

MALVY, LOUIS JEAN. *Mon crime.* Paris, 1921.

MARCELLIN, LÉOPOLD. *Politique et politiciens pendant la guerre.* 4 vols. Paris, 1922–24.

MARTET, JEAN. *Le Tigre.* Paris, 1930.

MAUNOURY, HENRY. *Police de guerre (1914–1919).* Paris, 1937.

DE MEAUX, VICOMTE. *Souvenirs politiques 1871–1877.* Paris, 1905.

MESSIMY, GENERAL ADOLPHE. *Mes souvenirs.* Paris, 1937.

MORDACQ, GENERAL JEAN JULES HENRI. *Le ministère Clemenceau, journal d'un témoin.* 4 vols. Paris, 1930–31.

MOTT, COLONEL T. BENTLEY. *Twenty Years as Military Attaché.* New York, 1937.

NEVINS, ALLAN (ed.) *The Letters and Journal of Brand Whitlock: the Journal.* New York, 1936.

NOULENS, JOSEPH. "Le gouvernement français à la veille de la guerre," *Revue des Deux Mondes,* February 1, 1931, pp. 608–21.

PAINLEVÉ, PAUL. *Comment j'ai nommé Foch et Pétain; la politique de guerre de 1917, le commandement unique interallié.* Paris, 1923.

PALAT, GENERAL BARTHÉLEMY. "Souvenirs de guerre 1914–1916," *Archives de la Grande Guerre et de l'Histoire Contemporaine.* 4e année, no. 45, pp. 1777–88.

PALÉOLOGUE, MAURICE. "Comment le service de trois ans fut rétabli en 1913," *Revue des Deux Mondes,* May 1 and 15, 1935, pp. 67–94, 307–44.

———. *La Russie des tsars pendant la grande guerre.* 3 vols. Paris, n.d.

———. "Sur le chemin de la guerre mondiale (février–mars 1913)," *Revue des Deux Mondes,* October 1, 1933, pp. 481–506.

PÉDOYA, GENERAL JEAN MARIE GUSTAVE. *La commission de l'armée pendant la grande guerre; documents inédits et secrets.* Paris, 1921.

PERSHING, JOHN J. *My Experiences in the World War.* 2 vols. New York, 1931.

POINCARÉ, RAYMOND. *Au service de la France.* 10 vols. Paris, 1926–33.

RECOULY, RAYMOND. *Foch; My Conversations with the Marshal* (translated by Joyce Davis). New York, 1929.

RIBOT, ALEXANDRE. *Journal d'Alexandre Ribot et correspondances iné-dites 1914–1922.* Paris, 1936.

——. *Lettres à un ami.* Paris, 1924.

SARRAIL, GENERAL MAURICE. "Souvenirs de 1914–1915," *Revue Politique et Parlementaire,* CVII (May–June, 1921), 161–81, 399–418; CVIII (July–August, 1921), 81–105, 221–48.

VON SCHOEN, WILHELM EDWARD. *The Memoirs of an Ambassador; a Contribution to the Political History of Modern Times* (translated by Constance Vesey). London, 1922.

SIXTE DE BOURBON, PRINCE. *L'offre de paix séparée de l'Autriche (5 décembre 1916—12 octobre 1917).* Paris, 1920.

STEED, HENRY WICKHAM. *Through Thirty Years, 1892–1922.* New York, 1924.

TARDIEU, ANDRÉ. *La paix.* Paris, 1921.

WEYGAND, GENERAL MAXIME. "Le Maréchal Foch et l'armistice," *Revue des Deux Mondes,* November 1, 1938, pp. 1–29.

BOOKS AND ARTICLES

ADAM, GEORGE JEFFERYS. *Treason and Tragedy: An Account of the French War Trials.* London, 1929.

ADAM DE VILLIERS, GEORGES. *M. Poincaré parle.* Paris, 1933.

ALLARD, PAUL. *L'oreille fendue; les généraux limogés pendant la guerre.* Paris, 1933.

BACH, AUGUST. "Frankreichs Entschluss zum Kriege," *Berliner Monatshefte,* XI (August 1933), 753–72.

BARTHÉLEMY, JOSEPH. *Le rôle du pouvoir exécutif dans les républiques modernes.* Paris, 1907.

BEER, MAX. *Zar Poincarew; die Schuld am Kriege.* Berlin, 1914.

BERGER, MARCEL, AND ALLARD, PAUL. *Les secrets de la censure pendant la guerre.* Paris, 1932.

BRÉAL, AUGUSTE. *Philippe Berthelot.* Paris, 1937.

BOURGET, JEAN MARIE. *Gouvernement et commandement; les leçons de la guerre mondiale.* Paris, 1930.

BUGNET, CHARLES. *Rue Saint-Dominique et G. Q. G. ou les trois dictatures de la guerre.* Paris, 1937.

CALLWELL, SIR CHARLES EDWARD. *Field Marshal Sir Henry Wilson; His Life and Diaries.* 2 vols. London, 1927.

CARRÈRE, JEAN, AND BOURGIN, GEORGES. *Manuel des partis politiques en France.* Paris, 1924.

CLAUSS, MAX. *Das Politische Frankreich vor dem Kriege.* Karlsruhe, 1928.

CONVERSET, COLONEL. *Les trois ans de diplomatie secrète qui nous me-nèrent à la guerre de 1914.* Paris, 1924.

COOPER, DUFF. *Haig.* 2 vols. London, 1935–36.

"COSMIN, S." [PHOCAS-COSMETATOS, S. P.]. *L'entente et la Grèce pendant la grande guerre.* 2 vols. Paris, 1926.

DEMARTIAL, GEORGES. *La guerre de 1914; la mobilisation des con-sciences.* Paris, 1927.

DESSAINT, JOSEPH. *Les enseignements de la guerre. Avant tout, un pouvoir central!* Paris, 1916.

DUGUIT, LÉON, AND MONNIER, HENRI. *Les constitutions et les princi-pales lois politiques de la France depuis 1789.* Paris, 1908.

DUPIN, GUSTAVE. *M. Poincaré et la guerre de 1914; études sur les responsabilités.* (New edition, revised). Paris, 1935.

ECHEMAN, JACQUES. *Les ministères en France de 1914 à 1932.* Paris, 1932.

ESMEIN, ADHÉMAR, AND NÉZARD, HENRY. *Eléments de droit constitu-tionnel français et comparé.* 2 vols. Paris, 1928.

FABRE-LUCE, ALFRED. *Caillaux.* Paris, 1933.

FAGUET, EMILE. *Problèmes politiques du temps présent.* Paris, 1907.

FAY, SIDNEY BRADSHAW. *The Origins of the World War.* (Second edition, revised.) New York, 1930.

GARNER, JAMES W. "The Presidency of the French Republic," *North American Review,* CXCVII (March 1913), 335–49.

GÉRIN, RENÉ. *Comment fut provoquée la guerre de 1914.* Paris, 1931.

———. *Les responsabilités de la guerre; quatorze questions par René Gérin—quatorze réponses par Raymond Poincaré.* Paris, 1930.

GHEUSI, PIERRE BARTHÉLEMY. *La gloire de Gallieni; comment Paris fut sauvé, le testament d'un soldat.* Paris, 1928.

GIRARD, HENRY. *Raymond Poincaré.* Paris, 1913.

GOOCH, GEORGE PEABODY. *Before the War: Studies in Diplomacy.* Vol. II. New York, 1938.

GOUTTENOIRE DE TOURY, FERNAND. *Poincaré a-t-il voulu la guerre?* Paris, 1920.

GUÉRARD, ALBERT. *Beyond Hatred; the Democratic Ideal in France and America.* New York, 1925.

GUEYDAN, B. E. *Les rois de la république.* 2 vols. Paris, 1925.

HANOTAUX, GABRIEL. *Contemporary France* (translated from the French). 4 vols. London, 1903–9.

———. *Raymond Poincaré.* Paris, 1934.

HELMREICH, ERNST CHRISTIAN. *The Diplomacy of the Balkan Wars 1912–1913.* Cambridge, Mass., 1938.

HERBILLON, COLONEL EMILE E. *Le général Alfred Micheler (1914–1918) d'après ses notes, sa correspondance et les souvenirs personnels de l'auteur.* Paris, 1934.

HUDDLESTON, SISLEY. *Poincaré; a Biographical Portrait.* London, 1924.

JACQUES, LÉON. *Les partis politiques sous la IIIᵉ république.* Paris, 1913.

JERROLD, LAWRENCE. "President Poincaré," *Contemporary Review,* CIII (February 1913), 179–83.

JÈZE, GASTON. "La présidence de la république," *Revue du Droit Public et de la Science Politique en France et à l'Etranger,* XXX (1913), 113–27.

JUDET, ERNEST. *Georges Louis.* Paris, 1925.

———. *Le véritable Clemenceau.* Berne, 1920.

LACHAPELLE, GEORGES. *Elections législatives des 26 avril et 10 mai 1914.* Paris, 1914.

LA CHESNAIS, P. G. "Les élections: statistique des résultats," *La Grande Revue,* LXXXV (May 10 and 25, 1914), 32–46, 253–62.

LEYRET, HENRI. *La république et les politiciens; lettres de province.* Paris, 1909.

———. *Le président de la république; son rôle, ses droits, ses devoirs.* Paris, 1913.

LÖWEGREN, GUNNAR. *Poincaré och Tredje Republiken.* Stockholm, 1936.

DE LUBERSAC, GUY. *Les pouvoirs constitutionnels du président de la république.* Paris, 1913.

MADELIN, LOUIS. "Un Lorrain: M. Raymond Poincaré," *Revue Hebdomadaire,* February 8, 1913, pp. 247–61.

MARCELLIN, LÉOPOLD. *Le règne des harangueurs.* Paris, 1928.

MARGUERITTE, VICTOR. *Les criminels.* Paris, 1925.

MARTIN, GASTON. *Joseph Caillaux.* Paris, 1931.

MASSIANI, MARTIAL. "M. Raymond Poincaré," *Fortnightly Review,* XCIII (new series, May 1913), 857–67.

MENNEVÉE, ROGER. "Le mariage de M. Poincaré," *Les Documents Politiques, Diplomatiques et Financiers,* XV (October 1934), 510.

———. "A propos des mémoires du Maréchal Joffre: la réaction maitresse des destinées de la France; l'affaire Du Paty de Clam," *Les Documents Politiques, Diplomatiques et Financiers,* XIV (October 1933), 498–510.

"MERMEIX" [TERRAIL, GABRIEL]. *Au sein des commissions.* Paris, 1924.

"MERMEIX" [TERRAIL, GABRIEL]. *Le combat des trois, notes et documents sur la conférence de la paix.* Paris, 1922.

————. *Joffre: la première crise du commandement (novembre 1915—décembre 1916).* Paris, 1919.

————. *Les négotiations secrètes et les quatre armistices avec pièces justificatives.* Paris, 1919.

MICHON, GEORGES. *La préparation à la guerre; la loi de trois ans.* Paris, 1935.

MIDDLETON, W. L. *The French Political System.* New York, 1933.

MORDACQ, GENERAL JEAN JULES HENRI. *Clemenceau au soir de sa vie, 1920–1929.* 2 vols. Paris, 1933.

————. *La vérité sur le commandement unique; comment il fut réalisé.* Paris, 1929.

MOTT, THOMAS BENTLEY. *Myron T. Herrick, Friend of France; an Autobiographical Biography.* New York, 1929.

PAIX-SÉAILLES, CHARLES. *Jaurès et Caillaux; notes et souvenirs.* Paris, n.d.

PAYEN, FERNAND. *Raymond Poincaré, l'homme, le parlementaire, l'avocat.* Paris, 1936.

PEVET, ALFRED. *Les responsables de la guerre.* Paris, 1921.

PINGAUD, ALBERT. *Histoire diplomatique de la France pendant la grande guerre.* 2 vols. Paris, 1938.

POINCARÉ, RAYMOND. *How France Is Governed* (translated by Bernard Miall). London, 1913.

————. *Questions et figures politiques.* Paris, 1907.

PORTER, CHARLES W. *The Career of Théophile Delcassé.* Philadelphia, 1936.

RENOUVIN, PIERRE. *Les formes du gouvernement de guerre.* Paris, n.d.

————. *Les origines immédiates de la guerre (28 juin—4 août 1914).* Paris, 1927.

RIBOT, ALEXANDRE. *Quatre années d'opposition. Discours politiques de M. A. Ribot (1901–1905).* 2 vols. Paris, 1905.

ROCHE, JULES. "La révision de la constitution," *Le Monde Economique,* March 30, 1912, pp. 385–90.

SAMNÉ, GEORGES. *Raymond Poincaré.* Paris, 1933.

SCHMITT, BERNADOTTE E. *The Coming of the War 1914.* 2 vols. New York, 1930.

SEIGNOBOS, CHARLES. *L'évolution de la troisième république.* Paris, 1921.

SIMONSSON, RAGNAR. *Millerands Presidentur. En studie över presidentmakt och parlamentarism i Frankrike.* Uppsala, 1938.
SOCIÉTÉ D'HISTOIRE MODERNE. *Les ministères français, 1912–1922.* Paris, 1922.
SONOLET, LOUIS. *La vie et l'œuvre de Paul Deschanel 1855–1922.* Paris, 1926.
SUAREZ, GEORGES. *Briand, sa vie, son œuvre, avec son journal et de nombreux documents inédits.* 4 vols. Paris, 1938–40.
––––––. *La vie orgueilleuse de Clemenceau.* Paris, 1930.
TICHELEN, JOSEPH VAN. *Le président de la république et le problème de l'état.* Liège, 1939.
ZÉVORT, EDGAR. *Histoire de la troisième république.* 4 vols. Paris, 1899–1901.
* * * , GENERAL. *La crise du commandement unique; le conflit; Clemenceau, Foch, Haig, Pétain.* Paris, 1931.

PERIODICALS

Le Correspondant, 1912–14. Paris.
L'Economiste Français, 1912–14. Paris.
La Grande Revue, 1913–20. Paris.
L'Œuvre, 1913–14. Paris.
L'Opinion, 1912–20. Paris.
Le Progrès Civique, 1919–20. Paris.
Revue des Sciences Politiques, 1912–20. Paris.
Revue du Droit Public et de la Science Politique en France et à l'Etranger, 1913–24. Paris.
Revue Politique et Parlementaire, 1913–20. Paris.
Saturday Review, 1913–14. London.
L'Action Française, 1913–14. Paris.
Le Bonnet Rouge, 1915–17. Paris.
La Croix, 1913–14. Paris.
L'Echo de Paris, 1913–14, 1919–20. Paris.
L'Eclair, 1913–14. Paris.
L'Excelsior, 1913, 1920. Paris.
Le Figaro, 1912–14. Paris.
Le Gaulois, 1913–14, 1919–20. Paris.
La Guerre Sociale, 1914. Paris.
L'Homme Libre, 1913–20. Paris.
L'Humanité, 1913–20. Paris.
L'Intransigeant, 1913–14. Paris.

Journal des Débats, 1912–14. Paris.
Le Journal du Peuple, 1919. Paris.
La Liberté, 1913. Paris.
La Libre Parole, 1913–14. Paris.
Le Matin, 1913–20. Paris.
Le Parlement et l'Opinion, 1920. Paris.
Le Radical, 1913–20. Paris.
La République Française, 1913–14. Paris.
Le Temps, 1913–20. Paris.
The Times, 1913–14. London.
La Victoire, 1920. Paris.

INDEX